'C' CLASS DESTROYERS

'C' CLASS DESTROYERS

by

Commander David Hobbs MBE RN (Retired)

Previous Page: *A classic picture of British destroyers at sea;* Contest *manoeuvring at high speed with other ships of the 6th Destroyer Squadron. (Syd Goodman Collection)*

First published in the United Kingdom in 2012 by Maritime Books, Lodge Hill, Liskeard, Cornwall, PL14 4EL

CONTENTS

ACKNOWLEDGEMENTS

I am grateful to Steve Bush of Maritime Books who located and made available the majority of the photographs that appear in this book. His input and encouragement throughout the various stages this work has gone through have been a great help and it would not have emerged as it has without them.

Photographs of the ships that did not serve in the Royal Navy are rare and I am grateful to Brian Hargreaves of the World Ship Society for making the photograph of the former HMS *Crown* available. I should also like to thank John Lambert and John Morris for providing both technical drawings and illustrations.

A number of people have made useful suggestions for which I am grateful but any errors and omissions that may come to light in the following pages are all mine.

INTRODUCTION

The 'C' class destroyers were among the Royal Navy's most important warships in the decade after 1945. Available in significant numbers, they incorporated the latest fire-control systems, a substantial torpedo armament and an adequate action information organisation but their anti-submarine capability soon fell below the standard required. This shortcoming was rectified in the modernisation applied to most ships which kept them viable against conventional submarines until the early 1960s. Apart from being available in quantity, they were relatively cheap to operate with a ship's company averaging 186 compared with about 247 for a 'Battle' class destroyer and nearly 300 for a 'Daring'. In a period of manpower shortages and severe financial constraint this made them attractive, especially for deployment to the foreign stations. The 'C's were among the last British warships to be deployed as squadrons of identical ships grouped together for service in a particular fleet.

The 'Ca' class saw action during the Second World War, not least in the hazardous Russian Convoy operations carried out by the Home Fleet; subsequently with the British Pacific Fleet immediately after the war and in operations with the Far East Fleet after modernisation. Between 1946 and 1959 the 'Ch' and 'Co' classes saw sustained operations in the Home, Mediterranean, British Pacific and Far East Fleets. The 'Cr' class saw little service with the RN. In the individual ship histories that follow there are descriptions of ships' participation in peace-keeping operations in the East Indies; the Palestine Patrol; the Korean War; the Malayan Emergency; Confrontation against Indonesia; the Cod Wars against Iceland; the Beira Patrol; Cold War anti-submarine preparations; the need for guard-ships at various locations to protect British interests; 'showing the flag' world-wide to promote British interests; the defence of Kuwait; action to end the East African Army Mutinies; the Yangtse Incident; anti-piracy patrols, the Suez Intervention and time spent in the strategic reserve. The list of their activities is, in itself, an illustration of the Royal Navy's achievements in the period. In order to avoid repetition, I have tried to bring out, when describing the careers of individual ships, different aspects of the achievements of the whole class. The overall picture that emerges is impressive.

The 'C' class was built to imperial measurements and I have used these throughout. In 1947 the mark numbers for British and Commonwealth equipment were changed from Roman to Arabic numerals. To avoid confusion and provide standardisation I have used the latter throughout the book.

David Hobbs
Crail, Scotland, 2012

DESTROYER NAMES IN THE ROYAL NAVY

HMS Hornet was launched by Yarrow in 1893 as one of the first group of prototype destroyers. She made 27.6 knots on trials and served in UK waters until sold in 1909　　　　　　　　　　　*(Syd Goodman Collection)*

The threat posed by torpedo-boats to battle squadrons operating off an enemy coast was recognised in the late nineteenth century as being so formidable that the Admiralty took prompt and effective steps to counter it. The Controller, Admiral 'Jackie' Fisher held talks with the heads of two firms that specialised in torpedo-boat construction, John Isaac Thornycroft and Alfred Fernandez Yarrow, in March 1892. Events moved swiftly after they decided that an enlarged vessel with higher speed and capable of the operating with the fleet to overwhelm enemy torpedo-boats was technically feasible. In true Fisher style the new vessels were to be called torpedo-boat destroyers, often abbreviated to TBDs. The first prototypes were HM Ships *Havock* and *Hornet* from Yarrow and *Daring* and *Decoy* from Thornycroft. They had coal-fired boilers, reciprocating machinery and were capable of

26 knots. Displacement was about 200 tons and armament comprised a single 12-pdr gun, a single 6-pdr aft and an 18-inch torpedo tube in the bow.

The immediate success of these ships led to rapid technological progress and large orders. They proved to be excellent sea-boats and the first turbine-powered TBDs, *Viper* and *Cobra* were ordered in 1899. Displacement doubled to 400 tons but speed increased to 35 knots. In a decade the destroyer rendered the torpedo-boat obsolete and took over all its functions. The first TBDs were given traditional Royal Navy small ship names and as they began to be built in distinct classes, names were allocated with a class theme, the first being the River class. Many of these names were new to the Service but were subsequently used by frigates in the Second World War. The last river class in the Royal Navy were fleet minesweepers completed in

the mid-1980s but, to this day, several Commonwealth navies keep what has become a tradition alive by naming escort vessels after rivers. Next were the Tribal class and then a resumption of small-ship names with an aggressive feel such as *Shark, Ardent, Contest* and *Spitfire*.

In 1913 the First Lord of the Admiralty, Winston Churchill, set up a committee under Captain H Lynes RN to look into the policy of naming destroyers and make recommendations. It proposed that all TBD classes should be classified by naming the ships in them with the same first letter and recommended that all existing ships should be renamed into classes starting with the letters 'A' to 'K' omitting 'J' which was felt to have insufficient potential. The Admiralty Board thought that wholesale renaming would cause confusion but did accept the concept, starting with a new 'L' class. Oil-fired boilers were introduced in 1910 and geared turbines allowed an increase in speed to 36 knots. During the First World War Britain built 240 destroyers, culminating with the magnificent 'V and W' classes which were arguably the world's best design at the time and which set the standard in the Royal Navy for the next two decades. The name torpedoboat destroyer was dropped from the Navy List in

1924 and from then these vessels have been known, simply, as destroyers.

At the end of the First World War the Royal Navy had 370 destroyers; this number was reduced to about 180 in 1934 by scrapping the older vessels as the fleet returned to a peace-time size. No new destroyers were ordered until the 1924/25 programme when the experimental *Amazon* and *Ambuscade* were ordered. These followed the layout of the 'V and W' group with four 4.7-inch guns in single mountings, two triple 21-inch torpedo mountings on a displacement of 1,200 tons and a top speed of 36 knots but incorporated all the lessons of wartime experience. Destroyer production in numbers started again after their completion with a new 'A' class of eight ships plus a slightly enlarged leader armed with a fifth 4.7-inch gun amidships. Further classes followed at yearly intervals but the 'C' class of 1931 was limited to a leader and only four other ships as an economy measure and all of these were transferred to the Royal Canadian Navy and renamed after Canadian rivers. In all sixty-eight vessels of the basically similar 'A', 'B' and 'D' to 'I' classes were in service with the Royal Navy by 1938 together with a number of older types. These ships were fast, reliable, good

HMS Vancouver *was a unit of the very successful 'V and W' class; launched in 1917 by Beardmore of Dalmuir she was re-named* Vimy *in 1928. She sank 2 U-boats in World War 2 and was finally broken up at Charlestown in 1948.*
(Australian Seapower Centre)

HMS Boadicea was a 'B' class destroyer built by Hawthorn Leslie on the Tyne and launched in 1930. She was torpedoes and sunk by German aircraft 12 miles south-west of Portland Bill on 13 June 1944 with only 12 survivors.
(David John Weller)

sea-boats and excellent platforms for using the destroyer's principle weapon, the torpedo; they were, however, small and had little margin for growth. They did not seem to compare well with larger fleet destroyers under construction for the German, Japanese, Italian or American navies which had heavy gun armaments as well as torpedoes.

To counter the threat the Admiralty produced new designs, the first of which was the 'Tribal' class of sixteen ships which broke the cycle of alphabetical class names. Heavier, at 1,850 tons, these ships had

One the Tribal class destroyers fitted as a leader. Cossack was built at Vickers Armstrong's Walker Yard on the Tyne and launched in 1937. She saw extensive service in the early years of World war 2 but was torpedoed by U-563 west of Portugal while escorting convoy HG 75 on 23 October 1941. Despite efforts to save her she foundered and sank on 27 October.
(T. Ferrers-Walker Collection)

Built as the 'M' class Marksman *and launched in 1941, she was renamed* Mahratta *in 1942 prior to completion. On 25 October 1944 when 280 miles west of the North Cape in the Barents Sea she was hit by a homing torpedo from U-956 and sank with only 16 survivors.* (Syd Goodman Collection)

a gun armament of four twin 4.7-inch mountings but only a single quadruple 21-inch torpedo mounting and were intended to support other destroyers with gunfire in a surface action. They gave good service but the lack of torpedo armament led to criticism and they were followed by slightly smaller fleet destroyers of the 'J', 'K' and 'N' classes with three twin 4.7-inch mountings and two quintuple torpedo mountings. The 'L' and 'M' classes were similar but replaced the open mountings with three fully-enclosed twin, power-operated 4.7-inch turrets which allowed the guns 50 degrees elevation. These were complicated and expensive to make and four 'L's were completed with four twin 4-inch mountings instead. The 'J' to 'N' classes were

designed with two, rather then three, boilers which allowed a shorter hull and a single funnel, the latter becoming a feature of British wartime destroyer construction. A weakness of all British destroyers in 1939 was an inadequate anti-aircraft armament. The standard 4.7-inch gun could only be elevated to 40 degrees and the lighter 2-pdr pom-poms and machine guns were useless against dive-bombers.

In the period of re-armament in the late 1930s, these large fleet destroyers were considered too complicated and expensive to build in larger numbers and the austere 'Hunt' class of about 1,000 tons and a speed of only 27 knots were ordered for escort work; over eighty of these were eventually built. In 1938 the Admiralty decided, however, that it need-

ed an 'intermediate' destroyer that could be built quickly in the largest possible number of shipyards but which would be capable of the full spectrum of destroyer duties.

Sketches were ready by December 1938 showing alternatives of two twin 4.7-inch mountings and four singles with two quadruple torpedo mountings and both multiple and single pom-poms. The latter, similar to the outfit of the 'A' to 'I' groups was selected as it was simple and easier to mass-produce. The machinery was to be the same as that in the 'J' class but fitted into a hull only 345 feet long. The design was approved in May 1939 but it was decided that the term 'intermediate' was ambiguous and the new destroyers were instead referred to as the Emergency Flotillas; the first was ordered on 3 September 1939 and comprised eight ships of the 'O' class. The similar 'P' class was ordered in October. Both had a new hull design which required new drawings and production tools so after the 'P's had been ordered, the Admiralty recast the

specification to use the hull of the 'J' class retaining the same machinery and armament. At 358 feet 3 inches, the hull was larger than the 'O's and 'P's and thus allowed a greater margin for the addition of radar, heavier anti-aircraft guns and other likely wartime additions. Work at the Admiralty Experimental Works at Haslar led to one hull change; a deeper squared-off transom was substituted for the original 'J' class design which gave a slight increase in speed and endurance at deep load. Since the new destroyers were to carry two single mountings forward rather than the two twins of the original 'J' design, the space originally occupied by B magazine was modified to provide extra fuel stowage, increasing the total from 484 tons to 615 tons, increasing the endurance by 1,000 nautical miles. The third and fourth Emergency Flotillas, the 'Q' and 'R' classes, ordered in April 1940, were built to this specification. More were to follow.

The ships which incorporated wartime experience and rectified the inadequate anti-aircraft armament

An earlier example of the wartime emergency destroyers than the 'C' classes, Troubridge *was the leader of the 6th Emergency Flotilla or 'T' class. She was built by John Brown of Clydebank and launched in 1942, sank a U-boat in 1944 and survived to be converted into a frigate in 1955 before being broken up at Newport in 1970.*

(Syd Goodman Collection)

broke from the alphabetical sequence like the 'Tribals' before them. They were named after battles and had two twin dual-purpose 4.5-inch gun turrets forward and a heavy battery of 40 mm Bofors guns in twin mountings aft. They had two torpedo mountings and a speed of 36 knots but traditionalists were shocked that they displaced over 2,500 tons. They were built in two batches ordered in 1942 and 1943. A third batch ordered in 1944 evolved into the post-war 'Daring' class with 'D' names and a smaller, specialist anti-submarine destroyer design, the 'Weapon' class saw limited production. Another lightweight class with names beginning with the letter 'G' was designed but cancelled before any were built in 1945. The Emergency Flotillas remained in production and underwent several changes in weapon and equipment fit in the light of war experience. This added a new version of the single 4.7-inch mounting which allowed 55 degrees of elevation, improved ammunition supply arrangements and a new bow, based on that of the 'Tribal' class, which produced less spray in rough seas but increased overall length to 362 feet 9 inches. The fifth Emergency Flotilla, the 'S' class was ordered in January 1941 followed by the 'T' class in March. The seventh to tenth Emergency Flotillas, 'U', 'V', 'W' and 'Z' classes ordered between June 1941 and February 1942 were effectively repeats of the 'S' class except that the 'Z' class introduced a new single 4.5-inch gun instead of the earlier 4.7 inch. This change standardised the 4.5-inch Mark IV gun in each of the Mark IV turrets in the 'Battles', the Mark V mountings in the 'Z's and the Mark VI turrets of the 'Darings'. It fired a heavier shell than the earlier 4.7-inch at 55lb instead of 50lb. The 'Z' class also featured the lattice mast introduced on the 'T' class

and a new combined high angle/low angle director capable of directing both surface and anti-aircraft fire designated the Mark 1 Type K. Earlier classes had two separate directors one for each function. A new, more advanced Mark VI director, designed originally for the secondary armaments of battleships and cruisers was in production and was specified for the 'Battle' class but could not be available for the tenth or eleventh Emergency Flotillas.

As the end of the alphabet was reached with the 'Z' class, subsequent Emergency Flotillas posed an obvious problem of nomenclature. Many of the 'A' to 'I' class ships were still in commission so starting again at 'A' would cause confusion. At first traditional destroyer names were allocated for the eleventh Flotilla until it was realised that a new 'C' class not only presented a number of adequate names but filled the gap left when the original 'C's were renamed when they became part of the Royal Canadian Navy. The variety of 'C' names was sufficient to consider different groups and it was decided to build a repeat 'Z' class with 'Ca' names as the eleventh Emergency Flotilla, followed by a twelfth with 'Ch' names, a thirteenth with 'Co' names and a fourteenth with 'Cr' names. The Chiefs of staff were making contingency plans for the war against Japan to last into 1947 and a fifteenth Emergency Flotilla with 'Ce' names was being considered in early 1945 but contracts were placed for 'Weapon' class ships instead. In all 96 Emergency destroyers were completed to the same basic design. Today they would be considered as ships of the same class built in successive batches. This book covers the last 32 ships, built as the eleventh, twelfth, thirteenth and fourteenth Emergency Flotillas, known collectively as the 'C' class.

DESIGN AND WEAPONS SYSTEMS

HMS. CAESAR (EX. RANGER) JOB Nº J 1809.
BUILT BY JOHN BROWN & CO. L.T.D. CLYDEBANK
ORDERED — 16/2/42
LAID DOWN — 3/4/43
LAUNCHED — 14/2/44
COMPLETED — 5/10/44.
SCRAPPED — 6/1/67.

DRAWN BY JOHN LAMBERT

'C' Group Design

All 'Emergency Flotilla' destroyers from the 'Q' class onwards had the same basic hull as the 'J' class. It was modified from the 'S' class onwards with a 'Tribal'-type bow and a transom stern. The former was introduced to keep the forecastle drier in rough sea conditions and the latter reduced hull resistance by 3%, effectively increasing the radius of action by 70 miles for the same amount of fuel. A deeper 'V'-type bilge keel was also adopted. Machinery comprised two Admiralty three-drum boilers installed back-to-back with their exhaust trunking leading up into the single funnel. Both boilers worked at up to 300 pounds per square inch pressure at 630 degrees Fahrenheit and delivered steam to two sets of Parsons single-reduction turbines developing a total of 40,000 shp which drove two shafts at up to 350 revolutions per minute. Maximum speed in the deep, fully loaded condition was 32 knots. Fuel capacity was increased from the 'Q' class onwards to 615 tons of furnace fuel oil (FFO) and this remained standard throughout the 'C' class giving an endurance of 4,680 nautical miles at 20 knots.

Incremental improvements in electrical power generation had led to the definitive specification for the 'Z' class which was repeated by the 'C' classes. These included two 155 kilowatt steam generators and three 50 kilowatt diesel generators. The latter were described in the staff requirement for this class as "giving sufficient power to fight the main armament when the boilers were out of action". Damage control arrangements included a 40 ton steam pump and two 20 ton electric pumps to cope with flooding. Early warship losses had indicated the necessity to provide alternative power sources for vital equipment such as pumps and fans. Ships also carried two portable 70 ton pumps which could be moved, with difficulty, to where they were needed most. Other changes found to be necessary and implemented on the 'C' class were the lowering of

cable runs and both the lowering and duplication of telemotor (hydraulic) pipes to the steering gear aft from the primary steering position under the bridge.

The 'C' group had common hull dimensions with an overall length of 362 feet 9 inches; a beam of 35 feet 8 inches and maximum draught of 14 feet 3¼ inches. Displacement of the 'Ca' class on completion was 2,530 tons. Stanchions were provided to allow fuel hoses from tankers or larger warships to be connected to an attachment point on the upper deck, allowing ships to refuel at sea. Replenishment at Sea (RAS) had helped escort vessels to extend their radius of action during the Battle of the Atlantic and by 1945 long-range, refuelled operations that lasted for weeks were common with food and ammunition being transferred at sea in addition to furnace fuel oil (FFO). Orders for the 'Ca' class were placed on 16 February 1942, only four days after the preceding 'Z' class were ordered and in April 1944 *Caprice* was the first ship of either class to be completed.

In the earlier destroyers of the Emergency Programme, the scheme of complement had been 179 officers and ratings but increases in close-range armament, radar, auxiliary machinery and the need for an action-information organisation led to this

HMS Cassandra *refuelling at sea from the aircraft carrier* Victorious. *The fuel hose is suspended from the carrier's starboard crane in bights, or loops, which evened out tension as the two ships rolled and moved.*

(Syd Goodman Collection)

figure being increased to 215, excluding canteen staff. Leaders had to cope with up to 237 and by 1945 accommodation could only be described as 'poor' with men sleeping on top of lockers in passageways and a minimal flow of air from fan trunking.

The Staff Requirement called for the ships to carry dry provisions and canteen stores for 90 days; flour for 30 days' bread-making and fresh vegetables capable of lasting 21 days. Catering was on the 'Broadside Messing' principle where food was prepared in mess decks and taken to a central galley for cooking. When ready, it was taken back to the mess decks where it was 'dished out' and then eaten off folding tables, with men seated at benches on either side, much as Nelson's sailors had done on *Victory*. Most ratings slung hammocks in their messdecks but by 1945 some had to sleep wherever they could find space. Officers' accommodation was amidships where easy access to the bridge was possible, even in rough weather.

As completed the first 'C' class ships had Type 86M wireless telegraphy (W/T) receivers and were capable of transmitting and receiving voice radio telephone (R/T) on four equipments in H/F, MF or VHF frequency ranges. An emergency battery-powered transmitter/receiver was stowed in a position that was remote from the W/T office. VHF transmitters for inter-ship nets and aircraft control were crystal-controlled. Most ships were fitted with a medium-frequency direction finder forward of the bridge and a high-frequency direction finder at the top of the lattice foremast. Navigational equipment included one Admiralty gyro compass and a standby magnetic compass, a bottom log to determine speed and an echo-sounder. An Admiralty Type JYA automatic plot was fitted in the small operations room under the bridge.

Radar included Type 293 surface and air warning set for target indication; Type 291 air warning set on a small main mast just aft of the after torpedo tubes; Type 285 on the director control tower and Type 282 on the Mark IV 'Hazemeyer' twin Bofors. Sonar was known as 'Asdic' in the Royal Navy

during and for a short while after World War II. The first ships were completed with Types 144 and 147.

The 'C' Class Weapons Systems

The Emergency Flotillas were designed to fulfil all the classic functions of British destroyers including attack on enemy surface ships with torpedoes at high speed and the defence of a task force against surface ships, aircraft and submarines. Less capable vessels such as corvettes, frigates, sloops and escort destroyers were capable of only part of this spectrum of capability.

The primary anti-ship weapon was the Mark 9 Torpedo. This was first deployed in 1930 and by 1945 had been developed into the Mark 9** version. The 'Ca' class carried two quadruple sets of torpedo tubes on the iron deck aft of the funnel. The Mark 9** was 21 inches in diameter, 23 feet 10½ inches long and weighed 3,731lb. They were aimed by visual sights, one on each wing of the bridge and the tubes could be rotated either electrically on command from the bridge or mechanically from the mounting itself. 'Aim-off' to compensate for the relative speed and course of the target ship was calculated by the Torpedo Officer using the appropriate sight. Torpedoes could be fired singly or in groups up to the full eight. They could be fired on a parallel track with the distance between torpedoes set by the speed of the firing destroyer through the water or, if the firing ship put on wheel they could open out in a 'fan' from the point of firing. Both methods had their points of merit and demerit. Parallel tracks might be best against a single ship at close range; the 'fan' might be best against a group of targets but the distance between torpedoes would increase with range, lessening the chance of hitting a single target. The classic destroyer attack involved a number of destroyers in formation attacking a ship together putting a number of weapons into the water and thus increasing the chance of hits, especially when they were launched from different angles to compound the target's problems in evading them. The last such action,

and arguably one of the most successful, was the sinking of the Japanese heavy cruiser *Haguro* 45 miles south-west of Penang by *Saumarez, Venus, Vigilant, Virago*, and *Verulam* of the 5th and 8th Emergency Flotillas. Torpedoes were always fired in a specific order with the aftermost tube fired first to avoid collisions or turbulence in the water caused by them running too close together.

The torpedoes were fired by an impulse charge cartridge fitted into a breech at the rear of the tube detonated electrically which discharged the weapon into the water at least ten feet clear of the ship. Each torpedo could be set with a specific running depth which might be varied when the target was identified as a small or large ship with a shallow or deep draught. The warhead was detonated by either contact or magnetic 'pistols' set before launch, the advantage of the latter being that the torpedo could be set to run under the target, detonating at the high-point of the magnetic signature under the keel where it would break the ship's back. The contact pistol was simpler and less prone to malfunction but had to hit the target to detonate the warhead.

The Mark 9** was a true 'ship-killing' weapon with a warhead comprising 805lb of 'Torpex', an explosive designed specifically for torpedoes. They could be set to run at 35 knots out to 14,000 yards or 41 knots out to 11,000 yards. Before weapons were launched the various settings would be ordered by the torpedo officer once the captain's attack plan was clear. The Mark 9** was powered by a radial diesel engine and contained a supply of the 'shale-oil' fuel and air. The engine relied on sea water to prevent it over-heating as it ran and developed 264 horse-power at 41 knots. Like all other British torpedoes it had two contra-rotating propellers to provide thrust (a single propeller would rotate the torpedo rather than move it forward; every reaction produces an equal and opposite reaction).

The most flexible weapons were the four medium guns in single mountings. These were 4.5 inch/ 45 calibre Mark IV guns in Mark 5 mountings, two forward and two aft designated 'A', 'B', 'X', and

'Y' mountings with 'B' and 'X' in super-firing positions. The Mark 5 mounting was a modification of the earlier CP Mark XXII fitted to the 'S' class onwards with 4.7 inch guns. The 4.5 inch gun was introduced in the 'Z' class and the 'C' classes to standardise ammunition with the same guns mounted in the Mark 4 and Mark 6 turrets of the 'Battle' and 'Daring' classes. It fired a heavier shell than the 4.7 inch and the shell and cartridge were separate making rapid reloading easier for the guns' crews, allowing them to keep up a high rate of fire. Earlier experience with heavy fixed ammunition showed that the crews rapidly became exhausted and the rate of fire dropped in long engagements. The Mark 5 mounting was capable of engaging both surface and air targets but with only 55 degrees elevation its use against aircraft was limited. This elevation was achieved by angling the rear of the loading tray to lie flush with the deck at maximum elevation and providing power ramming to help the loaders. The gun could be depressed to minus 5 degrees if necessary. The complete mounting weighed 33,562lb and its working circle was 188 inches. 'X' mounting could be trained through 360 degrees; the others were limited to some extent by superstructure.

The gun itself weighed 6,179lb and had rifling which twisted to the right. Nominal barrel life was 650 rounds. A number of shells were provided including practice, star-shell, semi armour-piercing (SAP) and high effect (HE). The last named were provided in the largest numbers. HE shells weighed 55lb and the separate brass cartridge cases 38½lb, of which 11lb was cordite propellant. The muzzle velocity of a new gun was 2,460 feet per second and that of a worn gun averaged 2,350 feet per second. Maximum range against a surface target was 20,750 yards and the theoretical ceiling in anti-aircraft fire at maximum elevation was 29,910 feet. Normal ammunition load was 400 SAP shells, 600 HE shells, 100 star-shell, 120 practice shells and 1,000 cartridges. In 1945 25% of the HE shells would have been fitted with variable-time (VT) fuses for anti-aircraft use; this percentage increased in the

HMS Cambrian *seen from astern showing the layout of depth-charge rails and throwers aft. The pale canisters either side of the rails are smoke canisters capable of forming a screen at short notice. As usual at sea, 'X' mounting is trained forward to limit the amount of salt spray on the gun breech and control instruments. 'Y' mounting was protected to some extent by the superstructure forward of it.* (Crown Copyright/MoD)

post-war years as greater numbers became available. Nominal rate of fire was 14 rounds per minute with the minimum time needed to load, fire, recoil and reload being 4.3 seconds. The 'Ca' class mountings were trained and elevated by hand following pointers which displayed information from the gun direction system. The 'Ch', 'Co' and 'Cr' classes had power-operated mountings using electric training and elevation metadyne remote power control (RPC) which allowed them to train and elevate to commands from the gun direction system at up to 20 degrees per second. RPC added topweight, however, and to compensate these three classes were completed with only one set of quadruple torpedo-tubes in the after position. To differentiate them from the earlier, hand-operated mountings, those in the last three classes were designated the RP50 Mark 5. When the 'Ca' class was modernised in the 1950s, RPC was added and their mountings were then designated Mark 5* Mod 1 with RPC. As alterations were made to all the 'C' group ships the number of mountings was reduced from the original four. Most had three, some two

and ships used for training had one or none. RPC mountings could be power-trained and elevated in local control by the captain of the mounting using a hand control 'joystick'.

Heart of the medium gunnery system was the Transmitting Station or TS which took information from the director and used an early form of analogue computer to derive firing data for the guns that would hit a moving target at the end of the shells' time of flight. For surface engagements a device known as the Admiralty Fire Control Clock or AFCC was used. A separate calculator was used to engage aircraft. The TS took visual or radar contacts and fed bearing, range and elevation to the director and guns. Radar Type 291 mounted on a short mainmast was fitted in the 'Ca' class and was used to detect aircraft out to an effective range of 35 miles but the primary target indication radar for the whole 'C' group was Type 293 with its distinctive 'half-cheese' aerial mounted on the foremast. It operated in 'S' Band with a peak power of 500 kilowatts and a pulse-repetition frequency (PRF) of 500 pulses per second. The scan rate could be set at 5,

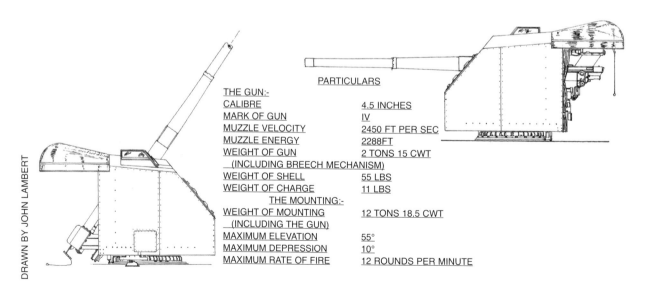

DRAWN BY JOHN LAMBERT

PARTICULARS

THE GUN:-	
CALIBRE	4.5 INCHES
MARK OF GUN	IV
MUZZLE VELOCITY	2450 FT PER SEC
MUZZLE ENERGY	2288FT
WEIGHT OF GUN	2 TONS 15 CWT
(INCLUDING BREECH MECHANISM)	
WEIGHT OF SHELL	55 LBS
WEIGHT OF CHARGE	11 LBS
THE MOUNTING:-	
WEIGHT OF MOUNTING	12 TONS 18.5 CWT
(INCLUDING THE GUN)	
MAXIMUM ELEVATION	55°
MAXIMUM DEPRESSION	10°
MAXIMUM RATE OF FIRE	12 ROUNDS PER MINUTE

PROVISION WAS MADE ON EACH SIDE OF THE GUNSHIELD FOR FIRING THREE 2-INCH ROCKET FLARES (NOT DRAWN)
SAFETY FIRING GEAR PREVENTED ROCKET DISCHARGE ON DANGEROUS BEARINGS.

10 or 15 revolutions per minute. As the speed of combat aircraft increased with the introduction of turbojet engines, 293 became less effective as its scan rate was too slow to track contacts moving at over 400 knots.

The supply of directors could not keep paced with demand and the 'Ca' class followed the 'Z' class in being fitted with the K Director Mark 1, known as the 'K' Tower. Earlier classes had two separate directors, one for surface and one for anti-aircraft fire and at least the 'K' Tower was an improvement since it combined both functions into a single unit. Some ships sailed without the director at first because supplies were not ready in time. The 'K' Tower contained separate gyro-stabilised surface and anti-aircraft visual sights. In the first ships it was hand-trained with the operators following pointers from the TS which laid them onto the target. By 1945 they were all modified to introduce power training so that the director could be slewed quickly onto GDS targets. The 'K' Tower was fitted with radar Type 285 M or P which used beam-switching to lock onto a surface contact when it was acquired. There was no beam-switching in elevation so although aircraft could be acquired, the director could not lock onto them and anti-aircraft fire was controlled by the layer using his visual sight.

The 'K' Tower was an adequate compromise in the short term but the Admiralty specified the Director Mark 6 to be fitted to the majority of warships as soon as supplies became available. It was designed to control the secondary armaments of battleships and cruisers and was numbered in the range of equipments for that use; hence the 'jump' from 'K' Mark 1 to Mark 6. Priority for Mark 6 deliveries was given to big ships and the 'Battle' class but the 'Ch', 'Co' and 'Cr' classes were fitted with them on completion after the war and the 'Ca' class was modernised with the improved Mark 6M.

The Mark 6 was extensively glazed to allow visual laying and training but was fitted with Radar Type 275. This comprised two dishes, each 4 feet in diameter and it operated in 'S' Band with a peak

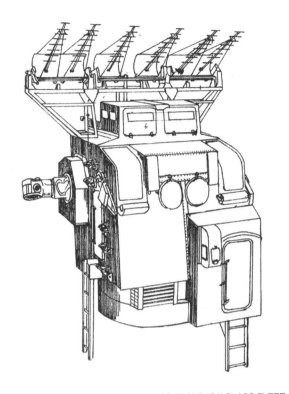

DRAWN BY JOHN LAMBERT

'K' TYPE DIRECTOR - FITTED ONLY TO 'Z' AND 'CA' CLASS FLEET DESTROYERS

power of 400 kilowatts and a PRF of 500 pulses per second. It used conical scanning to lock onto both surface and air targets and inputs to the TS used measurements in bearing and elevation to predict the aim of the guns, a system known as Goniometry. The director included a visual range-finder as a back-up but radar-ranging was sufficiently accurate that it was seldom used. The Mark 6 could detect a fighter sized target out to 35,000 yards and lock onto it inside 30,000 yards. The whole director trained to provide bearing information; the radar dishes rotated up to a maximum of 80 degrees to provide elevation information.

The modernised 'Ca' class was fitted with the improved Mark 6M director with less glazing and a distinctive Perspex dome on top for the director officer. It was installed with the Flyplane 5 fire-control system which departed from previous

British practice in measuring rates of target motion, a process known as Tachymetry, which gave more effective control in anti-aircraft fire. All up weight was 3 tons less than the Mark 6, at 8 tons of which the rotating mass weighed 5 tons. The guns used remote power control to follow the target and the director could indicate either visual or radar blind-fire information through the TS. Flyplane 5 could handle surface targets at up to 70 knots out to the maximum range of the guns; in anti-aircraft fire it could accept targets inside range limits of 500 out to 15,000 yards and a shell time of flight of up to 30 seconds against target speeds up to 700 knots. The director could track targets in bearing and elevation at rates up to 10 degrees per second and, if necessary, could be slewed onto a target at rates up to 45 degrees per second.

Close range armament varied in the 'Ca' class on completion but was standardised in modernisation and in the three follow-on classes. The majority had a twin 40mm Bofors power-operated mounting on top of the superstructure between the two sets of torpedo tubes. In the early ships this was a Mark 4 'Hazemeyer' unit fitted with Type 282 radar capable of ranging or locking onto a target. This was replaced in all ships by the Mark 5 controlled by a Simple-Type Director; the mounting could also be fired in local control by a trainer with a 'joystick' control. Whereas the Mark 4 was complicated and unreliable, the Mark 5 was robust, reliable and fitted widely throughout the Royal Navy in the post-war years. It fired fixed ammunition loaded into a gravity-fed slide on top of the breech mechanism in clips of four and was capable of firing 120 rounds per minute per barrel. Muzzle velocity was a nominal 2,890 feet per second and shell weight was 1.97 lbs fitted with a proximity fuse. Proximity fuses were usually set to detonate at 3,500 yards if they had not hit anything or been detonated before then but maximum effective range of the shell was 10,750 yards. The mounting could be trained at up to 35 degrees per second and elevated at up to 28 degrees per second. It could rotate through 360 degrees with maximum elevation 90 degrees and a

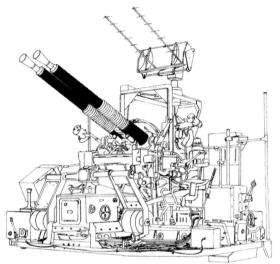

TWIN 40mm BOFORS MARK IV [HAZEMEYER] MOUNTING 1944 GENRAL ARRANGEMENT
THE MARK IV MOUNTING WAS FIRST CARRIED ABOARD THE DESTROYERS OF THE 5TH EMERGENCY FLOTILLA OR 'S' CLASS WHICH COMPLETED IN THE LATTER HALF OF 1943. THEY WERE CARRIED ON THE CENTRELINE & WERE FITTED TO THE LATER FLEET DESTROYER CLASSES

DRAWN BY JOHN LAMBERT

possible depression down to 15 degrees. The weight of the mounting was 6.397 tons. Two sailors stood next to the breeches to act as loading numbers, taking clips from 12 trays (48 rounds) on the mounting and transferring them to the gravity feed which could hold two clips at a time to maintain the rate of fire.

All 'C' class destroyers carried single 40mm Bofors guns in single Mark 7 mountings at some stage, usually on the signal deck by the bridge. This was hydraulically powered, derived from a wartime twin 20mm Oerlikon mounting fitted in some of the 'Ca' class on build. The Mark 7 was hydraulically powered and was fitted with the same type of gun as the Mark 5. It was laid and trained by a single 'aimer' with a gyro-gunsight and 'joystick'. The loader had access to six trays of ammunition with a clip of four in each. As in the Mark 5, ammunition numbers outside the mounting refilled

the trays as the loading number emptied them. The mounting weighed 3 tons. The Mark 9 mounting was very similar but electrically powered. On completion the 'Ca' class had magazine capacity for 1,400 Bofors rounds per gun.

Ships completed during the war were fitted with single 20mm Oerlikon Mark 4 mountings. This was a blow-back operated cannon aimed and fired by a single operator using a simple 'eye-shooting' sight. Shell weight was 0.44lb and rate of fire was 450 rounds per minute. Muzzle velocity was 2,730 feet per second and maximum range was 4,500 yards at 35 degrees elevation. The maximum effective range against an aircraft was about 2,000 yards but the small rounds were incapable of breaking up a kamikaze attack and, from 1945, the Royal Navy replaced the Oerlikon with Bofors guns in the majority of its ships. The mounting weighed only 970lb and ammunition feed was from a pre-loaded 80 round drum magazine, several of which were kept in ready-use lockers near the gun. The 20mm enjoyed something of a revival during the Confrontation against Indonesia in the 1960s when a number were fitted to warships to provide them with the ability to engage hostile small craft quick-

ly at close range. Magazine space for 2,400 Oerlikon rounds per gun was provided initially, later modified to accept Bofors ammunition.

The third major role of the 'C' group destroyers was the anti-submarine protection of a task force. All ships were built with sonar, known at the time in Britain and the Commonwealth as Asdic after the World War 1 Anti-Submarine Detection/Indication Committee that had sponsored its original development. They carried a large outfit of depth charges. The original sonar was Type 144 which operated between 14 and 22 Kilohertz; ships in company selected different frequencies to avoid mutual interference. The set had a search capability out to 3,000 yards and when contact was gained an attack setting gave more accurate ranges and bearings out to 1,500 yards. Contact 'paints' showed on a paper trace and by aligning a line of light along them range and bearing rates could be calculated. The main beam was 10 degrees wide and 10 degrees high. A separate 'Q' beam 3 degrees wide extended down from the sonar hull outfit at an angle of 60 degrees and was used to determine the target depth as it passed through the beam. Depths between 300 and 700 feet could be measured and the information

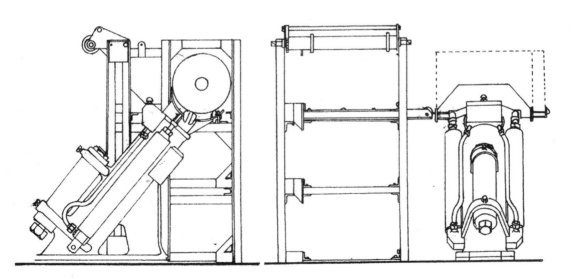

DC EQUIPMENT - MARK 1 STOWAGE RACK FOR THROWER MARK IV

DRAWN BY JOHN LAMBERT

was fed to the depth charge crews aft who set it on the pattern to be fired.

'Ca' class ships were designed to drop ten-charge patterns of Mark 7 depth charges as they passed over an enemy submarine; a technique that had the inherent drawback that sonar contact was lost underneath the destroyer and had to be regained after each attack. Depth charges were fired clear of the ship on the beam by Depth Charge Throwers Mark IV or rolled through a gate from rails near the stern. The former used a piston extended by an explosive charge to throw the depth charge about 60 yards clear of the ship. Earlier models had wastefully fired the Piston with the charge but in the Mark IV it stayed in the thrower, saving stowage space and weight. Both throwers and rails released Mark VII depth charges.

The Mark VII depth charge embodied considerable wartime experience and was the last anti-submarine weapon to be dropped, rather than fired by ahead-throwing weapons which allowed sonar contact to be maintained. It weighed 450lb with a charge of 290lb of Amatol, later changed to Minol. A different version with TNT filling was used in hot climates. A heavy version was produced by the simple expedient of adding a 150lb weight to make the depth charge sink more rapidly. The standard Mark VII sank at 7 feet per second, increasing to 9.9 feet per second at 250 feet. Lethal distance from the point of detonation was about 26 feet, depending on depth, for a Minol-filled charge with damage caused at about double that distance. The 'heavy' sank at 26 feet per second.

The standard wartime attack used the 'Ten Pattern' comprising two diamonds, 50 feet apart vertically, each diamond consisting of charges in each corner 60 yards apart and one in the middle. Any submarine caught within the volume of detonation or just outside would be destroyed. It was achieved using two rails and four throwers. The sequence to achieve it involved dropping a heavy charge from a rail first. Three seconds later two heavies were fired from the forward throwers and a light dropped from a rail. After a further 8 seconds

two light charges were fired from the after throwers and a heavy dropped from the rails and then the remainder as light charges from the rails. The 'Ch', 'Co' and 'Cr' had greater top weight because of the Mark 6 directors and remote power control for the 4.5 inch guns so the number of depth charges they could carry was reduced to 48 and they were limited to 'Five Patterns' with only one diamond. The system was incapable of engaging the type of fast submarine entering German service in 1945 and had already been outclassed by the ahead-throwing weapons fitted in frigates.

When ships were modernised with forward-firing anti-submarine mortars, Type 144 sonar was replaced by an improved version, the Type 164, capable of searching over similar ranges. The 'Q' beam was replaced by a separate sonar, the Type 147 which transmitted a fan-shaped beam 3 degrees deep in the vertical plane and 65 degrees wide in the horizontal plane transmitted from a 'sword-shaped' scanner fitted forward of the main sonar dome. This was capable of picking up contacts at about 800 yards and measuring their depth accurately. This information was fed automatically to the mortars and set on the projectiles shortly before they were fired. These developments in sonar and weapon technology meant that a ship could stand off, continuing to hold contact while engaging a target with ahead-throwing weapons set to detonate in a pattern at the target's depth, a vast improvement over the previous method.

The weapon associated with these improved sonars was the Mortar Mark 6 'Squid', first introduced in the Castle and Loch classes with conspicuous success in the last year of World War 2. It was three-barrelled and used cordite charges fitted into breeches at the base of each barrel to fire bomb-shaped charges ahead of the ship. Bombs were slid out of a hatch from the bomb-room onto a trolley on rails which carried them one at a time to the mounting which was rotated to the horizontal so that they could be rammed home. Two 'Squids' were mounted on top of the 'C' groups' after superstructure in place of 'X' 4.5 inch gun mounting in modernised

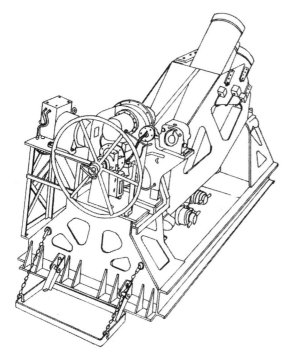

DRAWN BY JOHN LAMBERT

SQUID MARK IV ANTI-SUBMARINE MORTAR

270 yards from the mounting when it was mounted 9 feet above water level. For each additional foot that the mounting was fitted above the waterline, the range increased by one yard. The firing interval between barrels was 0.28 seconds. Normally the depth of detonation was set by the Type 147 sonar, but a shallow setting of 20 feet could be selected to engage radar or visual contacts of a 'snort' mast or periscope with a snap attack.

Some 'C' class destroyers were modified to act as minelayers. This involved the removal of the torpedo tubes and 'Y' 4.5 inch mounting and the fitting of rails on either side of the iron deck aft leading to chutes on either side of the transom stern from which the mines dropped into the sea. Twenty-five mines could be carried on each of the two rails. The conversion gave these ships a useful role, using their high speed to dash into enemy-held waters at night, lay their mines and withdraw before dawn. Typical mines were the Mark 17 buoyant type, of which the RN had 1,972 in storage in 1949. They could be laid in up to 1,000 fathoms and comprised 40 inch hemispheres welded to a central section 13.5 inches long. Mark 17s underwent several modifications and had explosive charges of between 320lb and 500lb of Amatol. They could be fitted with magnetic or contact detonators, the latter comprising the well tried and trusted 'Herz Horns' which sent an electric charge into the primer when it was 'broken' by impact.

When the 'Ca' class was modernised, the later ships were fitted 'for-but-not-with' the GWS 20 Seacat anti-aircraft guided missile system but only two ships, *Cavalier* and *Caprice*, were fitted taking the 'C' group into the missile age and spanning the era from the 2-pdr 'pom-pom'. The first version of Seacat to go to sea used command-guidance in which an 'Aimer' seated in a special director/sight, tracked the target through binoculars and guided the missile towards it by using a 'joystick' control by his right hand. He was able to gather the missile after launch and to track it by means of a flare at its after end. The basic GWS 20 was the first point defence missile system in the world to enter service.

ships; each had its own trolley on rails and bombs were stowed aft of the mountings in a specialised bomb-room. 'Squid' was the first anti-submarine weapon in the world to form part of a system with specialised sonars. The depth bombs were 56.5 inches long and 11.93 inches in diameter. They weighed 394lb, of which the explosive charge of Minol II weighed 207lb. They sank at 44 feet per second and each mortar's barrels were canted slightly so that the three bombs detonated in a triangle with sides of 120 feet. The two mortars were fired together producing two triangles 60 feet apart in depth, the apex of one forward and that of the other aft; the intention being to sandwich the submarine in the middle and cause lethal damage. The mortars were designed to fire dead ahead, over the bridge in the case of the 'C' classes, but the barrels could tilt up to 30 degrees from the vertical to compensate for the ship's roll and yaw. The middle barrel was angled for the bomb to splash into the water

The missile itself was a development of the 'Malkara' anti-tank missile and had a body 58.3 inches long and 7.5 inches in diameter. The wing-span was 25.6 inches and it weighed 138lb. Propulsion was a rocket booster which accelerated the missile to Mach 0.6 after which it glided towards the target, becoming more difficult to control as it slowed. Seacat's engagement envelope was a minimum of 1,500 yards, inside which it could not be controlled during the boost phase and a maximum range of 5,000 yards beyond which its speed reduced rapidly and it fell into the sea. The maximum practical height for an engagement was 3,300 feet. Missiles were stowed and handled onto the launcher in fibre-glass containers; the launcher itself had attachments for 4 Seacats and a central aerial that transmitted guidance signals. The first version of the missile was the Mod 0 which had rods weighing a total of 31lb spot welded at alternate ends wrapped around a 5lb explosive charge. As the missile passed close by the target, the fuse detonated the explosive charge which blew out the rods to form a continuous ring, like a chain-saw, which cut the target to pieces. This was a typical British warhead for the period but concerns about fusing led to the development of the Mod 1 Seacat which replaced the continuous rods with a 38lb High-Effect warhead surrounded by metal studs like a hand grenade, which relied on the close proximity of the blast and fragments to the target to destroy it.

After 1945 the 'C' class was fitted with a variety of equipments to keep them capable of fulfilling their wide range of roles. An early electronic warfare capability was provided by the FH 4 High-Frequency Direction-Finder, HF/DF, fitted to the top of the fore-mast. This gave a cathode-ray tube presentation that picked up both 'ground-wave' transmissions and those received from longer ranges that had bounced off the ionosphere, known as the 'sky-wave'. A skilled operator could refine a 'ground-wave' detection to reveal the 'wet' aerial of a submarine that had just surfaced and even the 'key-style' of an operator transmitting morse by hand. A single ship gaining FH 4 contact gave an 'intercept' bearing, two widely separated ships gave 'cross' bearings which accurately gave the position of the target.

A variety of navigational equipments was fitted including an Admiralty Gyro Compass, Decca navigator which used radio bearings in coastal waters to give an accurate position and Type 162 'Cockchafer' sonar which measured depth to the sea-bed and could be used to classify a submarine or wreck lying on the bottom. Radar Type 978 was used to give an accurate navigational picture at close range. It was used to detect other shipping and calculate its closest point of approach, CPA, and for blind pilotage in coastal waters whilst manoeuvring in reduced visibility.

The 'Ca' Class
The 11th Emergency Flotilla

The 11th Emergency Flotilla of destroyers which became the 'Ca' class was ordered on 16 February 1942. The eight ships were repeats of the 'Z' class which formed the 10th Flotilla, ordered only four days previously and *Caprice* was the first ship of either class to be completed. Originally the eight ships of the 11th Flotilla were allocated random traditional destroyer names but these were rationalised to names beginning with 'Ca' during build. The designed armament comprised:

- 4 x 4.5 inch guns Mark 4 in Mark 5 mountings with 250 rpg.
- 2 x 40mm Bofors mark 4 'Hazemeyer' in twin Mark 4 mounting with 1400 rpg.
- 6 or 8 20mm Oerlikon in twin Mark 5 and single Mark 7 mountings with 2400 rpg.
- 2 x quadruple Mark 8 torpedo tubes with 8 Mark 9** torpedoes but no reloads.
- 4 depth charge throwers; 2 rails and up to 108 depth charges

Although the Admiralty had stated its intention that, from 1944, all destroyers were to be fitted with Mark 6 directors, production of these was limited and priority was at first given to capital ships, cruisers and the 'Battle' class. The 'Ca' and 'Z' classes were, therefore designed to take the interim K Mark 1 director and even then production was inadequate to fit every ship on build. Another 'bottleneck' was the provision of close-range armament and there were several differences between ships on completion as some were fitted with what was available rather than what was intended. *Caprice*, for instance, was completed with a quadruple 2-pdr

instead of the twin Bofors; one of the last to be fitted to a new-built warship.

The hulls of all 'Ca' class destroyers were riveted in the same manner as the preceding emergency flotillas and machinery was the same, allowing mass production techniques to be used and giving the economy of scale. This standardisation made it relatively easy for sailors to be transferred between ships without the need for extensive re-training. In the immediate post-war years the 'Ca's were deployed to foreign stations because they were economical to operate, had an armament adequate for peace-keeping or constabulary tasks and ship's companies that were considerably smaller than the larger Battles and Darings.

All the 'Ca's spent a number of years in the reserve fleet and were among the first ships to be 'cocooned' by spraying polyvinyl chlorate over external fittings such as gun mountings and radar aerials to make them airtight and prevent rust. Desiccants were usually sealed inside the cocooned structures to maintain a dry atmosphere. The reserve fleet was concentrated in groups at a number of ports, not all in Dockyards, where maintenance parties provided routine maintenance such as running boilers and turning the main engines so that the ships could be brought out of reserve at short notice and re-commissioned if required. An extensive reserve fleet was maintained until 1957 because the Royal Navy's wartime requirements considerably exceeded the number of ships that could be maintained in commission in peace-time. Among the most recent of the emergency flotillas, the 'Ca's were considered worth retaining and the Admiralty decided to keep them for fleet operations as destroyers rather than make them available for

conversion to fast anti-submarine frigates under the Type 15 and 16 programmes. By 1950 their weapons were considered obsolescent for modern warfare however, and in 1951 a staff requirement for their modernisation was issued by the Admiralty.

The primary function of destroyers in the post-war RN was the escort and support of the carrier task forces that formed the core of the operational fleet. The main threats were air and submarine attack but destroyers had to be capable of contributing to surface action as well. The modernisation was extensive but retained the same well-proven hull and machinery. To save top-weight the old bridge was removed and replaced by a new aluminium structure that included a new, enlarged operations room below the bridge itself. In four ships, *Carron, Cavalier, Carysfort* and *Cavendish*, the bridge was an open structure similar to the Daring class; the other four, *Caprice, Caesar, Cassandra* and *Cambrian*, had enclosed bridges modelled on contemporary frigate designs. The old radar and sonar outfits were removed together with the K Mark 1 director and 25 tons of lead cabling. The after torpedo tubes were removed together with 'X' 4.5-inch mounting and all the close-range armament. The ships were then re-built with a modern Flyplane 5 fire-control system and a Mark 6M director with its distinctive twin antennae for the Type 275 radar and remote power control for the three remaining 4.5inch mountings. The after deck house was extended forward into the space vacated by the after tubes with a twin Mark 5 Bofors mounting fitted onto the forward part and two Mark 6 'Squid' three-barrelled anti-submarine mortars mounted aft with their associated bomb-handling arrangements. The Squid magazine at the after end of the deck house carried 60 rounds, enough for ten double salvoes.

A new lattice mast was stepped which carried Type 293Q radar for air and surface target acquisi-tion and Type 974/8 for navigation. A pole extension at the top of the mast carried UHF/DF and ESM aerials. Sonar Types 164 and 174 replaced the earlier fittings and were linked directly to the depth setting mechanism on the Squids to make an effective system. As completed after modernisation the 'Ca's armament comprised three 4.5-inch mountings, a twin Mark 5 Bofors mounting aft and single Mark 7 Bofors mountings in each of the bridge wings. Four 21-inch torpedoes with no reloads were retained in the forward mounting and there were the two Squid mountings aft. In addition to the improvements to the armament the opportunity was taken to modernise the accommodation arrangements, introducing cafeteria messing with separate sleeping messdecks fitted with bunks rather than space to sling hammocks. Accommodation remained tight, however, especially in the ships fitted as leaders.

Cavendish, Cavalier, Carysfort, Cambrian and *Caprice* were further modernised and fitted for the GWS 20 Seacat close-range guided missile system during refits between 1963 and 1966. This involved the removal of the twin Mark 5 40mm Bofors and its replacement by a deckhouse and missile handling room, on top of which the director was situated. The remaining set of torpedo tubes had to be removed to compensate for the additional top-weight. In the event only *Cavalier* and *Caprice* were actually fitted with Seacat launchers, the remaining three carried a single Mark 7 40mm Bofors in place of the launcher which was intended as a temporary measure but they were withdrawn from service before the full system was installed.

The Royal Navy underwent a period of contraction after the 1966 Defence review and the end of Confrontation against Indonesia. This led to several 'Ca's being withdrawn from service earlier than intended; their departure being viewed by many as the end of the 'classic' destroyer type in service with the RN.

'Ca' Class data as built:

Displacement:	1,781 tons light 2,510 tons full load
Dimensions:	Length 362 feet 9 inches Beam 35 feet 8 inches Draught 12 feet 6 inches forward, 15 feet 11 inches aft
Gun Armament:	4 x 4.5-inch QF Mark 5; Twin 40mm Bofors Mark 4; 4 x 20mm Mark 5; 2 x 20mm Mark 7 (Variations in close-range weapons between individual ships).
Torpedo Armament:	8 x 21-inch in 2quadruple mountings 4 x Mark 9** torpedoes in each with no re-loads.
A/S Weapons:	4 depth-charge throwers; 2 depth-charge rails at stern up to 108 depth-charges carried.
Machinery:	Two shaft Parsons single-reduction turbines Two Admiralty three-drum boilers 40,000 shp giving up to 34 knots
Complement:	186 (wartime maximum 225 in a leader)
Oil fuel:	588 tons FFO plus 27 tons diesel
Endurance:	1,450 miles @ 31 knots 3,900 miles @ 20 knots 5,500 miles @ 15 knots

Variations after modernisation:

Displacement:	2,053 tons light 2,675 tons full load
Gun Armament:	3 x 4.5-inch Mark 5 with RP mountings. Twin 40mm Bofors Mark 5 (replaced by GWS 20 Seacat in some ships) 2 x Bofors Mark 7
Torpedo Armament:	4 x 21-inch in one quadruple launcher Mark 8 (removed in ships with Seacat)
A/S Weapons:	Two Mark 6 'Squid' three-barrelled mortars
Complement:	202 (243 wartime maximum for a leader)

Chapter 1

HMS CAESAR

A port bow view of Caesar *taken in Plymouth Sound in July 1945. The angled structure on the side of 'B' gun-shield is a launcher for rockets used to illuminate relatively close range targets at night.* (Crown Copyright/MoD 1945)

Contracted to John Brown & Co on Clydebank and given the Job Number J1605, the name originally allocated to this ship was *Ranger* but it was changed to *Caesar* before she was launched. The first steel was laid down on 3 April 1943 and she was launched on 12 February 1944. She was completed on 5 October 1944, initially without a director control tower because deliveries had not kept pace with the number of ships under construction. She was commissioned on the same day, Contractor's sea trials having been carried out in the Clyde areas from August. She was fitted out as a 'leader' with extra accommodation for a Captain (D) and his small staff and became leader of the 6th Destroyer Flotilla serving with the Home Fleet. In mid October she left Greenock to commence a work-up to operational

efficiency with the Home Fleet at Scapa Flow which was completed satisfactorily by early November.

On 9 November 1944 she sailed with a force comprising the escort carrier *Pursuer*, the cruiser *Euryalus* and the destroyers *Nubian, Venus* and *Zephyr* for Operation 'STEAK', an attack on enemy shipping in the leads off Trondheim. The weather proved to be too bad and the force returned to Scapa Flow, sailing for the second time on 12 November. By 14 November the leads were found to be empty but the armed trawler *VP 6413* and a radio station ashore were attacked by *Pursuer's* aircraft and destroyed.

On 30 November 1944 *Caesar, Cambrian, Caprice* and *Cassandra* took part in Operation 'ACUMEN', the cover for Convoys JW 62 to and

Another view of Caesar *in July 1945 showing the depth-charge rails and throwers aft that were intended to drop a full 10-charge pattern. The Mark 4 Bofors is pointed directly at the camera.* (Crown Copyright/MoD 1945)

RA 62 from North Russia together with the escort carriers *Campania* and *Nairana*. There were 30 merchant ships in the outbound convoy, 20 American and 10 British. Fighters from the two carriers shot down 3 enemy aircraft that attempted to shadow the convoy on the outbound journey and Swordfish flew night anti-submarine patrols off the Kola Inlet while the force waited for RA 62 to sail. The return convoy comprised 28 merchant ships, most of them in ballast, and left the Kola Inlet on 10 December; Swordfish from *Campania* sank *U-365* on 13 December. *Caesar* and the other destroyers arrived back in Scapa Flow on 18 December but sailed again later in the month for several short-range anti- U-boat patrols.

Subsequently, *Caesar* operated in the sea areas off Liverpool, the Clyde and Londonderry on a series of short-duration anti-submarine sweeps. In the spring of 1945 the Admiralty made plans to allocate fresh destroyer flotillas to the British Pacific Fleet and the 6th Destroyer Flotilla was

ordered to prepare for service in the Pacific. On 3 April 1945 *Caesar* arrived in Devonport Dockyard to have her director fitted and to undertake a short refit. The work was completed on 1 June 1945 and she carried out a brief visit to Dartmouth which lasted until 4 June after which she worked up in Scapa Flow before sailing from Rosyth to join the British Pacific Fleet. The war against Japan was expected to last into 1946 and the Admiralty was concerned to keep a steady stream of replacements heading east; thus the destroyers of 6 DS made steady, largely independent, progress, stopping to refuel in Gibraltar, Malta, Alexandria and Aden. *Caesar* arrived at Colombo on 7 August in company with *Cavendish*. By then the first atomic bomb had been dropped on Hiroshima and three days later the bulk of the British Pacific Fleet left operations off the Japanese coast to return to Australia for replenishment. Hostilities ended on 15 August 1945, known at first as VP-Day and subsequently as VJ-Day. *Caesar* moved to the main East Indies

Fleet base at Trincomalee on 5 September.

All previous plans were changed as the BPF and East Indies Fleets were tasked to take the surrender of Japanese forces in their areas, repatriate allied former prisoners of war and internees and restore law and order in British possessions. The Dutch and French were not immediately in a position to restore order in their colonies in the East Indies and Indo-China and it fell to the British to do so until the colonial powers were able to send forces. In both areas force had to be used against nationalist groups who sought independence. Against this background, the Royal Navy had to send ships home that had spent the longest periods away from the UK and 'hostilities-only' men had to be demobilised, causing disruption in most ships companies. British colonies in Malaya, Singapore and Hong Kong had to be re-occupied and law and order restored. Destroyers proved ideal ships for constabulary operations as they were large enough to

put landing parties ashore but able to move freely among the many islands and archipelagos. *Caesar* arrived in Sydney on 19 August, four days after VJ Day, and had minor repairs carried out by the BPF Fleet Maintenance Group after which she remained part of 6 DF which was allocated to the East Indies Fleet. Singapore was re-occupied by British forces on 2 September 1945 and *Caesar* paid a short visit to the naval base on 14 September on her way to Trincomalee. She returned to Singapore on 22 October and was based there until February 1946. On 1 November she formed part of a task group with the heavy cruiser *Sussex* and her sister-ships *Carron* and *Cavalier* which covered the landing of the 5th Indian Division at Surabaya in the Dutch East Indies. British forces provided stability in the region after the surrender of the Japanese until the Dutch colonial government was in a position to take over.

Constabulary operations included visits to Penang

HMS Caesar *in the Johore Strait with hands about to fall in for entry in Singapore Naval Base. Note the curved rails on which trolleys carried the 'Squid' mortar bombs from the handling room aft to the mountings. The mountings were turned onto their sides to allow the bombs to be pushed into the barrels while firing charges were inserted into the breeches.* (Syd Goodman Collection)

and Colombo and in March 1946 *Caesar* underwent a maintenance period in Trincomalee before returning to the UK in May. On 10 May 1946 she arrived in Aden with *Petard* and *Carron* during a period of tension caused by civilian unrest and riots; no shore leave was given. On 20 May she made a brief visit to Malta during her return passage to the UK to drop off mail for the ships in company and then continued to Gibraltar to refuel.

Caesar underwent a refit in Devonport Dockyard between June and November 1946, on completion of which she was placed in Category 'B' Reserve at Devonport, moored with hundreds of other ships in the River Tamar. In 1951 she moved to Penarth until 10 April 1954 when she was moved to Rosyth for a refit which ended in February 1955, after which she was re-cocooned and returned to reserve status at Penarth. In the 1950s the Royal Navy maintained a large Reserve Fleet and ships from it were regularly brought forward and steamed to test the ability of the organisation to regenerate them in an emergency. *Caesar* was brought out of reserve and re-commissioned on 24 January 1956 and put through a trials programme that tested the soundness of hull and machinery. She reduced to reserve again in February.

On 6 November 1957 she was taken under dockyard control in Rosyth and work started on her as part of the 'Ca' class modernisation programme. The work took three years and she eventually emerged on 22 November 1960 to re-commission as leader of the 8th Destroyer Squadron for service in the Far East Fleet. She was one of the four 'Ca' class destroyers to be fitted with an enclosed 'frigate-style' bridge and retained the forward set of torpedo tubes with a twin Mark 5 40mm Bofors mounting forward of the Squid mortars. In December she worked up to operational efficiency under the Flag Officer Sea Training (FOST) at Portland. When this was complete she sailed for Portsmouth and secured outboard of the cruiser *Gambia* on Fountain Lake Jetty on 14 December 1960. On 18 December a fire broke out in *Gambia's* superstructure and *Caesar's* fire party

was called away at 0750 to help extinguish it. An hour later the fire was under control and *Caesar* recovered her fire party and moved to a different part of the dockyard. She sailed from Portsmouth for the Far East on 18 April 1961, stopping at Gibraltar, Malta and Colombo to refuel, and arrived in Singapore Naval base in late May. From Singapore she sailed to join the Far East Fleet off Japan during its summer cruise. She stopped at Hong Kong to refuel and visited the small Japanese port of Tokuyama.

After the port visit she joined a task force comprising the cruiser *Belfast*, her sister-ship *Carysfort*, the frigates *Crane* and *St Brides Bay* and *RFA Wave Master* to take part in the Royal Australian Navy fleet exercise 'TUCKER BOX'. This took the task force across the Java and Timor Seas and the Torres Straits to the east coast of Australia. After the exercise *Caesar* visited Melbourne from 28 August before returning to Singapore. In October 1961 she took part in Exercise FOTEX 61, an important, multi-national annual naval exercise which included ships of the RN, RAN and USN. The aircraft carriers *HMS Victorious* and *USS Ticonderoga* were escorted by *Caesar, Cavalier, Caprice* and the RAN destroyers *Quiberon* and *Vampire*.

During the early part of 1962 *Caesar* acted as the Senior Officer's ship of the task unit involved in anti-piracy patrols off North Borneo until she was relieved by the survey ship *Dampier* which was carrying out hydrography tasks in the same area.

In 1963 the RN re-organised its destroyer and frigate squadrons from typed groups, usually comprised of ships of the same class, into mixed groups known as Escort Squadrons. On 7 March 1963 *Caesar* became the leader of the 26th Escort Squadron. The new system was intended to allow more flexibility in operations since destroyer and frigate squadrons were no longer operating together as close-knit groups. It soon became apparent, however, that the escort squadrons were no more likely to work together and their individual ships, each on general service commissions that included time in the Home and Far East Fleets, were soon

HMS Caesar's enclosed 'frigate-type' bridge is seen clearly in this photograph as she comes alongside an aircraft carrier for a jackstay transfer. Note the strong-point just forward of 'B' mounting and the shot-mat on the upper deck just below it. The carrier always fires the Coston gun-line to avoid damage to aircraft on deck so that here all personnel but the First Lieutenant on Caesar have taken cover.   *(Syd Goodman Collection)*

spread all over the world. After a work-up for the Commonwealth warships designated JET 63, in April 1963 *Caesar* joined the aircraft carriers *HMS Hermes, HMAS Melbourne* and *USS Yorktown* for the next big exercise, designated Exercise 'SEA SERPENT'. She formed part of a task force that included the cruiser *Lion* and the destroyer *HMAS Voyager*. In all 57 warships from the South East Asia Treaty Organisation, SEATO, took part and

they anchored in Manilla Bay in the Philippines on 8 May 1963 at the end of the exercise. When the assembly of ships separated, *Caesar* operated with *Hermes* as her plane-guard escort. *HMS Ark Royal* joined the Far East Fleet in July 1963 and she joined *Hermes, Caesar, HMA Ships Vampire* and *Voyager* and other Commonwealth and USN warships in the next big annual exercise, designated FOTEX 63.

On 16 March 1964 *Caesar* re-commissioned after

HMS Caesar *with the submarine* Anchorite *alongside her at the end FOTEX 63. The destroyers astern of her are the Australian* Vampire *and* Voyager *and the aircraft carrier* Hermes. *(Crown Copyright/MoD 1963)*

a refit in Singapore with a new ship's company flown out from the UK. A work up to operational efficiency began on 31 March and lasted until 10 April when she sailed to take part in Exercise 'HIGH-UP'. By then the Far East Fleet was heavily involved in the Confrontation with Indonesia and she carried out a patrol of north-eastern Malaysian waters sailing to Chukai, Kuantan and Tumpat in the latter part of April. In May 1964 *Caesar* visited Penang and passed an Operational Readiness Inspection, ORI, carried out by the staff of the Commander Far East Fleet, COMFEF. Most of June was spent patrolling off Tawau in Sabah, North Borneo at the end of which she ferried a contingent of Ghurkhas back to Singapore. Between 24 July and 9 August 1964 she took part in Exercise FOTEX 64 with other Commonwealth and international warships. On 13 August she visited Bangkok

with *Loch Killisport*, sailing at high speed on 16 August to carry out a further patrol of eastern Malaysia. These patrols were intended to intercept and then search vessels that were suspected of trying to land weapons or supplies to terrorist groups ashore. *Caesar* arrived back in Singapore on 21 August.

On 26 August 1964 *Caesar* sailed in company with *Victorious* and *Cavendish* for exercises with a USN task force comprising the nuclear-powered warships *Enterprise, Long Beach* and *Bainbridge* which were circumnavigating the globe and visiting Western Australia. While *Victorious* and *Cavendish* visited Fremantle, *Caesar* visited Bunbury; after sailing, the three rejoined each other and headed for the Sunda Strait. As they approached Indonesian waters there was panic in the Indonesian capital, Jakarta, where the population feared air strikes.

South of Java the guided missile destroyer *Hampshire* and the frigates *Dido* and *Berwick* joined the task force but the Indonesians attempted to close the Strait by declaring it to be a danger area in use for a naval exercise. Undaunted, on 12 September the British task force sailed through the narrow Lombok Strait, east of Bali, asserting their legal right of innocent passage through international waters. The ships closed up at action stations with all guns manned and stood by to repel possible attacks by Indonesian warships or aircraft as they passed through the narrow strait. At one stage an Indonesian submarine was sighted on the surface and the ships prepared to open fire if it displayed hostile intent. In the event the Indonesians decided that it would be wiser to leave the task force unchallenged and the submarine sent a message of good wishes. The British ships emerged unscathed from the Lombok Strait and altered course for Singapore.

In late September *Caesar* carried out an assisted maintenance period; her ship's company moved into *HMS Terror*, the barracks ashore while the ship was taken into an Admiralty floating dock for a 'bottom-clean'. By mid October she was back on patrol again, this time in the Malacca Straits until 16 November when she sailed for Hong Kong. Unfortunately Typhoon Kate passed through her track and she sustained damage which forced her to return to Singapore for repairs. When these were complete she carried out further patrols in the Singapore and Malacca Straits areas and underwent an inspection by the staff of FO2 Far East on 16 December. She sailed for Hong Kong for the second time on 18 December and encountered rough weather again which delayed her arrival by one day until 23 December. She spent Christmas in Hong Kong and sailed for the USN exercise areas off Subic Bay in the Philippines in January for exercises with *Victorious* and American warships. On passage back to Singapore EM J C Hughes died on

HMS Caesar's *Mark 6M director with its distinctive Type 275 fire-control radar aerials stands out clearly in this photograph, as do the Type 293, 974 and IFF Mark 10 aerials on the fore-mast.* (National Museum of the Royal Navy)

board on 17 January 1965; he was buried with full naval honours at the Ulu Pan Dang Military Cemetery on 20 January. A day later *Caesar* resumed patrols in the Malacca and Singapore Straits interspersed by a maintenance period in Singapore during February. On 5 March she began the harbour training period for Exercise FOTEX 65, the biggest yet in the series of multi-national exercises. She sailed for the sea-phase of the exercise itself on 12 March and arrived back in Singapore for a short maintenance period on 26 March.

On 5 April she sailed with *Victorious, Ajax, Zest* and *RFA Tidepool* for Japan, visiting Nagasaki on 12 April and carrying out exercises with American warships in the Okinawa areas from 21 April. She left for Hong Kong on 24 April and by early May she had resumed patrol duties. These were her last operational days at sea, however, and she left Singapore for the last time to return to the UK on 26 May 1965. She re-fuelled from *RFA Wave Victor* at Gan on 1 June and again at Aden on 5 June. She passed through the Suez Canal for the last time on 11 June and stopped at Gibraltar to buy 'rabbits' between 18 and 21 June.

HMS *Caesar* arrived back in Portsmouth on 24 June 1965 to be de-stored and de-commissioned and was subsequently towed to Chatham. She was immediately put up for disposal and arrived at Blyth to be broken up on 6 January 1967; the first of her class to be scrapped.

Chapter 2

HMS CAMBRIAN

An overhead view of Cambrian *in October 1944 showing the positions of weapons, directors and boats. The picture emphasises how very heavily armed the 'C' class were for their modest size.* *(Syd Goodman Collection)*

Originally to have been named *Spitfire*, *Cambrian* was re-named before launch. She was ordered from Scotts at Greenock and allocated the shipbuilder's yard number 614. The first steel was laid down on 14 August 1942 and she was launched on 10 December 1943. She commissioned into the Royal Navy on the day she was completed, 14 July 1944 and then carried out post-build trials in the Clyde areas. These were completed in Augus. She joined the Home Fleet based in Scapa Flow to work-up to operational efficiency. On 23 October 1944 she was one of 8 destroyers, together with the cruiser *Bellona* that escorted the fleet aircraft carrier *Implacable* for Operation 'ATHLETIC', strikes on Rorvik, Bodo and Lodings in the Norwegian littoral during which Barracudas dropped 27 tons of bombs in 40 sorties. Two days later the Barracudas carried out the Royal Navy's last operational airborne torpedo attack and sank 6 German merchant ships. On 1 November she sailed for Operation 'GOLDEN', the escort of Convoy JW 61A to North Russia together with the escort carrier *Campania*, the heavy cruiser *Berwick* and the destroyers *Caprice*, *Cassandra*, *Saumarez*, *Scourge* and *Serapis*. Within the convoy were two troopships carrying nearly 11,000 Russian former Prisoners of War and other nationals, including 30 women, home to the Soviet Union. The return convoy, RA 61A, left the Kola Inlet on 11 November 1944 and arrived in the Clyde on 17 November without incident. Its escort had been joined by two additional destroyers, *Savage* and *Scorpion*.

Cambrian formed part of the escort for a further convoy to North Russia, JW 62 outbound and RA

HMS Cambrian *is seen here as she was completed in 1944 with a modified Western Approaches paint scheme. Note the 20mm Oerlikon in the starboard bridge wing and the Mark 4 'Hazemeyer' Bofors between the torpedo tubes. As usual, 'X' mounting is trained forward to lessen the effect of salt spray on the gun breech and equipment inside the gun-shield.*
(Crown Copyright/MoD 1944)

62 return between 27 November and 14 December 1944 after which she was used on shorter range escort duties. These included escorting the US troopship *West Point* through the Irish Sea on 16 February as she arrived from the USA and again as she departed outbound on 20 February. *Cambrian* and *Cavendish* were both damaged by heavy seas in the latter operation.

A short refit was carried out at Leith, the port of Edinburgh, between May and July 1945 to prepare her for service in the British Pacific Fleet. She sailed to the Mediterranean to work up off Malta in August. She was at Alexandria on VJ-Day but continued her passage east, arriving at the newly liberated naval base at Singapore on 15 November, rejoining the remainder of 6 DF, and was used on constabulary duties, patrolling the waters around the Dutch East Indies. She was in Trincomalee in February 1946 and subsequently returned to the UK through the Suez Canal and Mediterranean.

After de-storing at Chatham she paid off and was taken in hand by the dockyard for refit. Shortages of labour caused the refit to be suspended for three months from March to June 1947 but it was finally completed on 23 July when she was placed into reserve at Chatham. She remained there until March 1955 when she was towed to Liverpool for an interim modernisation during which 'X' mounting was replaced by a twin 'Squid' mortar installation with its associated handling equipment and bomb room. On completion of the work she recommissioned for steaming trials in April 1956 and then paid off again for a period in reserve at Liverpool. On 12 November 1956 she was towed the short distance to Barrow-in-Furness by the tug *Prosperous* and laid up again, pending a Dockyard slot to carry out a full modernisation refit. This became available in April 1958 when she was moved to Devonport but shortage of labour posed a problem again and the work had to be suspended on several occasions and post-refit sea trials were not carried out until September 1962. She finally recommissioned on 3 January 1963 for a general service Home/Far East commission as part of the new 21st Escort Squadron. She was the last ship of her class to complete modernisation and was one of the four ships to be fitted with an enclosed bridge built over an enlarged operations room. All torpedo tubes were removed and she was fitted 'for but not with' GWS 20 Seacat with the prominent missile handling room forward of the Squid launchers. She was never fitted with the missile launcher itself, however, and had a single 40mm Bofors gun mounted instead. When she sailed for sea trials at Portland her first task, as she left Plymouth Sound, was to respond to a distress call from the frigate *Pheasant* which had broken loose from its tug off Trevose Head while it was on its way to the scrapyard at Troon.

Cambrian joined other units of 21 ES in Gibraltar in June 1963 and sailed with them for the Far East but detached to act as plane-guard for the aircraft carrier *Ark Royal* off Mombasa on 19 June followed by a passage to Singapore. In July she took part in Exercise FOTEX 63 with *Albion, Lion, Cambrian, Duchess, Duncan, Plymouth, Salisbury, HMA Ships Quiberon* and *Vendetta* and *HMNZS Otago*. Later in 1963 *Cambrian* was involved in making an Admiralty instructional film on refuelling at sea together with the *RFA Tideflow*.

On 12 January 1964 the African population of Zanzibar revolted against the Arabs and Asians who held power on the prosperous island and murdered many of them. The British High Commissioner was trapped in his residence and unable to communicate with London. On hearing the news the C-in-C Middle East, Lieutenant General Sir Charles Harrington, ordered preparations to protect British citizens and Rear Admiral J Scotland the Flag Officer Middle East ordered the aircraft carrier *Centaur* which was off Aden to embark 600 men of 45 Commando Royal Marines. No alongside berth was available and the carrier had to embark the men, 24 Land Rovers and 70 tons of stores and ammunition while anchored a considerable distance offshore. She also embarked 5 armoured cars and men of the 16/5 Lancers, hundreds of jerry cans full of vehicle fuel and 2 Belvedere helicopters of 26 Squadron RAF in addition to her normal air group of Sea Vixen fighters, Gannet AEW aircraft and Wessex helicopters. She sailed with *Cambrian* as plane-guard on 20 January 1964 and headed south at high speed.

On the day she sailed men of the Tanganyikan Rifles mutinied in Dar es Salaam and pillaged the city causing consternation and two days later

A port-side view of Cambrian *taken in 1963. By then she had been modernised and was fitted for-but-not-with GWS 20 Seacat with the tall missile handling room forward of the 'Squid' mountings where the twin Bofors had been sited. A Mark 7 single Bofors is fitted in lieu of the Seacat launcher as there were not yet enough available to equip every ship planned to receive the weapon. Note that all torpedo armament has been removed to reduce topweight.*

(Steve Bush Collection)

British troops had to be flown into Uganda to restore order at the request of the Ugandan government and, on 24 January, quell a mutiny by the 11th Battalion of the Kenyan Army at the request of the Kenyan government.

On 24 January, *Centaur* with her improvised battle group arrived off Dar es Salaam and a boat from *Cambrian* brought Brigadier Sholto-Douglas off from shore. He reported continued, unchecked rioting, looting and murder in the city and at about the same time a signal arrived from C-in-C Middle East ordering 'Disarm Tanganyikan Army Colito Barracks soonest'. Captain Steiner of *Centaur* had made contingency plans to land marines at dawn, supported by *Cambrian*'s guns in an overwhelming display of force. In order to minimise casualties, *Cambrian* was ordered to lay down a diversionary bombardment with air burst 4.5 inch shells onto an uninhabited area north of the barracks, shifting the

aim onto the barracks itself if it was found to be necessary. Shooting into a darkened target area without a forward observer from tidal waters was no easy task but the destroyer accomplished her task well. At 0630 Royal Marines of Z Company 45 Commando flew into the assault in Wessex helicopters of 815 NAS and captured the barracks after an initial show of resistance which ended when an anti-tank missile was fired into the guardroom. Mutineers further inland were cowed by Sea Vixens which flew low over them and surrendered without further resistance. After this classic demonstration of sea power, *Victorious* and *Albion* arrived, allowing *Centaur* and *Cambrian* to sail for a brief show of strength off Mombassa before returning to Singapore on 12 February 1964.

By then the Confrontation with Indonesia was at its height and constant patrols by ships of the Far East Fleet were required in the waters off Malaysia,

Singapore and Borneo. Even when they were alongside, ships had to maintain constant vigilance to counter potential attacks by swimmers with limpet mines. Armed boat patrols were maintained in Singapore Naval Base throughout the day and night.

After the Rhodesian Unilateral Declaration of Independence (UDI) in 1965 the United Nations imposed sanctions against the illegal regime and Security Council Resolution 217 called for an international embargo on all shipments of oil to Rhodesia. When it became clear that shipments were still arriving, the British government instituted the Beira Patrol in March 1966. It was to become a major commitment which continued for nine years. The first ships on task were the aircraft carrier *Ark Royal* and the frigate *Rhyl* which had been on route from Mombassa to Singapore. Later in the month *Eagle* replaced *Ark Royal* and *Cambrian* together with the frigate *Plymouth* oper-

ated close inshore for a time and intercepted the tanker *Joanna V* among others which were turned away from their destination. Earlier in the month *Cambrian* collided with *RFA Tidepool* in the Malacca Strait while coming alongside to replenish at sea.

Although she saw most operational activity in the Middle and Far East Stations, *Cambrian* returned to the UK for the home elements of her general service commissions. She collided with a Port Auxiliary Service lighter in Portsmouth on 18 December 1966 and took part in Portsmouth Navy Days in August 1967. Before returning to the Far East she took part in anti-submarine exercises with Britain's first nuclear-powered submarine, *Dreadnought*, off the west coast of Scotland; this must have stretched her aging anti-submarine sensors to, or perhaps beyond, their limit. Her next passage to the Far East had to be via the Cape as the Suez Canal had been closed after ships were sunk in

HMS Cambrian *as she finally appeared with an enclosed bridge, fitted-for-but-not-with Seacat and no torpedo tubes.*
(Crown Copyright/MoD)

it during the 1967 fighting between Egypt and Israel. She stopped in what was still an RN base at Simonstown near Cape Town for a visit before carrying out more patrols off Beira interspersed with a visit to Mombassa; by 1967 patrols were usually carried out by one or two frigates or destroyers on their way out to or returning to the UK from the Far East Fleet.

On 21 January 1968 *Cambrian* sailed from Mombassa to exercise with *Euryalus* and *Zest* which were maintaining a British presence off Mauritius after rioting had broken out in the capital. When the latter suffered machinery defects, *Cambrian* was ordered to replace her but on 24 January she was diverted to Rodriguez Island, 350 miles east of Mauritius, to restore order after food riots broke out following a cyclone. Order restored she departed for Hong Kong. An eventful few months followed with visits to Fremantle and Geraldton in West Australia but the ship's material state was giving cause for concern and she added a visit to Auckland, New Zealand to her programme so that dockyard assistance could be provided by the nearby Devonport Dockyard in March. From New Zealand she sailed to Manus Island, formerly one of the British Pacific Fleet's wartime bases, and from there to Yokohama in Japan. On return to Singapore *Cambrian's* ship's company moved ashore into *HMS Terror* and she underwent an assisted maintenance period in *AFD 31* which

ended in June. Later in June she sailed for the UK via Simonstown where she carried out a boiler clean but after leaving, on 15 July, a defective condenser contaminated the ship's feed-water supply and she had to put into James Bay in St Helena for a week to carry out temporary repairs. With these complete she sailed for Portsmouth via Gibraltar and arrived on 1 August 1968.

In September 1968 she took part in Exercise 'SILVER TOWER', a major NATO maritime command and control demonstration with the aircraft carrier *Eagle* and a large number of British and allied warships and auxiliaries. In October she took over the role of Gibraltar guard ship until December when she returned to Portsmouth. In January 1969 she visited her 'adopted' port of Cardiff for a farewell visit and in the weeks after that carried out a series of anti-submarine training exercises off the west coast of Scotland. *Cambrian* returned to Portsmouth flying her paying-off pennant on 3 March 1969. After de-storing she paid off for the last time on 24 March and in April was towed to Chatham where all useful equipment was removed. She was subsequently sold for scrap to the Welsh yard of Thomas Ward at Briton Ferry and arrived there under tow on 6 September 1971. Work on her didn't start until January the following year, however, but it was declared to be complete on 1 September 1972.

Chapter 3

HMS CAPRICE

HMS Caprice *seen from the air at high speed in January 1945, still very much as completed.*

(Syd Goodman Collection)

Laid down on 28 September 1942 by Yarrow and Co. at their Scotstoun Yard and originally to have been named *Swallow*, *Caprice* was re-named on the slip before being launched on 16 September 1943. She was the first and, at the time of writing, the only ship to have been allocated this name in the Royal Navy. Completed 5 April 1944, she carried out trials and worked up to operational efficiency at Tobermory in April and May 1944 for service with the 6th Destroyer Flotilla in the Home Fleet. She had an active war from the outset and sailed as part of the escort for Operation 'VICTUAL', convoy JW59 to North Russia on 17 August in company with the escort carriers *Vindex* and *Striker*, the cruiser *Jamaica* and the destroyers *Marne*, *Meteor*, *Milne* and *Musketeer*. The escort detached from the convoy off the Kola Inlet on 24 August and picked up the return convoy RA59A

four days later. The convoy returned to UK waters unscathed on 4 September 1944. In October she formed part of the escort for the new fleet aircraft carrier *Implacable* for Operation 'ATHLETIC', a search for the battleship *Tirpitz* and strikes against shipping in Norwegian waters during which Barracudas torpedoed and sank the 2,693 ton *SS Karmoy* in the last airborne torpedo attack carried out by the Royal Navy. Other ships in the screen included the cruiser *Bellona* and the destroyers *Venus*, *Scourge*, *Savage*, *Verulam* and *Cassandra*.

On 1 November 1944 she sailed with the escort carrier *Campania*, the cruiser *Berwick* and *Cambrian*, *Cassandra*, *Saumarez*, *Scourge* and *Serapis* as the ocean escort for Operation 'GOLDEN', convoy JW61A to North Russia. Included in the convoy were the troopships *Empress of Australia* and *Scythia* repatriating 11,000 Russians

HMS Caprice *leaving Malta in April 1959 on passage to join the 8th Destroyer Squadron in the Far East Fleet. She had recently completed an extensive modernisation and has an enclosed 'frigate-style' bridge; 'Squid' anti-submarine mortars in 'X' position on an enlarged deck-house that continues forward over the place formally occupied by the after torpedo tubes. The close-range armament comprises one twin Mark 5 Bofors and two singles in the bridge wings.*   *(National Museum of the Royal Navy)*

who had been liberated by the allies in Normandy. The ocean escort sailed for the return voyage with convoy RA61A on 10 November; the two troopships carrying Russian sailors travelling to the UK to man warships, including the battleship *Royal Sovereign*, that were to be lent to the Soviet Navy by the RN. The warships returned to Scapa Flow on 27 November. Turnaround time was short and on 30 November 1944 *Caprice* sailed as part of the ocean escort for Operation 'ACUMEN', convoy JW62 to North Russia. The powerful force comprised, in addition to *Caprice*, two escort carriers *Campania* and *Nairana*, the cruiser *Bellona* and the destroyers *Caesar, Cassandra, Cambrian, Onslow, Obedient, Offa, Onslaught, Oribi* and *Orwell*. During the operation aircraft from the two carriers flew for 180 hours on searches, 70 of them night, sank *U-365* and shot down 2 enemy aircraft. *Caprice* returned to Scapa Flow on 14 December 1944. From 24 December 1944 to 15 April 1945 she formed part of the escort for twenty-four

TA/AT series convoys from the Thames to Antwerp and back that carried military supplies in support of the allied land campaign before being selected, with the other ships of her Flotilla for service with the British Pacific Fleet.

She was refitted at Portsmouth between 11 May and 29 July 1945 and, after a short work-up, sailed for the Far East on 5 August. With the end of the war ten days later she delayed for a while in Malta before moving to Singapore where she arrived on 2 October, a month after the liberation. After replacing destroyers that returned to the UK she was used to patrol the Dutch East Indies and to assist with their re-occupation by allied and then Dutch forces. After VJ-Day this area was transferred from the American South-West Pacific Command to Admiral Mountbatten's South East Asia Command and British forces took the surrender of Japanese, repatriated former prisoners of war and tried to prevent insurgents from seizing control. The situation was made worse because the Dutch were in no posi-

tion, at first, to resume control and the local population resolved to fight rather than be subjected to Dutch colonial rule once more. There was no shortage of Japanese weapons available to them and the situation was complicated by a declaration of Indonesian independence by Dr Soekarno in August 1945. Eventually large numbers of British and Indian troops had to be landed to restore order until the Dutch returned and warships were used to examine shipping to ensure that illegal cargoes of arms were not shipped in for the nationalists. They also protected troop movements and moved political officers safely between islands. Singapore Dockyard was not restored to its full capability until 1947 so ships of the BPF that needed technical support had to use maintenance facilities in Ceylon, Australia or South Africa until then.

Caprice did not spend long in this difficult environment and she left for the UK in early 1946, arriving in Portsmouth Dockyard on 2 May. She was de-stored and laid up in reserve in Pembroke

Dock on 31 July, remaining there supervised by a small care and maintenance party for just over ten years before being towed to Yarrow's Shipyard at Scotstoun on the Clyde for modernisation in September 1956. The work took three years and she re-commissioned on 17 February 1959 for service with the 8th Destroyer Squadron in the Far East Fleet (FEF). She had the 'standard' modernisation but was one of the four 'Ca' class to be fitted with an enclosed bridge. By then destroyer squadrons had replaced the earlier flotilla designations but, with reducing numbers, they had become administrative rather than tactical units and their individual ships seldom worked together. *Caprice* worked up at Portland in March 1959 and sailed for the Far East in April. She was diverted to the Persian Gulf to replace the frigate *Loch Fada* temporarily on patrol. On 29 August 1959 she replaced *Cavalier* as guard-ship for the RAF installations on Gan Island during civil unrest in the Maldive Islands. In October *Caprice* and *Cavalier* visited Tokyo,

HMS Caprice was one of only two 'Ca' class destroyers that were actually fitted with the Seacat close-range anti-aircraft missile system, the other was Cavalier. She is seen here with dummy rounds on the Seacat launcher. All torpedo tubes had been removed to compensate for the extra topweight of the missile handling room and magazine.

(Tim Meredith)

A stern view of Caprice *showing details of the Seacat system including the entry into the handling room through the open door. The GWS 20 Seacat director is over the door.*   *(Syd Goodman Collection)*

returning first to Hong Kong and then Singapore in November. In January 1960 *Caprice* underwent an assisted maintenance period in Singapore which included a docking in the King George VI dry dock.

Caprice was in Hong Kong in November 1960 for the annual fleet sailing regatta against the Royal Hong Kong Yacht Club; other ships in harbour included the C-in-C Far East Station's despatch vessel *Alert, Bulwark, Cardigan Bay, Hartland Point* and *Crane*. In December 1960, while she was on passage to Singapore from Hong Kong, *Caprice* responded to an SOS from the Panamanian ship *Galatea* which was aground on the Pierson Reef, 250 miles away near North Borneo. Heavy seas were breaking on the vessel's windward side but *Caprice's* whaler succeeded in rescuing 20 people in a humanitarian operation that spread over 2 days, 10 people being taken off in each. The lieutenant in charge of the whaler and its coxswain were subsequently awarded Queen's Commendations for their acts of bravery.

In August 1961 *Caprice* took part in Exercise 'TUCKERBOX' in the Hervey Bay areas off eastern Australia together with the cruiser *Tiger* and *Cassandra, Loch Killisport,* several RFAs and much of the RAN including the aircraft carrier *Melbourne*. Later, in October 1961 she took part in the annual Flag Officer's Tactical Exercises, FOTEX 61 with the aircraft carriers *Victorious* and the *USS Ticonderoga*, her sister-ships *Caesar* and *Cavalier* and the Australian destroyers *Quiberon* and *Vampire*. On completion of this exercise she joined other Commonwealth warships in Melbourne for a celebration of the RAN's 50th birthday. In November she visited Auckland and took part in exercises with ships of the RAN and RNZN.

Caprice remained in the Far East for four years, refitting and re-commissioning on station during that time with a new ship's company. In February 1962 she took part in the large Commonwealth naval exercise 'JET 62' with the aircraft carriers *Centaur* and *INS Vikrant*, escorts which included *Rhyl, Plymouth* and *HMAS Yarra* together with

warships from several Commonwealth countries. 'FOTEX 62' which took place in July included the aircraft carrier *Ark Royal* together with *Caprice, Cassandra* and *Carysfort* and *HMAS Yarra*. She visited Sydney and Brisbane in January 1963 before leaving the Far East and moving to the Mediterranean Fleet.

In 1963 *Caprice* was allocated to the 21st Escort Squadron (ES) in the Mediterranean and then on the West Indies Station. ES proved no more practical than the earlier system and individual ships spent no more time working together so the RN eventually reverted to numbered destroyer and frigate squadrons. During her time in the West Indies, *Caprice* served as guard ship at Georgetown in British Guiana between May and July 1963 and on a patrol intended to deter and intercept illegal immigrants trying to enter the Bahamas until the end of August.

She returned to the UK for refit in November 1963 and became one of only two ships of her class to be fitted with the GWS 20 'Seacat' anti-aircraft guided-missile system although several others had been fitted 'for-but-not-with'. Her remaining torpedo tubes were removed to compensate for the increase in top weight. A shortage of manpower led to her being paid off into reserve at Rosyth when the refit was completed in June 1964 but when the frigate *Blackpool* was lent to the Royal New Zealand Navy in July 1966 her ship's company transferred to *Caprice* and re-activated her to complete their commission. She was allocated to 1 DS in the Far East Fleet and was used on patrol duties based on Singapore during Confrontation against Indonesia. She left the UK on 25 January 1968 for her last commission, the first part of which was to be in the Far East Fleet. With the Suez Canal still blocked she sailed via Gibraltar and Simonstown and then spent a month on the Beira Patrol with a short break in the middle. She arrived in Singapore on 6 April 1968 and then visited Tokyo in May. In September she sailed for Exercise 'CORAL SANDS' which lasted into October and constituted the largest Commonwealth amphibious exercise

HMS Caprice *being towed out of Plymouth Sound on her way to the breaker's yard by the tug* RMAS Robust *in October 1979.*   *(Syd Goodman Collection)*

ever held, ending with a ceremonial entry into Sydney Harbour by the largest fleet assembled there since the Second World War. Among the RN ships involved were the aircraft carrier *Hermes* together with *Albion, Triumph, Intrepid, Defender, Diana, Caprice* and a number of other escorts from the RN, RAN and RNZN.

After that Caprice made her way back to the UK, arriving at Portsmouth on 23 December 1968. She partially de-stored and reduced to reserve again, this time at Gibraltar. Despite her age, however, she was re-commissioned with a reduced ship's company in 1971 for duty as a sea-training ship for engineer officers, based in Devonport. Her ability to return to active service was demonstrated by participation in several exercises, among them Exercise 'WESTWARD HO' in the eastern Atlantic during July 1972 with *Ark Royal, Bulwark, Blake, Fife,*

Achilles, Jaguar and *Lynx*. In January 1973 she began acting as a navigation training ship, operating out of Portsmouth but between 12 February and 2 March 1973 she carried out a patrol off Iceland in support of British fishing vessels during the second 'Cod War'. During this period she helped in the search for the survivors of a sunken Icelandic fishing boat for several days after it was lost. In mid-March she returned briefly to her engineering and navigation instructional duties and then visited Swansea on 29 March. After that, she returned to Devonport to de-commission for the last time on 2 April 1973. She was de-stored and re-usable equipment was removed after which she was moored in the River Tamar and placed on the disposal list. She was eventually sold for scrap and arrived at Queensborough on 5 October 1979.

Chapter 4

HMS Carron

HMS Carron *painted in the Admiralty Standard camouflage scheme in which she was originally completed. Her armament comprised two sets of quadruple torpedo tubes; four 4.5 inch gun mountings; a twin Mark 4 'Hazemeyer' Bofors; several 20mm Oerlikon and depth charges aft.* *(Syd Goodman Collection)*

HMS *Carron* was ordered from Scott's of Greenock as Job Number J1141 in March 1942, laid down on 26 November and launched on 28 March 1944. She was originally to have been named *Strenuous*, but was re-named before launch. Shortages of equipment led to her being completed on 6 November 1944 without the director for her main armament. She carried out contractor's sea trials in October and worked up for service with 6 DF in the Home Fleet at Scapa Flow. On 6 December she was one of a number of ships ordered to locate a U-boat that had sunk the frigate *HMS Bullen* with a homing torpedo off Cape Wrath, the North-West corner of the Scottish mainland. The weapon hit amidships and broke her in half but 97 men were rescued by the destroyer *Hesperus*. The U-boat, *U-775*, evaded the search and managed to get away.

On 10 January 1945 *Carron* sailed as part of the force that carried out Operation 'SPELLBINDER' in company with the escort for the escort carriers *Premier* and *Trumpeter* to intercept and attack an enemy convoy off Egersund in Norway. Aircraft from the carriers shot down a shadowing Junkers 88, sank the German minesweeper *M1* and damaged a 3,350 ton merchant ship off Nord Byfjord. The operation included the laying of a minefield off Utsira Island by the fast minelayer *Apollo* screened by *Zealous* and *Carron* which covered the operation with a smoke-screen. For the remainder of the war in Europe she was employed escorting a series of short range convoys, mainly in the Irish Sea, with frequent stops to refuel in Liverpool, the Clyde and Londonderry.

Together with her sister-ships in the 6th Destroyer Flotilla she was selected for duty with the British

HMS Carron *carrying out post-modernisation trials in the Thames off Sheerness Dockyard. Two 'Squid' anti-sub-marine mortars have replaced 'X' mounting on a larger after deck-house and only the forward torpedo tubes remain. All depth charge fittings aft have been removed and a Mark 6M director has replaced the earlier K Mark 1.*

(Syd Goodman Collection)

Pacific Fleet and she was taken in hand by Devonport Dockyard from 25 June 1945 for a refit during which her director was fitted and her close-range armament improved to suit her for operations in the Pacific. The war ended while she was carrying out a work-up but it was decided that she was still needed by the BPF to replace long-serving units which would be returning to the UK. She sailed with *Cavalier* on 25 August 1945 to join the remainder of 6 DF in the BPF, joining the other 'Ca' class destroyers at Singapore on 22 October after a passage through the Mediterranean, Suez Canal, Aden and Trincomalee. She was used to patrol the Dutch East Indies and was in Soerabaya in October and Batavia, their capital, in December 1945. On 23 February 1946 she was deployed to Bombay with a number of other ships to deal with

a mutiny in ships of the Royal Indian Navy. She joined other destroyers in sinking the old river gun-boat *Tarantula* during target practice off Trincomalee on 1 May 1946 and sailed for the UK flying her paying-off pennant two days later in company with *Carysfort, Caesar* and *Petard*. No shore leave was given during a refuelling stop at Aden due to civilian unrest and riots at RAF Khormaksar. She passed through the Suez Canal on 15 May and arrived back in Chatham Dockyard on 29 May after stopping in Gibraltar to repaint the whole ship's side in a single day. After de-storing and de-commissioning she was placed in reserve in September 1946. She was steamed to Gibraltar for a refit in 1947, returning to Chatham with the steaming party that had run *Carysfort* in September 1947 after which she was placed back into reserve.

She spent less time laid up than the majority of her sisters and was the first of her class to be taken in hand for modernisation in November 1952. This took place in Chatham Dockyard and started with the removal of the old bridge structure, weighing 19½ tons, over 25 tons of lead-covered cable, the after torpedo tubes and much of the original armament in early 1953. During this period there was a small fire on board but it did not delay the work. She was then re-built with a lighter aluminium bridge structure based on the Daring class design with an open bridge over a larger operations room. Two Mark 6 'Squid' mortars were installed instead of 'X' mounting aft and the deck-house structure was extended forward into the space that had contained the after torpedo-tubes. The three 4.5-inch mountings were fitted with remote power control and a new Mark 6M director was installed aft of the bridge together with the new 'Flyplane 5' gunnery control system. The close-range armament comprised a twin Mark 5 40mm Bofors forward of the Squids and two single 40mm Bofors, one in each bridge wing. The sonar was updated to form part of the weapons system with 'Squid' and numerous other improvements were made to bring the ship up to the standard required for contemporary fleet operations. The forward torpedo tubes were retained.

After completion of the work, *Carron* re-commissioned on 8 June 1955 and carried out post refit trials in the Thames estuary off Sheerness and was present at Chatham Navy Days in August 1955 but not open to the public. She deployed for a 'shakedown' deployment to the Mediterranean Fleet dur-

HMS Carron *in the River Dart while serving with the Dartmouth Training Squadron. Note that a training bridge and chart-room have replaced 'B' mounting and a deck-house has replaced the two 'Squid' anti-submarine mortars aft. It was used as a classroom.* (Steve Bush Collection)

ing the autumn and returned to Chatham in December. Surprisingly, after the effort and expense of bringing her up to contemporary capability as a fleet destroyer, she was allocated to the Dartmouth Training Squadron (DTS) with a reduced ship's company and used to train young officers. 'B' mounting was subsequently removed and replaced by an instructional bridge, forward of and lower than the actual bridge at the forward end of an extended operations room structure which was converted into classrooms. It was used to instruct cadets in navigation and the duties of the officer of the watch at sea. The new Dartmouth Training Squadron replaced the aircraft carrier *Triumph* and comprised *Carron* and the frigates *Venus* and *Vigilant*. In October 1957 the 4.5-inch mountings and Squids were removed to reduce the amount of maintenance required, leaving her with only the Bofors mountings for continued service with the DTS.

A number of warships normally engaged on trials and training duties were pressed into service for patrol duties off Iceland in support of British fishing vessels during the First 'Cod War' between September 1958 and March 1961, *Carron* among them. She carried out a patrol between 11 and 29 September 1959. She had her full complement of cadets on board, for many of whom this was their first trip to sea, and she hit a gale in the North Sea soon after sailing but the patrol was completed without any serious incident. *Carron* continued to

serve in the DTS until the end of 1959 when she was refitted and converted for use as a navigational training ship to operate as a tender to the Navigation and Direction School, *HMS Dryad* in Portsmouth, commencing her new duties in July 1960. In this role she took officers training to be navigators to sea for short periods to practice their skills and provided basic instruction in techniques such as coastal chart work and anchorage planning for classes of Sub Lieutenants before they were appointed to their first ships. This work was mainly carried out along the south coast but she made occasional cruises throughout the UK and to northwest Europe. She assisted in the rescue of a ditched Whirlwind helicopter crew off Portland in August 1960 and in 1961 carried out evaluations of new life-rafts and survival suits during foul-weather trials in the North Atlantic. By 1963 a number of newer frigate hulls that were surplus to requirements in the operational fleets and which required less manpower than *Carron* to run were becoming available so she paid off into un-maintained reserve at Portsmouth on 5 April 1963. After de-storing and the removal of equipment that could be re-used in other ships was completed on 30 April, *Carron* was placed on the Sales List but no foreign navy showed any interest in her and she was sold to T W Ward for scrap on 10 March 1967 and towed to Inverkeithing three weeks later, arriving on 4 April 1967 after which she was broken up for scrap.

Chapter 5

HMS CARYSFORT

HMS Carysfort *in her original configuration, painted in the Admiralty Standard Scheme, photographed in April 1945. 'X' and 'Y' mountings are following the director which is trained on the camera.* *(Steve Bush Collection)*

The order for *Carysfort* underwent several changes before the ship was even laid down. She was originally ordered from Cammell Laird & Co of Birkenhead on 16 February 1942 and to have been named *Pique*. In August 1942 the contract was transferred to J Samuel White of Cowes and the name changed to *Carysfort*. She was eventually laid down on 12 May 1943 and launched on 25 July 1944 by Mrs G A Bassett, the wife of the Admiralty's Deputy Director of Dockyards. As with others of her class, supply shortages forced her to be completed without a director and she commissioned to this interim standard on 20 February 1945, ten days after completion, for service in the Home Fleet with the 6th Destroyer Flotilla. She was the last of her class to be completed and worked up to operational efficiency in March

before sailing on 26 March for Operation 'PRE-FIX', a series of attacks on shipping in Trondheim Leads, Aalesund and towards Kristiansand North by aircraft from the escort carriers *Searcher, Queen, Nairana* and *Puncher*. They were escorted by the cruisers *Dido* and *Bellona* and the destroyers *Onslow, Carysfort, Serapis, Zealous, Zest* and HM Canadian destroyers *Haida* and *Iroquois*. Bad weather limited the effectiveness of the strike but carrier-borne fighters shot down several enemy aircraft over the target areas.

On 6 April she sailed with the escort carriers *Puncher, Queen* and *Searcher* for Operation 'NEW-MARKET' which was intended to attack U-boat depot ships in Kilbotn, near Harstadt, Norway, but despite cruising for several days waiting for an improvement, bad weather prevented aircraft from

HMS Carysfort *entering Portsmouth flying her paying-off pennant on 28 May 1946. Days later she was reduced to extended reserve.*
(National Museum of the Royal Navy)

taking off and the operation was cancelled. After a brief docking, *Carysfort* carried out experiments with taking on ammunition at sea in company with *LST 3019* on 15 April 1945. Her work-up exercises included being towed by the cruiser *Bermuda* and escorting the battleship *Rodney* while she carried out main and secondary armament shoots.

On 4 May 1945 she sailed with the escort carriers *Trumpeter*, *Searcher* and *Queen* for Operation 'JUDGEMENT', another air strike on the U-Boat depot ships at Kilbotn, which was to be the last offensive operation by the Home Fleet during the Second World War. In addition to the carriers, the force included the cruisers *Norfolk* and *Diadem* and the destroyers *Opportune*, *Savage*, *Scourge*, *Zambesi* and *Carysfort*. Avenger bombers from the carriers sank the 5,035 ton depot ship *Black Watch*, *U-711* alongside her and the 840 ton cargo vessel *Senja*. The flak-ship *Harald Haarfagre* was left on fire by strafing fighters but only two aircraft were

lost. Two days later the force was diverted from its return to Scapa Flow to proceed to Copenhagen in support of British units that were to take the surrender of German forces in Denmark; the task was given the code name Operation 'CLEAVER'. Other tasks followed and on 9 May 1945 she patrolled the Skagerrak to prevent U-boats from escaping the defeated Germany. She returned to Scapa Flow on 10 May and on 21 May was off Greenock where the troopship *Largs Bay* was embarking Norwegian troops. On 22 May both ships sailed for Tromso, arriving on 26 May when the Norwegians landed and took over from the German garrison which surrendered. *Carysfort's* First Lieutenant seized the opportunity to re-paint the ship in peacetime grey and on 27 May she was opened to visitors and entertained a number of local dignitaries. She returned to Scapa Flow on 31 May, leaving on 3 June for a boiler clean in Rosyth. After allocation to the BPF she entered Portsmouth

Dockyard on 16 June to de-ammunition in preparation for a refit during which her director was to be fitted and the close range armament improved.

Post-refit trials and a work-up were carried out from 19 September 1945 and she sailed for the Far East on 28 September. She worked up to operational efficiency off Malta during October with *Norfolk, Chaplet*, motor-torpedo boats and aircraft from the Fleet Requirements Unit at RNAS Hal Far. She passed through the Suez Canal on 1 November and proceeded to Trincomalee via Aden and Colombo, arriving on 17 November. By 4 December 1945 she was carrying out her first patrol in the strait between Java and Sumatra seeking to prevent arms being landed to support the insurrection against Dutch rule. On 12 December she joined Captain D6 in *Caesar* with *Carron* and *Cavalier* for exercises off Singapore before proceeding to Soerabaya in Java where she stood by to bombard insurgent positions ashore in support of British infantry. The town was captured a day later and *Carysfort* put a landing party ashore to help

patrol the streets. On 18 December she moved to Semerang on the north coast of Java and landed a team of engineers to get the local power station back into operation. For several days she bombarded road-blocks and other insurgent positions inland, finally leaving the area on 5 January 1946 to patrol the Java Sea between Java and Borneo to prevent junks from taking supplies to the Indonesians. On 9 January she returned to Singapore in company with *Carron* and *Cavalier* before proceeding to Trincomalee where she carried out an assisted maintenance period secured alongside *Beachy Head*. Visits to Johore and Selanghor in Malaya in February were followed by exercises with *Cavendish* and *Loch Glendhu* after which *Carysfort* visited Batavia, the capital of the Dutch East Indies. Next she carried out a number of visits to 'show the flag' and restore stability; on 21 February while she was off Macassa in Celebes with *Crane*, the American ship *Sea Satyr* steamed passed the British warships and hit a mine while entering harbour. On 27 February *Carysfort* was ordered to leave

HMS Carysfort as she appeared in September 1959. She was one of the four modernised 'Ca's to have an open bridge based on the Daring class design which allowed a larger operations room beneath it.
(National Museum of the Royal Navy)

Macassa and proceed 'with all convenient despatch' to Palembang on the east coast of Sumatra where British forces were insufficiently strong to take action against local extremists. Japanese troops, under British control, were still being used to protect the oil refinery at Pladjoe and they reported after dark that Indonesians were landing from boats near them and appeared likely to attack. Prompt steps were taken to counter the threat but no attack developed and the movements appear to have been some sort of demonstration. *Loch Tarbert* relieved *Carysfort* on 7 March and she sailed for Singapore, arriving a day later. She returned to Trincomalee on 16 March and sailed a day later to transport passengers to Cochin in India. In April she operated as plane-guard for the aircraft carrier *Colossus* which had transferred to the East Indies Fleet from the BPF and was operating off Ceylon. The ever present threat from wartime mines which had broken adrift was emphasised on 26 April when a marksman, closed up for the purpose on *Carysfort* shot and detonated a floating mine nearby. On 1 May *Carysfort* took part with other warships in the live firing practice that sank the old gunboat *Tarantula* and on 3 May 1946 *Caesar, Carysfort, Carron* and *Petard* all left Trincomalee for the UK flying paying-off pennants. They passed through the Suez Canal on 15 May and on 19 May, while steaming off the coast of North Africa, another mine passed between *Carysfort* and *Petard* and had to be detonated by a marksman from the former. She arrived back in Portsmouth on 28 May and de-stored prior to paying off into reserve, moored in Portchester Creek.

She was brought out of reserve and re-commissioned by a steaming party on 21 July 1947 to accompany a group of Minesweepers that had been sold to the Greek Navy on the outbound voyage as they were towed to Piraeus, arriving on 1 September. Her return voyage took her through a storm off Sicily and arrived in Gibraltar, where she was to be refitted, on 7 September after which her steaming party sailed *Carron* back to the UK leaving *Carysfort* in dockyard hands. In November a

steaming party brought *Cavalier* out to Gibraltar for refit and transferred to *Carysfort* to sail her back to the UK on completion of her post refit trials. She sailed on 5 December and carried out a full power trial during which she achieved 33 knots for three hours. On 18 December she arrived back in Portsmouth and reduced to reserve again.

After a short refit in Portsmouth in 1950, a contract was placed with Yarrow in 1953 to modernise *Carysfort* at their Scotstoun Yard in Glasgow and she was downgraded to un-maintained reserve to await the work. Nearly a year elapsed before work started however, and she was towed to Scotstoun for work to commence on 23 January 1954.

She re-commissioned for operational service on 14 December 1956 and was allocated to 6 DS for rotation between the Home and Mediterranean Fleets as part of a new policy intended to lessen the time ship's companies spent deployed away from their homes and families. She took part in the usual routine of fleet exercises and port visits and in 1957 carried out a six week patrol in the coastal waters off Cyprus, preventing gun-runners from smuggling supplies ashore to EOKA terrorists. The opportunity was taken to take parties of soldiers to sea and to land parties of sailors to carry out patrols in the Troodos mountains with the Army. The UK leg of the commission took place in the latter part of 1957 and the early part of 1958 and included visits to Antwerp, Hartlepool and a major visit to London from 20 February 1958 in company with *Contest* and *Cavendish*. A further stint in the Mediterranean followed, during which she was refitted in Malta. On 28 November 1958 *Carysfort* returned from the Mediterranean in company with the frigate *Torquay* and re-joined the Home Fleet for a series of anti-submarine exercises in the Clyde exercise areas. She was open to the public at Portsmouth Navy Days in March 1959 together with *Tyne, Gambia, Troubridge, Plover* and *Zest*. The First 'Cod War' against Iceland had begun in September 1958 and *Carysfort* carried out two patrols in support of British fishing vessels, the first between 10 and 28 May and the second between 23 July and 11 August

1959.

After a short refit she re-commissioned again on 8 September 1959 and was allocated to 8 DS in the FEF as a replacement for *Cheviot*. She sailed from the UK on 20 November 1959 and acted as guard-ship at Gan for a few days in January 1960. On 18 January she visited Calcutta in company with *Belfast, Cavalier* and *RFA Gold Ranger*. After sailing on 22 January she exercised with the Pakistan Naval destroyer *Jahangir*, formerly her sister-ship *Crispin*. She arrived in Singapore and exercised in the local areas before sailing to Trincomalee in February for participation in Exercise JET with the aircraft carriers *Centaur* and *Vikrant* together with a number of other Commonwealth warships. During the exercise a Sea Venom fighter from *Centaur* ditched and its pilot and observer were rescued by *Carysfort*. From March to June she underwent a refit in Singapore and, after working up, sailed on 5 August for Exercise FOTEX 60 in company with *Belfast, Caesar, Crane, St Brides Bay* and *RFA Wave Master*. When the exercise was over she carried out a series of port visits in Australia and New Zealand which included Darwin, Cairns, Brisbane and Auckland. The opportunity was taken between visits to exercise with RAN and RNZN warships. On 20 October 1960 she was in Sydney and underwent a short docking and 'bottom scrape' in the Captain Cook dry dock in Garden Island Dockyard. She returned to Singapore via Darwin and subsequently visited Hong Kong, Penang and Bangkok.

On 9 May 1961 she paid off in Singapore and a new ship's company took over and re-commissioned her on 15 May 1961. Much of the Far East Fleet's activity at this time was centred on demonstrating its ability to defend British and Commonwealth interests and trade in the region. *Carysfort* took part in Exercise FOTEX 62 and visited Inchon in South Korea, Yokohama in Japan and Okinawa before returning to Singapore to prepare for her departure from the Far East Fleet after three years on the Station. After passing through the Mediterranean she arrived in Gibraltar for a long refit on 25 October 1962.

She emerged from the refit to re-commission on 14 May 1964 and sailed for the UK to work up at

HMS Carysfort *off Portsmouth in March 1967. She has been fitted for-but-not-with Seacat and has a single Mark 7 Bofors fitted on the launcher position after of the missile handling room structure.* (Syd Goodman Collection)

Portland, carrying out visits to Santander, Antwerp and Londonderry while serving with the Home Fleet. At the beginning of September 1964 she joined *Lion, Agincourt, Diamond, Eskimo, Galatea, Londonderry, Pellew, Relentless, Rhyl* and *Salisbury* in the Firth of Forth for a Review to celebrate the opening of the Forth Road Bridge on 4 September 1964. After that she returned to the Far East Fleet, arriving in Singapore on 12 February at the height of the Confrontation with Indonesia. She carried out several patrols against Indonesian incursion in Malaysian waters and handed over the task of guard-ship at Tawau to *HMAS Yarra* in June 1965. In December she took part in Exercise 'CALPURNIA' with *Lion, Agincourt, Penelope* and *Troubridge*. In 1966 she acted as guard-ship in the Seychelles during riots that followed a labour dispute, being relieved by *Mohawk* to return to Devonport for refit.

Carysfort re-commissioned at Devonport on 20 January 1967 and worked up subsequently at Portland. On 18 March she was allocated to the force spraying detergent on the oil spilling from the wrecked tanker *Torrey Canyon* off the coast of Cornwall together with *Barrosa* and *Clarbeston*. By 21 March the situation had deteriorated and it was decided to use naval aircraft to bomb the wreck in order to ignite the oil in the hope of burning it off. *Carysfort, Aurora, Eskimo, Daring, Chichester, Barrosa* and *Delight* formed a five-mile cordon around the wreck to keep other shipping clear. Later in 1967 she acted as plane-guard for *Eagle* and then became guard-ship at Gibraltar during a period of tension with the Spanish Government over sovereignty. In January 1968 she deployed to the South Atlantic, visiting Freetown en route. After a further stop at Simonstown she carried out a Beira Patrol and then visited Mauritius for its Independence Day celebrations on 15 March 1968 and then proceeded to Singapore via Gan to rejoin the Far East Fleet. She visited Tonga and Fiji in June 1968 and was at Nelson in New Zealand on 18 June for ceremonies to mark the adoption of a new white ensign by the Royal New Zealand Navy. From there she carried out a fortnight's self-maintenance period in Sydney and then carried out exercises with Australian warships. After a further visit to New Zealand waters for exercises with the RNZN she returned to Singapore via Townsville, New Caledonia and Darwin. It was now time for *Carysfort* to leave the Far East for the last time, having spent most of her operational life there. She sailed via the South Pacific for a further Beira Patrol and was in Simonstown in October 1968. She arrived back in Devonport on 14 November 1968.

Early in 1969 she carried out submarine training exercises with boats in the Faslane areas including *Onyx*. Later in January she deputised for the navigation training ship *Ulster* and took classes of Sub Lieutenants to sea for training. She returned to the Faslane areas for a CASEX with *Finwhale* and *Olympus* later in February and then visited Liverpool where she was open to visitors. After sailing she carried out a CASEX with *Dundas* and the new SSBN *Renown* after which she returned to Devonport in March flying her paying-off pennant. She paid off formally at sunset on 31 March 1969 having de-stored at the end of an effective and varied life in the RN. She was immediately placed on the disposal list. By then much of her equipment was considered to be obsolescent and of little further value and on 23 October 1970 she was sold to John Cashmore Ltd for scrap, arriving at Newport to be broken up on 13 November 1970.

Chapter 6

HMS CASSANDRA

HMS Cassandra *painted in the two-tone grey paint scheme used in the immediate post-war period. She is seen here still very much as completed in terms of armament and equipment.* (Crown Copyright/MoD)

Ordered from Yarrow at Scotstoun and originally to have been named *Tourmaline*, she was renamed *Cassandra* before being laid down on 30 January 1943. She was launched on 29 November 1943, having been 'adopted' by Surbiton after a successful Warship Week raising funds through National Savings. She was completed on 28 July 1944 and commissioned after the completion of Contractor's Sea Trials but had to leave the builder's yard without her director because of wartime supply shortages. After storing she sailed for Scapa Flow to work up in July 1944 and joined 6 DF in August. In October 1944 she sailed for Operation 'ATHLETIC' with the new fleet aircraft carrier *Implacable* during which her aircraft attacked coastal shipping successfully with bombs and torpedoes. The screen comprised *Bellona,*

Venus, Scourge, Savage, Verulam, Caprice, Zambesi, Cambrian and *Cassandra*. In November 1944 she sailed with the escort carrier *Campania* for Operation 'GOLDEN' as ocean escort for Convoy JW61A to North Russia together with *Berwick, Cambrian, Caprice, Saumarez* and *Scourge*. This convoy contained troopships that were carrying former Russian prisoners of war back to Russia after their liberation in Normandy. She returned with the same ships escorting RA61.

On 30 November she sailed with the escort carriers *Campania* and *Nairana* as part of Operation 'ACUMEN' to escort convoy JW62 to North Russia. Other ships in the screen included *Bellona, Caesar, Cambrian, Caprice, Onslow, Obedient, Offa, Onslaught, Oribi* and *Orwell*. They arrived in the Kola Inlet without having been attacked by the

enemy on 7 December 1944. The escort carried out an offensive sweep against U-boats known to be in the area on 10 December but when the return convoy, RA62, left Kola that day it was immediately attacked by U-boats and aircraft. At 0601 on 11 December 1944 *Cassandra*, which was stationed to the rear of the convoy, was hit in the bow by a torpedo from *U-365* and the whole section forward of 'B' mounting broke off and sank. Sixty-one sailors were killed outright and another died later of his injuries. Twenty-one men were injured. The soundness of the design's watertight sub-division and good damage-control saved the ship, however, and the frigate *Bahamas* managed to pass a line to the stricken vessel and subsequently towed her stern-first to Murmansk where she was docked on 5 January 1945. The damaged area was cut away and a temporary bow fitted. A shortage of steel plate in Russia slowed the work which was not completed until June 1945 and she finally sailed for the UK on 14 June 1945 accompanied by *Onslaught*. She

arrived at Rosyth Dockyard on 18 June to de-store and land all her ammunition and then sailed to Gibraltar where a permanent replacement bow, built for the purpose by Yarrow, was fitted from 11 August 1945. The priority for such work was low and it was not completed until the end of 1946.

In December 1947 *Cassandra* returned to Devonport where she joined the Reserve Fleet and laid up on the River Tamar. On 14 April 1947 she was taken into Dockyard hands for her director to be fitted and the implementation of a number of class alterations and additions. When the work was completed in October she rejoined the Reserve Fleet in Devonport with a small working party carrying routine maintenance. In 1949 she was towed to Sheerness Dockyard by the tug *Cautious*, arriving on 21 November. On 2 March 1955 the same tug towed her to Liverpool where she underwent interim modernisation work, including the installation of twin Squid mountings and the associated bomb-room in place of 'X' mounting. The work

HMS Cassandra *laid up in reserve with her armament, bridge and funnel cap cocooned.* *(David Hobbs Collection)*

HMS Cassandra *in the Johore Strait with hands fallen in for entering Singapore Naval Base. Interestingly, she has neither a leader's black band on the funnel nor a pennant number painted on the hull. The paying-off pennant could date this photograph to 1961.*   *(Steve Bush Collection)*

was completed in November and she subsequently carried out steaming trials before being laid up in un-maintained reserve at Penarth awaiting her full conversion. In November 1957 she was towed to Yarrows on the Clyde where a full modernisation was carried out although the work was slowed by shortages of manpower and equipment. She re-commissioned on 18 July 1960 for service with 8 DS in the Far East Fleet, nearly sixteen years after she had last seen operational service. On 17 October she sailed from the UK for Singapore, taking the normal route through the Mediterranean, Suez Canal and Indian Ocean.

On 26 June 1961 she was with the aircraft carrier *Victorious* on passage from Singapore to Hong Kong when the force was ordered to proceed to the Persian Gulf 'with all despatch' after Kuwait was threatened with invasion by Iraq. On passage they were refuelled by *RFA Wave Ruler* off Northern Sumatra and *Cassandra* was re-fuelled twice by *Victorious*. Before they arrived in the Gulf they

were joined by the aircraft direction frigate *Lincoln*. They arrived on 8 July to participate in Operation 'VANTAGE' and, together with Royal Marines landed from *Bulwark* and troops subsequently flown in from Aden and East Africa, the task force provided a show of British strength that deterred Iraqi aggression. They were relieved in late July by *Centaur* and her battle group, although by then the crisis was over.

In September she took part in Exercise TUCKER-BOX, an Australian-planned training period that covered an area from the Coral Sea to Sydney. RAN ships involved were the aircraft carrier *Melbourne* and the destroyers *Vendetta, Vampire, Queenborough* and *Anzac*; the RN input comprised *Tiger, Caprice, Cassandra, Loch Killisport* and several RFAs. The planned fleet entry into Sydney at the conclusion of the exercise had to be cancelled, unfortunately, because of bad weather. In March 1962 she took part in FOTEX 62 with a large number of Commonwealth warships including *Ark*

HMS Cassandra *showing off her classic destroyer lines as she approaches another ship to carry out a replenishment at sea.* *(Syd Goodman Collection)*

Royal, Bulwark, Tiger, Carysfort, Cavalier, Plymouth, Eastbourne, HMA Ships Parramatta, Yarra and *HMNZS Taranaki.* A sports day at *HMS Terror,* the RN barracks in Singapore Naval base, on 6 June 1962 went well until it was washed out by a thunderstorm.

Back at sea in July 1962 *Cassandra* and *Caprice* collided whilst manoeuvring in close company and

Cassandra suffered considerable damage to her bow. Repairs were carried out in the King George VI dock in Singapore Dockyard and the ship finally sailed, with her third bow, on 17 October 1962 for Exercise TUCKERBOX 62 after which she visited Sydney, Newcastle, Magnetic Island and Townsville with many sailors able to visit the Great Barrier Reef. She returned to Singapore in compa-

ny with *Caprice* to carry out a self maintenance period. A visit to Hong Kong saw *Cassandra* taking part in a bombardment exercise followed by a landing exercise on Lantao Island.

Like several of her sister-ships *Cassandra* spent periods as guard-ship at Gan in the Maldive Islands. In November 1962 a representative from the Commonwealth Relations Office had visited Male, the Islands' capital after which islanders staged a hostile demonstration against the handful of British citizens. Five Britons, including two women schoolteachers, were evacuated to the frigate *Loch Fada* and *Cassandra* relieved her on station. The dispute arose out of the removal of the civilian population from Gan Atoll, 300 miles from Male, when

it was leased to the RAF for use as a staging post in 1959. After three weeks on station *Cassandra* was, in turn, relieved by *Blackpool*.

Cassandra returned to Singapore for a week and then sailed for what her Report of Proceedings described as a "backwards around the world cruise". In January 1963 she visited Guam and then joined *Cavalier, Llandaff* and *RFA Wave Sovereign* in the Central Pacific to form a line along the route of the Queen's flight to Australia and New Zealand from Fiji to provide SAR cover which, fortunately, was not needed. Resuming her passage home, *Cassandra* visited Honolulu and San Francisco, opening to visitors in the latter. After passing through the Panama Canal, she rescued some

Amidships detail of Cassandra *in 1960. The overlapping, riveted hull plates show up clearly, as do the 'wind-scoops' fitted into some scuttles. The round plate below the after end of 'A' mounting is an escape hatch.*

(T. Ferrers-Walker)

Cuban 'boat people' and diverted to land them in Key West before proceeding as originally planned to Bermuda. After short re-fuelling visits to the Azores and Gibraltar, *Cassandra* entered the Mediterranean for a docking in Malta after which she joined the newly-formed 21st Escort Squadron. She subsequently visited Barcelona with *Devonshire* where both ships put on very successful children's parties. Subsequent visits to Gibraltar and Casablanca were followed by exercises with the Moroccan Navy before *Cassandra* finally sailed for the UK. She arrived at Portsmouth on 6 May 1963. Since leaving the UK she had steamed 53,807 miles and visited 25 ports in five continents; fired 1,100 rounds of 4.5 inch ammunition and drunk 140,400 cans of beer in 12 months.

In January 1964 she sailed with the aircraft carrier *Hermes* screened by *Lion, Berwick, Devonshire* and *Llandaff* for Exercise 'PHOENIX', a test of the Home Fleet's defences against high-flying jet bombers. In May she visited Belfast and among many visitors were men who had been on board when she was torpedoed in 1944. In June she deployed into the Mediterranean again to take part in the last Mediterranean Fleet Assembly, led by the last Flag Officer Flotillas (Mediterranean) flying his flag in *Lion*. Other ships present were *Aisne,*

Falmouth, Surprise, two submarines and *RFA Wave Baron*.

In March 1965 she took part in the large NATO Exercise 'PILOT LIGHT' with *Ark Royal, Tiger, Lion, Brighton, Falmouth*, and *Murray* together with warships from Canada, Norway, the Netherlands and the United States. On completion of the exercise, the allied warships visited Bergen. After that she returned to Rosyth and then Portsmouth on 18 June 1965 where she was de-stored, de-commissioned and placed on the Disposal List. In a life of just over twenty years, she had spent only six of them in operational service and had been extensively modernised but there was no overseas interest in buying her as a 'runner' and on 3 March 1967 she was sold to Thomas Ward for scrap, arriving at Inverkeithing on 28 April 1967 for demolition. Like several of her sisters, her short operational life hardly seems to have justified the cost of maintenance and modernisation but she had played a useful role in the reserve fleet and her short commission after modernisation had been an active one that many remember with pride. Her part with *Victorious* in 1961 in Operation 'VANTAGE' was a classic demonstration of how sea power supports the interests of our island nation.

Chapter 7

HMS CAVALIER

A slightly weather-battered Cavalier *leaving Liverpool, in 1945, after her K Mark 1 director was fitted. Note the number of depth charges stowed aft.*
(Syd Goodman Collection)

The contract that eventually led to *Cavalier* was originally placed with John Brown of Clydebank for a destroyer to be named *Pellew*. Due to the pressure of work at the yard, however, the contract was transferred to J S White of Cowes and the name changed before she was laid down on 28 February 1943. Construction was delayed slightly by damage to the shipyard in an air raid but she was launched on 7 April 1944. She was completed on 22 November 1944 without her director and commissioned for service with the 6th Destroyer Flotilla in the Home Fleet. She was the first, and remains the only RN warship ever to have been allocated the name and was adopted by the town of Morpeth in Northumberland.

After completion she carried out contractor's sea trials and moved to Portsmouth to take on stores

and ammunition, leaving for Scapa Flow on 2 January 1945 to commence a work-up. After several short-range screening operations she sailed in company with the escort carriers *Premier* and *Puncher* on 11 February 1945 for Operation 'SELENIUM', a series of strike operations off the Norwegian coast which were adversely affected by bad weather. The screen comprised *Devonshire*, *Cavendish*, *Scourge* and *Zebra* in addition to *Cavalier*. On 22 February she sailed with the same aircraft carriers for Operations 'SHRED' and 'GROUNDSHEET', further strikes in the Norwegian littoral. This time the screen comprised *Dido*, *Myngs* and *Scorpion* in addition to *Cavalier*. Operation 'SHRED' had to be aborted because of bad weather. On 23 February she was detached with *Myngs* and *Scorpion* to reinforce the escort of

HMS Cavalier *returning to Portsmouth flying her paying-off pennant on 16 June 1946.*

(National Museum of the Royal Navy)

convoy RA64 which had been dispersed by extremely bad weather that damaged some of the escorts. They 'rounded up' the convoy, which had encountered Force 12 winds, and 31 of the original 34 merchant ships arrived safely in the Clyde. The escorts returned to Scapa Flow on 27 February. In April and May she acted as escort for high-speed troopships as they entered the North West approaches loaded with US troops. On 6 May she began a search for surfaced U-boats that had been ordered to surrender. A day later she carried out torpedo firing exercises with other destroyers in Scapa Flow and was hit by a practice weapon that damaged both propellers and the port 'A' bracket. Following an underwater inspection in Scapa Flow, she was towed to Rosyth for repairs in June and the opportunity was taken to fit her director tower and refit her for service in the BPF. During post-refit trials she visited her adopted town, Morpeth on 25 August 1945

Cavalier sailed for the Far East on 30 August 1945, arriving at Malta on 7 September for a further period of work up to operational efficiency. She passed through the Suez Canal on 17 September

and arrived in Trincomalee on 2 October. In November she patrolled the sea areas off Java and on 10 November bombarded Indonesian insurgents at Surabaya after they had been warned that they were about to come under fire. After a brief visit to Singapore she sailed with *Sussex, Caesar* and *Carron* to cover the passage of a convoy taking the 5th Indian Infantry Division to Surabaya. In February 1946 *Cavalier* formed part of Force 64 which was used to put down a mutiny by the Royal Indian Navy in Bombay, after which she visited a number of ports in India as a display of British strength as the Sub Continent moved towards independence, before returning to Singapore at the end of April. She left Singapore on 20 May and returned to the UK, arriving in Portsmouth on 16 June 1946. Once she was alongside her ship's company was run down and stores and ammunition were removed before she was reduced to reserve status on 6 September 1946.

In 1948 she was 'cocooned' for a long period in reserve, but remained capable of being brought forward at short notice for operational service if needed. In May 1955 she was brought out of reserve,

refitted at Portsmouth and then modernised by Thornycroft at its Southampton shipyard between 1955 and 1957. She emerged with a new bridge similar to that fitted in the Daring class and the other features standardised in the 'Ca' class modernisation package and re-commissioned for active service on 15 June 1957. She worked-up at Portland and Malta before joining 8 DS in the Far East Fleet, replacing *Comus*.

She arrived in Singapore on 31 October 1957 and was to spend the next six years serving in the Far East Fleet. She spent Christmas and the New Year in Hong Kong before visiting Saigon on 3 February 1958 after which she carried out an anti-piracy patrol off Borneo before returning to Singapore on 20 February. In March she sailed for a series of visits to Australian ports starting with Fremantle where she joined *HMAS Melbourne* for a subsequent series of exercises. Next she visited Melbourne and Hobart before crossing the Tasman Sea to exercise with the RNZN and visit Auckland. On 12 April she visited Suva in Fiji and then joined the aircraft carrier *Warrior* and other ships in a task force assembled to secure and patrol the area around the British hydrogen bomb tests at Christmas Island, Operation 'GRAPPLE'. *Cavalier's* commission book for the period describes the detonation as "a great inferno in the sky, red and glowing and yet beautiful, bursting and growing, white, red and huge". She left the area on 2 May in company with *Ulysses* and returned to Hong Kong via Ocean Island and Manus in the Admiralty Islands which had been a BPF base in 1945 and still had a small RAN staff.

After a period in Hong Kong, *Cavalier* sailed in company with *Cheviot* to take part in Exercises 'SHOWBOAT' and 'JET' but over 100 of her ship's company went down with influenza and participation in the latter was cancelled; instead she went to Pulau Tioman to recuperate, eventually returning to Singapore on 5 July. After a dockyard-assisted maintenance period she deployed to the Persian Gulf to relieve *Cossack* at short notice in September and then returned to Singapore. She visited

Bangkok in November, spent Christmas in Hong Kong again and then returned to Singapore on New Year's Day 1959 and de-commissioned.

Cavalier remained alongside in Singapore while her old ship's company flew back to the UK and their replacements flew out to re-commission the ship on 9 January 1959. Six days later she sailed in company with *Cheviot* and the Australian destroyer *Quiberon* for a week of exercises in the Singapore areas during which they carried out anti-submarine training and live shoots against targets towed by Beaufighter aircraft from RAF Seletar. She was in Hong Kong for part of February and then returned to the Malacca Straits for exercises with *Ceylon, Cheviot, Chichester* and the Australian *Queenborough* and *Quiberon*. On 21 February she fired a 21-gun salute for the Duke of Edinburgh who joined the force in the Royal Yacht *Britannia* before entering Singapore. Subsequent visits were made to Penang and Langkawi. In March 1959 *Cavalier* landed her ammunition in Singapore prior to a refit and entered the King George VI dock on 6 April. When the dock was flooded on 8 May, a leak was discovered in her hull and it had to be emptied while rectification work was carried out. After the successful completion of work, she visited Cochin before exercises with *Ceylon, Cheviot,* the submarine *Anchorite* and the Indian frigate *Brahmaputra*. In August she acted as guard-ship at Gan in support of British interests in the Maldive Islands after which she carried out exercises with the aircraft carrier *Centaur* in company with *Ceylon, Llandaff, Solebay* and *RFA Tidesurge* before returning to Singapore. In September she visited Saigon again and hosted a dinner for members of the British, Canadian and Australian Embassies and the Indian Consul. A month later she acted as plane-guard for *Centaur* and then visited Tokyo with her sister-ship *Caprice*. In November she returned to Singapore for an assisted maintenance period before returning to Hong Kong for a third consecutive Christmas.

In January 1960 she returned to Singapore and then moved to Gan for a further spell as guard-ship before carrying out exercises with the RAN from

February. After visits to Fremantle, Adelaide and Hobart she arrived in Sydney on 24 March for a five-day visit. After exercises with the RAN she visited Darwin and then returned to Hong Kong on 7 April and then proceeded to Manilla for the multinational Exercise 'SEALION'. After that she returned to Singapore for a docking and to de-commission. She re-commissioned on 24 June 1960 with a new ship's company flown out from the UK in what was now a well-drilled routine intended to save the time, wear and tear on ships if they had to return to the UK and back to change their people. The system ended a few years later when 'trickle drafting' was introduced.

Cavalier carried out an intensive work-up after re-commissioning and then sailed for the USN exercise areas off Subic bay in the Philippines where she acted as plane-guard for the US aircraft carrier Ticonderoga before moving on to visit Guam and ports in Japan. After a further spell of assisted maintenance in Singapore she took part in Exercise 'PONY EXPRESS', a major exercise that involved six nations, sixty warships and over a hundred naval aircraft. In May she visited Kobe and Manilla before returning to Hong Kong. Another new ship's company took Cavalier over and re-commissioned her at the end of 1961 before taking part in Exercise JET in March 1962 together with the aircraft carriers Centaur and INS Vikrant screened by Belfast, Rhyl, Caprice and Plymouth. The warships that had taken part gathered at the end of the exercise for a de-briefing at Langkawi after which Cavalier accompanied Centaur to Aden for the colony's Armed Forces Week. In mid April she returned to Singapore and, after a spell alongside, sailed for Hong Kong with Carysfort. Visits to Japan and South Korea followed and then she returned to Singapore for a refit that was to last until October 1962. Late in the year she sailed for Fremantle to represent the RN for the Commonwealth Games at nearby Perth and during the passage responded to a distress call from the merchant ship Horizon which had a crew member suffering from pneumonia and internal bleeding.

Cavalier's doctor radioed instructions while she made a high speed dash to the ship 1,200 miles west of Fremantle and, despite high seas, transferred the patient by boat. A 24 knot dash to the port followed during which she re-fuelled from RFA Wave Ruler and eventually the seaman was landed in time for hospital staff to save his life.

On 8 December 1962 an armed rebellion against the formation of Malaysia broke out in Brunei, Sarawak and North Borneo. Cavalier was on her way back from Australia and was ordered to proceed to Singapore 'with despatch'. She slowed as she entered the Changi Channel but still created a sizeable bow-wave which caused excitement among those with boats moored nearby. She entered Singapore Dockyard on 9 December and took on board Land Rovers and trailers together with about 90 Royal Marines of 42 Commando plus a similar number of Gurkhas together with their ammunition and stores. After a further high-speed dash they were landed in Labuan and Cavalier assumed the duty of senior officer in the area and communications relay ship until the arrival of the cruiser Tiger. Christmas 1962 was spent in Singapore and in early 1963 she was given the task Royal Search and Rescue Ship; this entailed being positioned close the flight paths of the Royal Flights when the Queen visited Fiji, Australia and New Zealand. The task included visits to Suva and, eventually on 20 February, Auckland in New Zealand where a maintenance period was carried out in Devonport Dockyard. On 6 March she sailed back to the UK across the Pacific with visits to Tahiti, Christmas island, Pearl Harbor, San Diego and La Libertad in El Salvador before passing through the Panama Canal on 29 April 1963.

On 1 May Cavalier carried out a humanitarian patrol off the island of Haiti on which a revolution was causing considerable distress before moving on to Bermuda where she refuelled in the Dockyard before crossing the Atlantic. She arrived back in Portsmouth after six years away on 26 May 1963 to be greeted by cheering crowds on the Round Tower and foreshore. After being de-stored she de-com-

missioned and was towed to Chatham where she was placed in reserve. In May 1964 she was towed to Gibraltar for a refit but whilst on passage she was hit by the Liberian tanker *Burgan* which damaged her bow and she had to be towed back to Portsmouth for immediate repair. A replacement bow section twenty-five feet long was fabricated and fitted at Devonport. The ship was then towed to Gibraltar for refit, this time successfully. The refit included the removal of the remaining torpedo tubes and the twin Mark 5 Bofors mounting and the fitting of a GWS 20 Seacat launcher and director. She was one of only two 'Ca' class destroyers to be fitted with Seacat although others were fitted 'for but not with'. She was re-commissioned in September 1966 and returned to Portsmouth under

her own power but during post refit trials a number of serious defects were found, most seriously the fire control system which had not been properly refitted and which did not work. After a difficult period working up at Portland she had to be taken in hand at Devonport for her defects to be rectified.

This work was completed in May 1967 and after more time at Portland she arrived in Portsmouth to prepare for service with the Far East Fleet. She sailed on 5 June 1967 having to take passage via the Cape of Good Hope since the 'Six Day War' between Egypt and Israel had closed the Suez Canal. After a brief maintenance period in Simonstown she sailed on 10 July for two Beira Patrols separated by a short maintenance period. After a visit to Mombasa she acted as plane-guard

HMS Cavalier *after her further modernisation with the full GWS 20 Seacat anti-aircraft missile system installed. She is turning away from the camera at speed 'dressed' with a jack forward and white ensigns at the foremast and aft.*
(Crown Copyright/MoD)

HMS Cavalier *entering Portsmouth towards the end of her long career. She has four dark blue dummy Seacat rounds on the launcher and hands are fallen in for entry into harbour.* *(Tim Meredith)*

for the aircraft carrier *Eagle* before arriving in Singapore on 6 October. By November she was in Hong Kong and underwent Captain 'D's harbour and sea inspections, doing well in both. A self-maintenance period back in Singapore extended over the Christmas period and she sailed with the aircraft carrier *Eagle* for flying exercises off Gan in January 1968. In February she visited Adelaide prior to exercises with the RAN and subsequently visited Melbourne in company with *Troubridge*. After further visits to Newcastle and Jervis Bay she visited Sydney for a week from 11 March. After that she visited Hobart and then Mauritius and Diego Suarez in April before carrying out another Beira Patrol until 30 April. She visited Simonstown for a maintenance period until 18 May when she sailed for the UK with refuelling stops in Freetown and Gibraltar. *Cavalier* arrived in Devonport on 30 May 1968 where she joined the new Western Fleet, an amalgamation of the former Home and Mediterranean Fleets.

After a defect rectification period in Devonport, she acted as plane-guard for the aircraft carrier *Hermes* off Portland in July and then joined *Chichester* and *Jaguar* for Exercise 'FORTHEX' in the Firth of Forth. In September she took part in Exercise 'SILVER TOWER', a major NATO exercise intended to demonstrate the ability of national forces to integrate into an effective coalition organisation at short notice. *Cavalier* returned to Devonport in August and then sailed for the Mediterranean in October, visiting Gibraltar, Marseilles and Toulon before taking part in another major NATO exercise, 'EDEN APPLE' in November. It was intended to give practice to the navies of the UK, USA, Greece, Italy and France in co-ordinating their naval air and anti-submarine forces in the region. RN forces included *Hampshire, Kent, Barossa, Cavalier, Arethusa, Juno, Sirius, Mohawk, Zulu, Jaguar, Leopard, Troubridge* and the submarines *Valiant, Oracle, Osiris, Grampus, Alliance,* and the *RFAs Olwen, Olmeda, Tidepool, Resource* and *Lyness*. The aircraft carrier *Eagle* was in refit at the time but her air group participated from the NATO air base at Decimomannu in Sicily. In all some 50 ships took part in one of the largest NATO exercises to date and *Cavalier* gathered in Naples with other warships for the subsequent de-brief on 16 November.

In January 1969 she took over for a period as guard-ship at Gibraltar which ended on 21 February when she paid off for a refit in Gibraltar Dockyard.

She moved to Portsmouth to complete the refit and re-commissioned at South Railway Jetty on 6 March 1970 and worked up for operational service in March and April. In May she visited Cherbourg to take part in a ceremony to commemorate wartime resistance fighters. In June she visited Falmouth and then undertook a 'Meet the Navy' tour of UK ports that included Liverpool, Llandudno, the Clyde and Portree. In August she visited Copenhagen and in August acted as plane-guard for the aircraft carrier *Ark Royal*. Late on 8 September she was diverted to go to the aid of the coaster *St Brandon* in the Bristol Channel which was on fire and abandoned in heavy seas and high winds. Despite the difficulties *Cavalier* got a boarding party across and managed to tow the ship into Milford haven after 52 hours hard work. The ship's company were later rewarded with an £11,000 salvage award for their outstanding seamanship. After this incident she re-joined *Ark Royal* and took part, with her, in Exercise 'NORTHERN WEDDING', another massive NATO exercise which included over 180 warships. Another element of the RN input was the Royal Yacht *Britannia* which was used to simulate a convoy in a bid to make wider use of her as a fleet asset. In the event storm damage to her paintwork proved so expensive to refurbish that she was never used in such a role again.

After the exercise *Cavalier* visited Oslo on 26 September and after a brief return to Chatham spent October acting as a target for potential submarine commanding officers doing their 'Perisher' course in the Clyde areas. She visited Peterhead for a few days and then joined the aircraft carrier *Eagle* in the Moray Firth during November to act as plane-guard; she was ideal for this task since she was one of the fastest ships in the fleet and one of only a handful that could match the top speed of the big fleet carriers. In December she sailed to Gibraltar for a brief spell as guard-ship and then spent Christmas in Malta while she carried out a short self-maintenance period. January 1971 saw *Cavalier* taking part in Exercise 'MEDTRAIN', a

weapons and command training period in the Gibraltar areas, after which she returned to Portsmouth in February for a docking. March and April were spent working up at Portland. In late April she visited Llandudno and then represented the Royal Navy at the Battle of the Atlantic Anniversary event in Liverpool. The next few days were spent carrying out fleet exercises followed by a visit to Copenhagen before returning to Chatham on 21 May. She visited Belfast on 2 June and Aberdeen on 8 June before carrying out a fishery protection patrol south of Iceland. This was a period of relative peace between the first and second 'Cod Wars' and she carried out a goodwill visit to Reykjavik on 17 June. After a visit to Peterhead on 5 July *Cavalier* was due to carry out a full power trial and the opportunity was taken to meet *Rapid* after a discussion between the two commanding officers had decided to settle the friendly rivalry between the ships to see which was the fastest. There was considerable interest in the 'race' which took place on 6 July 1971, not least because the two ships were both over 25 years old and no destroyers built subsequently could match them. After a run of 65 nautical miles, *Cavalier* crossed the finishing 'line' first approximately 30 yards ahead of her friendly rival. Both ships entered Rosyth Dockyard where the losers toasted the winners' health in *Rapid's* wardroom.

August was spent training in the Portland areas with visits to Guernsey and Alderney after which she sailed to Gibraltar to take over the duty of guard-ship again. In October she took part in Exercise 'DEEP FURROW', an amphibious training period for NATO warships, including *Bulwark* with 41 Commando Royal Marines and 845 Naval Air Squadron embarked, in the Eastern Mediterranean. Visits to Piraeus, Rhodes and Crete were carried out either side of the exercise and *Cavalier* returned to the UK via Malta. She arrived at Chatham on 5 November 1971. Another large-scale NATO exercise, 'HIGHWOOD' followed a short maintenance period and lasted until 9 December. She was back in Chatham for Christmas

HMS Cavalier *photographed from the air during her 'race' with* Rapid *in July 1971.*   *(Syd Goodman Collection)*

and carried out a period of weapons training at Portland in January 1972. Her last months in operational service included a number of visits to UK ports and in February she visited Cardiff, Birkenhead, Southampton, London and Newcastle. A self-maintenance period in March was followed by a final spell as Gibraltar guard-ship in April, Exercise 'EASY LIFE' and a visit to Livorno in Italy from 24 April. In June she visited the town of Chatham and then Rotterdam before returning to Chatham Dockyard flying her paying-off pennant on 6 July 1972.

While she de-commissioned and de-stored attempts were made by a Trust to preserve her as one of the few remaining British destroyers that had

fought in the Second World War. It eventually purchased *Cavalier* for £65,000 on 21 October 1977. Preservation proved difficult - she was moved at first to Southampton, then the Tyne. Eventually she was procured by the *HMS Cavalier* (Chatham) Trust for £43,350 in January 1999 and towed from Tyneside to Chatham which, by then, had ceased to be a Royal Dockyard and part of it had become Chatham Historic Dockyard Trust. Her case was one of several that were instrumental in establishing a national policy on the preservation of historic vessels and she was subsequently awarded over £1 million from the Heritage Lottery Fund. In 2012 she is open to the public in Number 2 Dry Dock at Chatham and her future seems to be reasonably assured.

Chapter 8

HMS CAVENDISH

HMS Cavendish *in her original condition, painted in the Admiralty Standard Scheme photographed in February 1945. Note the gush-chute rigged at the forecastle break.* (Crown Copyright/MoD 1944)

Ordered from John Brown of Clydebank in February, allocated the job number J1606 and originally to have been named *Sibyl*, she was renamed *Cavendish* before being laid down on 19 May 1943. She was launched on 12 April 1944 and completed on 13 December 1944 without her director tower which had been delayed by production difficulties. On completion of storing she moved to join 6 DF in Scapa Flow where she worked up before sailing for her first operational sortie on 13 January 1945. This was Operation 'GRATIS' in which she formed part of the screen for the escort carriers *Premier* and *Trumpeter* from which aircraft laid mines off Haugesund in Norway. The remainder of the screen comprised *Dido, Opportune, Zest* and *Zodiac*. In February she was employed on screening operations with the Home

Fleet before sailing on 11 February for Operation 'SELENIUM' with the escort carriers *Premier* and *Puncher* with *Devonshire, Cavalier, Scourge* and *Zebra* forming the rest of the screen. The operation was divided into two elements; the first included an attack on shipping in Hustadviken Lead and the second minelaying by aircraft off Skatestromen near Skaten Lighthouse on the coast of Norway. On completion of this operation she returned to screening activities in the North Sea and North West Approaches. In April 1945 she escorted the battleship *Nelson* as far as Gibraltar on the first leg of her deployment to the Far East and in early May 1945 she was ordered to search for U-boats that had been ordered to cease hostilities. *U-516* surrendered to *Cavendish* on 10 May 1945.

Together with other ships of the 6th Destroyer

HMS Cavendish *on completion of her modernisation in 1956. Note the whip aerials; open bridge with the Mark 6M director above it; 'Squid' anti-submarine mortars in 'X' position and the enlarged after deck house which has replaced the after bank of torpedo tubes with the twin Mark 5 Bofors at its forward end. The forward torpedo tubes have been retained.* (Steve Bush Collection)

Flotilla, she was allocated to the British Pacific Fleet so underwent a refit to prepare her for service in the Far East in Devonport Dockyard, which included fitting her K Mark 1 director, between late May and July. She arrived in Colombo on 8 August 1945, shortly before the end of the war and, like her sister-ships, spent some months patrolling the East Indies and supporting British peace-keeping operations ashore. She returned to the UK in the summer of 1946 to de-store and de-commission after which she was placed in reserve in Portsmouth, subsequently moving to Harwich. During a refit in 1950 the engines refused to turn and a subsequent investigation found that nuts and bolts had been scattered through vital parts of the machinery. A police investigation was carried out but insufficient evidence was found to charge anyone with malicious damage. After repairs and the completion of this refit she returned to reserve at Harwich but in 1953 she was reduced to a lower grade of readiness prior to her extensive modernisation. On 10 February 1954 she was towed to the Tyne where she was to be modernised by Vickers-Armstrong at their Walker Naval Yard. This followed the standard 'Ca' class lines with an open bridge based on the Daring design. The work was completed in April and she re-commissioned on 24 April 1956.

After working up *Cavendish* joined the Plymouth Local Flotilla for a spell before being allocated as leader of the Home Fleet's 6th Destroyer Squadron in September 1956 to replace *Battleaxe*. She was in Portsmouth for a leave period in September 1956 when her ship's company were recalled for Operation 'MUSKETEER', the Anglo/French intervention in Suez. She sailed as leader of 6 DS and joined *Comet* and *Contest* in the Eastern Mediterranean where they formed part of the screen for the aircraft carriers *Eagle, Albion* and *Bulwark*. By 13 November she was in Port Said after the cease-fire with a large number of warships that constituted Task Force 345. When the British troopships began to sail from Egypt in convoy she left Egyptian waters in company with *Eagle* and *Barrosa*. After the fighting a United Kingdom Salvage Unit (UKSU) remained in the Canal Zone to raise the wrecks that had blocked the canal.

Warships were stationed 25 miles north of Port Said, outside Egyptian territorial waters, to act in support of the UKSU at short notice should it become necessary. The frigates *Torquay* and *Wizard* fulfilled the task at first, relieved by *Cavendish, Corunna* and *Barrosa* on 29 December 1956. The requirement for the patrol ended and the ships sailed for other duties on 4 January 1957.

Cavendish and 6 DS returned to peacetime duties with the Home and Mediterranean Fleets after the Suez Crisis. In February 1958 the Squadron, comprising *Cavendish* (Captain D6), *Contest* and *Carysfort*, visited London before deploying to the Mediterranean in March. In July 1958 *Cavendish, Dunkirk, Salisbury* and *Torquay* escorted the aircraft carrier *Eagle* during Operation 'FORTITUDE', a major Anglo/American operation to fly British troops from Cyprus to Jordan and land US Marines in the Lebanon to counter aggression from Iraq and Syria. *Eagle's* battle group was placed about 50 miles off Haifa and flew 'round the clock' fighter patrols to defend RAF transport aircraft against interception. This part of the operation was completed on 23 July but the RN continued to provide a presence in the Eastern Mediterranean for a considerable time afterwards. *Cavendish* returned

HMS Cavendish *carrying out a shoot with the director and 4.5-inch guns trained to port. Note the gun's crew around the breech of 'Y' mounting in anti-flash gear, helmets and their action working dress trousers tucked into their socks. The barrels of the Mark 5 twin Bofors are pointed vertically upwards.* (Crown Copyright/MoD)

HMS Cavendish, *with* Carysfort *astern, carrying out officer-of-the-watch manoeuvres at high speed.*
(Crown Copyright/MoD)

to the UK on 28 November 1958 for a spell with the Home Fleet. Between 15 April and 10 May 1959 she carried out a patrol in support of British fishing vessels off Iceland during the first 'Cod War' with Captain D6 on board acting as officer in tactical command, OTC, of all British ships in the area.

She took part in a Home Fleet visit to Stockholm on 2 June 1959 with the flagship *Tyne, Carysfort, Contest, Exmouth* and other ships. A visit to Aarhus in Denmark followed on 12 June. After a refit *Cavendish* re-commissioned on 13 October 1959 for service in the Far East Fleet, replacing *Cheviot* in 8 DS. Her voyage east included a visit to Massawa during which she was present for a graduation ceremony at the Imperial Ethiopian Naval

Academy and fired a 21 gun salute to the Emperor. During her time in the Far East *Cavendish* visited Hobart in May 1960, acted as plane-guard for the aircraft carrier *Albion*, exercised with units of the RAN and RNZN and visited Auckland in September. She was back in Singapore in May 1961 from where she sailed to Gibraltar for refit which lasted from June 1961 to August 1962 after which she re-commissioned for a general-service commission. Her refit had included the removal of the twin Mark 5 40mm Bofors and the installation of a Seacat handling room in a structure that replaced the after torpedo tubes but she was only fitted 'for but not with' a launcher; a single Mark 7 40mm Bofors being fitted instead. After post-refit

trials she sailed for the UK to work up at Portland and spent Christmas 1962 in Portsmouth. She left the UK to return to the Far East Fleet for service in 25 ES on 28 January 1963, passing through the Mediterranean and Suez Canal before being diverted to carry out guard-ship duty at Mali in the Maldive Islands. After arriving in Singapore on 20 March she carried out an anti-piracy patrol off North Borneo before returning to the UK in June.

On 12 August she sailed from Plymouth in company with *Tiger*, *Llandaff* and *Tartar* for Exercise 'RIPTIDE', a NATO training period in the North Atlantic and Bay of Biscay which included the nuclear-powered cruiser *USS Long Beach* among the participating warships. In September 1963 she took part in Exercise 'UNISON' which was intended to practice convoy protection techniques. The aircraft carrier *Hermes* took part flying the flag of Admiral of the Fleet Lord Mountbatten, the Chief of the Defence Staff and the exercise ended off

Portland with the participating ships *Tiger*, *Cavendish*, *Rothesay*, *Llandaff*, *Gurkha*, *Berwick*, *Decoy*, *Leander*, *Brave Borderer* and *Brave Swordsman* steaming past the flagship. In November 1963 she visited Cork and Londonderry before taking part in several Home Fleet exercises. In January 1964 she began a maintenance period in Devonport before sailing for the Far East leg of the commission in April as part of 21 ES. She spent May and June in the Middle East with periods in Aden and Bahrain. She also acted as plane-guard for the aircraft carrier *Centaur* while her aircraft carried out strikes against rebel tribesmen in the Radfan area north of Aden and her helicopters flew troops and stores into the front line. *Centaur's* aircraft flew a total of 560 sorties which played a key role in ending the armed insurrection. After more time in Aden and a visit to Mombassa she arrived at Singapore somewhat later than planned on 13 July 1964.

An assisted maintenance period followed, for

HMS Cavendish *towards the end of her career. The second set of torpedo tubes were landed to compensate for the* weight of the Seacat system.   (Crown Copyright/MoD)

which she was secured alongside the maintenance ship *Hartland Point*. After that she took part in FOTEX 64. The high-point of the commission was a visit to Australia with the aircraft carrier *Victorious*. During a four day visit to Fremantle 18,500 visitors toured *Cavendish* in four days. After leaving Fremantle on 8 September she passed through the Lombok Strait in company with *Victorious* and *Caesar*, *Hampshire, Dido* and *Berwick* to prove their right of innocent passage on the high seas on 12 September and subsequently took part in anti-infiltration patrols off Borneo and Malaysia. These delayed her departure from the Far East but she was still able to return to the UK on 22 October 1964 for a planned refit.

On 6 January 1965 it was announced that she would not re-commission after the refit as intended but would, instead, be placed at extended notice pending a decision on her future. She was laid up in 'G' moorings in Fountain Lake with other ships of the Reserve Fleet in Portsmouth. On 6 August it was decided that she would not be retained in service and she was placed on the Disposal List. On 3 June 1966 she was towed from Portsmouth to Chatham where re-usable items were removed and, after a relatively short operational career, she was sold to Hughes Bolckow on 2 August 1967 for scrap. She arrived at Blyth under tow on 17 August and was subsequently broken up.

The 'Ch' Class
The 12th Emergency Flotilla

The twelfth Emergency Flotilla was given names beginning with 'Ch' from the outset and ordered on 24 July 1942. They retained the same hull and machinery as the previous class and were to be the last class of British destroyers with all-riveted hulls but they incorporated some major differences in armament and fire control. Supplies of Mark 6 directors fitted with Type 275 radar were improving and all eight ships were fitted with them in build although this delayed their completion until after the war was over. The new director proved to be considerably heavier than the K Mark 1 and the original optical range-finder in this type of director was eventually removed during modernisation to save about 1,600lb in top-weight. The same Mark 5 mountings for the 4.5 inch guns, with 55 degrees elevation, were retained but from the 'Ch' class onwards they were fitted with remote power control, RPC, rather than the manual laying and training in the 'Ca' class. This added another 8 tons at upper deck level and compensations had to be made to keep stability within limits. The 'Ch' class had 170 tons more weight at upper deck level than the original emergency destroyers of the 'Q' class and these ships can fairly be said to have reached their design limit.

The most obvious compensation was the removal of the forward set of torpedo tubes but additionally two depth-charge throwers were removed and the number of depth charges embarked was lowered to 48 which were to be dropped in five instead of ten-charge patterns. The twin 40mm Bofors Mark 4 'Hazemeyer' mounting was replaced as soon as possible after completion by the lighter and more robust Mark 5 mounting with a Simple-Type Director. The original requirement for the close-range armament called for a mix of light 20mm and 2pdr pom-pom weapons but most were fitted with two or four 40mm Mark 7 Bofors single mountings soon after the war in the light of the BPF's experience. The fore mast was slightly enlarged to take Type 293 target indication radar and most ships were completed with Type 291 air-warning radar on a short main-mast aft. Arctic heating arrangements were removed with other small weight reductions wherever possible to keep topweight within acceptable limits.

Extra equipment needed more sailors to man it and internal arrangements were cramped and uncomfortable. The flotilla leaders *Chequers* and *Childers* had ship's companies of 240 which meant that some men had to sleep on mattresses on top of lockers. The ships retained hammocks and broadside messing throughout their service lives. Even with their expanded ship's companies the 'Ch's, like the 'Ca's were economical ships to operate, however, in the constrained financial climate after 1945.

The 'Ch's were never modernised to the same extent as the 'Ca' class because they were built with better fire control and RPC from the outset. Their anti-submarine capability was improved by a limited modernisation carried out in the early 1950s when 'X' 4.5-inch mounting was removed and replaced by a double Mark 6 'Squid' mortar installation with its associated weapon handling equipment and magazine. Two ships, *Chaplet* and *Chieftain* were further modified for minelaying with rails on either side aft capable of carrying 25 mines each. Before any mines could be embarked 'Y' gun mounting, all Squid depth-bombs and the torpedo tubes had to be landed to maintain stability within

acceptable limits. By the late 1950s the Royal Navy was contracting and the number of destroyers was drastically reduced as new anti-submarine frigates joined the fleet. All the 'Ch' class were withdrawn by 1962 but many had given over a decade of operational service and actually spent longer in commission than some of the modernised 'Ca' class.

Of interest, the Admiralty sought to help with Royal Canadian Navy plans at the end of 1944 to expand in order to play a greater part in Pacific operations. The RCN was, therefore, offered the whole 'Ch' class on completion but felt that it would not have enough manpower to be ready in time for the planned completion dates. The plan was changed in 1945 and the RCN agreed to take over the whole of the later 'Cr' class instead.

'Ch' Class data:

Displacement:	1,900 tons light 2,535 tons full load
Gun Armament:	4 x 4.5-inch Mark 5 with RPC Twin 40mm Bofors Mark 4 2 x 40mm Bofors Mark 7 2 x 20mm Oerlikon Mark 7
Torpedo Armament:	4 x 21-inch tubes in one quadruple launcher 4 x Mark 9** torpedoes with no re-loads (removed from ships converted to minelayers)
A/S weapons:	Two depth-charge throwers and rails aft Up to 48 depth-charges carried Replaced by 2 x Mark 6 'Squid' mortars after modernisation

Other data as for the 'Ca' class.

Chapter 9

HMS CHAPLET

HMS Chaplet *photographed in August 1945, shortly after her completion. Note the Mark 6 director and the absence of the forward bank of torpedo tubes which had to be removed to compensate for the extra weight of the new director and remote power control for the 4.5 inch guns. Compared with the 'Ca' class there are less depth charges aft and she could only drop a 5-charge pattern. Close-range weapons include a twin Mark 4 'Hazemeyer' Bofors in the 'bandstand' forward of the torpedo tubes; 2pdr 'pom-poms' in powered mountings aft of the funnel and 20mm Oerlikons on the bridge wings.* (Crown Copyright/MoD 1945)

HMS *Chaplet* was ordered in July 1942 from Thornycroft and laid down at their Woolston Yard on 29 April 1943. She was launched on 18 July 1944 and completed only days after the end of the Second World War on 24 August 1945, the lengthy period between launch and completion being due in large part to the delayed delivery of equipment such as the Mark 6 director. She commissioned for the first time on the day of her completion and sailed for Portsmouth to carry out sea trials and to work-up to operational efficiency. On completion she sailed for the Mediterranean Fleet and was allocated to the 14th Destroyer Flotilla. Following a re-organisation of flotillas in 1946 it

was re-numbered to become the 1st Destroyer Flotilla.

After the end of the war in Europe in May 1945 a considerable number of Jewish refugees attempted to reach Palestine, then a British mandated territory, to begin a new life. Their number far exceeded the immigration quota agreed by the United Nations and from the autumn of 1945 the Mediterranean Fleet was ordered to patrol the waters off Palestine with the aim of intercepting ships carrying illegal migrants. The 1st Destroyer Flotilla with its 'Ch' class destroyers was heavily involved from the outset until 1948 when the British mandate ended and the state of Israel came into existence. Migrant

HMS Chaplet *sailing from Malta in 1946 photographed from a different angle. The masts of Ricasoli W/T Station are visible ashore and two Algerine class minesweepers are at buoys close to the wreck of the tanker* Ohio, *made famous by her arrival in Grand Harbour after the 'Pedestal' Convoy in 1942.* (T. Ferrers-Walker Collection)

ships were detained and their people taken to camps, first in Palestine and then in Cyprus, until places could be found for them in the legal quota allowance. The ships were usually released and immigrants knew they were likely, eventually, to be allowed entry so there was always an incentive for the voyages to continue. The ships made every effort to defeat boarding parties and the RN limited the use of firearms for humanitarian reasons. This arduous and unpleasant task continued for over two years.

Chaplet's first interception took place on 18 May 1946 when an RAF patrol aircraft guided *Charity* and *Chaplet* to intercept *Fede* and *Fenice* both flying Italian flags and full of young Jewish illegal

immigrants said to be 'in high spirits'. The ships were escorted to Haifa where their passengers were taken into police custody. The ships were not detained and thus able to return to Italy. On 18 October 1946 *Fenice*, then renamed *Alma*, made another run. She was spotted by an air patrol and intercepted by *Chequers* 140 miles north west of Haifa. *Chequers* shadowed her through the night and then passed the task of making the arrest to *Chaplet* and the minesweepers *Moon* and *Rowena*. Bad weather prevented a boarding at first but she was eventually arrested by parties from *Chaplet* and *Moon* 12 miles off Haifa when she stopped, claiming her engine had broken down. The time in close company had been used to good effect and no

resistance to the arrest was offered; *Moon* towed her into port where 513 men, 261 women and 40 children were landed. Four days later they were taken to a camp in Cyprus in a transport ship escorted by *Chivalrous*.

On 28 September 1947 *Chaplet* took over the task of shadowing *Paducah* and *Northland* as they emerged from the Dardanelles packed with Jewish migrants from Eastern Europe. The task was subsequently handed on to *Haydon* and *St Austell Bay*. By that stage shadowing operations covered not just the coast off Palestine but the length and breadth of the Mediterranean. On 2 October 1947 *Chaplet* intercepted the Panamanian-registered *Paducah* off Tel Aviv and escorted her into Haifa. On 31 January 1948 *Childers* and *Chaplet* intercepted the *Sylvia Starita* 70 miles north west of Cape Carmel and escorted her into Haifa. The wooden motor vessel *Cicilio* was located by aircraft and intercepted by *Cheviot* on 10 February 1948. *Chaplet* and

the tug *Marauder* joined her in the evening. Boarding parties were resisted fiercely until *Chaplet* put a Palestinian police officer onto *Cicilio* after which the migrants agreed to be towed into Haifa by *Marauder*.

Chaplet remained with 1 DS until 1951 when she returned to Portsmouth and paid off into Category A reserve with a small maintenance party on board. In the early 1950s the Commander-in-Chief Mediterranean asked for his Fleet's minelaying capability to be enhanced and as consequence several destroyers, including *Chaplet*, were modified for the role. The work was carried out in Chatham Dockyard, starting on 6 June 1953, as part of an interim modernisation which included the removal of 'Y' mounting and the fitting of mine rails along either side of the iron deck aft and chutes off which the mines were dropped on each quarter. If no mines were carried, 'Y' mounting and the torpedo tubes could be replaced to give the ship a better sur-

HMS Chaplet *as leader of the Plymouth Local Squadron in July 1959. She is 'dressed' with a jack forward and a Norwegian flag at the foremast. Hands are not fallen in but men in working dress are stowing wires and fenders in the blast screen forward of 'B' mounting.* (Syd Goodman Collection)

HMS Chaplet *at anchor with armourers working on 'A' and 'B' mountings; the latter is at its maximum elevation of 55 degrees.*
(*David Hobbs Collection*)

face action capability. In the same dockyard period 'X' mounting was removed and replaced by two 'Squid' anti-submarine mortars and a mortar handling room and the light anti-aircraft weapons were replaced by single Bofors mountings, one on each bridge wing. Improvements were also made to the sonar and radar outfits. No mortar bombs could be carried if the ship had an outfit of mines on deck.

She re-commissioned on 21 January 1954 and rejoined 1 DS in the Mediterranean Fleet after working up. Together with the other ships in her squadron, *Chieftain* and *Chevron*, she carried out patrols in the waters off Cyprus during 1955/56 searching for small craft that were used to smuggle arms and ammunition to EOKA terrorists ashore. The ships operated at night, fully darkened, using Type 974 navigational radar to search for suspect vessels. When one was located *Chaplet* would close as quietly as possible and illuminate it with a 20-inch searchlight, inviting the target vessel to

stop and be searched. During the day ships would anchor in remote locations with armed guards ready in case terrorists tried to swim out to the ship and attach limpet mines.

In October 1956 the squadron comprised *Chieftain, Chaplet* and *Chevron* and formed part of the task force gathered in the Mediterranean for Operation 'MUSKETEER', the Anglo/French operation to re-take control of the Suez Canal from the Egyptian Government that had nationalised it. Initially *Chaplet* formed part of the escort for convoy MES1 as it moved east towards Egypt, refuelling from *Wave Laird* on 2 November. On 6 November, the day of the allied amphibious landings at Port Said, *Chaplet* joined *Duchess, Diamond* and *Decoy* and gave supporting fire for the landing craft as they carried out their assault. The four destroyers steamed ahead of the LSTs engaging targets of opportunity until they reached the 3-fathom line when they fanned out, two ships each to port

and starboard, opening their arcs to give broadside support to the men on the beach. *Chaplet* fired in support of 40 Commando Royal Marines for 45 minutes from 0400 and thereafter as requested by the headquarters ship *Meon* during which she fired 69 rounds of 4.5-inch ammunition.

Chaplet remained with 1 DS in the Mediterranean until May 1957 when she was relieved by *Solebay*. She returned to the UK and replaced *Orwell* in the Plymouth Local Squadron. Local squadrons in the 1950s had reduced ship's companies and were used for a variety of trials and training tasks; it was a method of keeping ships at high readiness at less cost than full commission and, in her case, provided occasional capability as an exercise minelayer. Her operational days were not quite over and she carried out two patrols in the First 'Cod War' during 1959. Between 12 and 28 May she deployed

with Captain 'D' Plymouth who acted as Officer in Tactical Command of the British operation in support of its fishing vessels. This patrol involved two incidents; on 16 May the trawler *Samuel Hewitt* was fired on by the Icelandic gunboat *Odinn*. *Chaplet* moved to the trawler's aid and stood by her until *Odinn* withdrew. Six days later *Odinn* moved aggressively against the trawler *St Just*; *Chaplet* moved between them in support and was hit by the gunboat although not seriously. She returned, this time without Captain 'D', between 30 September and 16 October 1959 for a second patrol which was to be her last operational deployment.

From February 1960 *Chaplet* provided sea-going experience for junior ratings and artificer apprentices from the training schools *Raleigh* and *Fisgard* at Torpoint. In September 1961 she paid off into un-maintained reserve at Devonport and was placed

HMS Chaplet *laid up in the River Tamar awaiting disposal in April 1962. She has no fuel or ammunition on board and is consequently high in the water but she has not been stripped of boats or equipment other than life-rafts. Note the white paint mark on the waterline at the bow. This was applied to all ships in the reserve fleet to show at a glance whether they were taking in water and slowly sinking at their moorings. The Type 15 frigate alongside is* Ulysses.

(David Hobbs Collection)

on the Disposal list in November after being laid up in the River Tamar. Despite being economical to run and having a useful range of capabilities there was no foreign interest in buying her and approval was given to scrap her in July 1963. After four years moored on the trots in the River Tamar she was sold to Hughes Bolckow on 6 November 1965 and subsequently towed to Blyth where she was broken up.

Chapter 10

HMS CHARITY
(PNS SHAH JAHAN from 1958)

HMS Charity *carrying out sea trials on 12 November 1945 a week before her nominal completion date. She is paint-ed in the Admiralty Standard Scheme and already has the 14th Destroyer Flotilla marking on her funnel. Note the canvas-covered boat on the iron deck between the 'Hazemeyer' and 'pom-pom' 'bandstands' arranged to look like the absent, forward torpedo tubes.* (Syd Goodman Collection)

HMS *Charity* was laid down at Thornycroft's Woolston Yard just over two months after *Chaplet* on 9 July 1943. She was launched on 30 November 1944 and completed 19 November 1945. After her initial sea trials in the Solent, she worked up at Malta and joined 1 DS, taking part in patrol operations in the Eastern Mediterranean and off the coast of Palestine to try to stem the flow of illegal Jewish immigrants into the British mandated territory of Palestine. On 18 May 1946 she inter-cepted the Italian-flagged *Fede* and *Fenice* after they were detected by RAF reconnaissance aircraft and escorted them to Haifa together with *Chaplet*. She escorted a transport from Haifa to Cyprus on 22 September 1946 in which there were 611 illegal immigrants from the *Ariella* which had been arrest-

ed the day before by the minesweeper *Rowena* after a most difficult boarding in which the RN had to use tear gas to clear a space for the party to get on board.

On 29 March 1947 she assisted the disabled immigrant ship *San Philipo* together with *Haydon*, *St Brides Bay* and *Octavia*. When intercepted the ship was seen to be dangerously unstable but refused assistance at first; when it finally put out an SOS the warships closed in and *Haydon* put a sal-vage party across with a diesel salvage pump and hoses. They managed to clear the water from the boiler and engine rooms but she remained listed 25 degrees to starboard. No more could be done until the passengers were evacuated from the holds and both *Charity* and *Octavia* went alongside and began

As bow view of Charity *as completed. Note the optical range-finder above the port Type 275 radar aerial in the Mark 6 director and the 20mm Oerlikon in the port bridge wing.* *(Syd Goodman Collection)*

to take them off. *Charity* took on 556 migrants including 49 pregnant women, 18 children plus a doctor and 2 nurses. *Octavia* took on 265 including 65 women and 4 children. Others refused to leave and stayed in *San Philipo*. *Octavia's* passengers were subsequently transferred to *St Brides Bay* leaving her free to tow the stricken ship into Haifa, arriving just as terrorists set fire to an oil refinery there. There could be no doubt that *San Philipo* was dangerously overcrowded and the UN authorities subsequently praised the sailors in the RN ships involved in the incident for their "magnificent, tireless, good humoured and humane action".

The next incident occurred on 2 April 1947 when boarding parties from *St Brides Bay* and *Haydon* met fierce opposition when they tried to arrest *Guardian* aka *Theodor Herzl* and had to open fire on violent 'thugs' among the migrants on the advice of a Palestinian policeman, killing 2 and wounding a third who died later. Fourteen other casualties were transferred to *Charity*, together with a wound-

ed officer from one of the boarding parties, and taken at high speed to Haifa for hospital treatment. The largest and most widely publicised incident was the voyage of the *President Warfield* which passed into Israeli folk-lore as *Exodus 1947* and subsequently portrayed in the film '*Exodus*'. She sailed originally from Marseille, stopping at Sete, ostensibly for the Black Sea with 4,229 men women and children on board from Eastern Europe on board. At sea she was shadowed by the RN but an arrest could not be made until she entered Palestinian territorial waters. The RN shadowing force eventually included the cruiser *Ajax* and *Chequers* (Captain D1), *Childers*, *Chieftain*, *Charity* and *Cardigan Bay*. Preparations for boarding had to include the construction of platforms to get over obstructions placed on *Warfield's* upper deck and when the first attempts were made the decks were crammed with people. Eventually several boarding parties were transferred and, after some heavy fighting at close quarter, the ship was

arrested and taken to Haifa, led in by *Charity* on 18 July 1947. The Commanding Officers of *Charity*, *Chieftain* and *Childers* were mentioned in despatches for their parts in the incident and a number of other awards were made including several Distinguished Service Medals for ratings in the boarding parties.

On 15 December 1948 she was reduced to reserve during one of several post-war manning crises and served as an accommodation ship and headquarters for the Senior Officer Reserve Fleet in Malta. When the manpower situation stabilised she recommissioned for service in the Mediterranean Fleet on 16 May 1949. On 29 June 1949 the submarine *Teredo* carried out a mock attack on her at periscope depth but misjudged her position and collided with *Charity* causing slight damage to her sonar dome and fuel tanks 7 and 8. Later in the year she transferred to 8 DS in the Far East Fleet and underwent a docking in Hong Kong in October 1949.

Charity was involved in the Korean War from the outset and in July 1950 formed part of a task unit

with *Belfast* and *HMAS Bataan* off the west coast of Korea. In August *Belfast*, *Cossack* and *Charity* were instructed to join *Kenya* in a bombardment of an area which was believed to be in use as a base by the North Korean Army. The bombardment took place on 5 August close to a lighthouse in the centre of a channel eleven miles south of Inchon. *Charity's* role was to prevent any communist attempt to interfere with the bombardment from the south while the cruisers fired successfully at targets inshore. On completion *Belfast*, *Cossack* and *Charity* returned to the naval base at Sasebo, near Nagasaki. On 7 September *Charity* spotted a number of mines on the surface while she was on patrol with *Jamaica* 25 miles to seaward of Chinnampo. They could have been carelessly laid moored mines or others intended to float but they resembled Russian Mark 26 mines and marked the beginning of a period when enemy mines caused considerable concern to the United Nations forces.

Later in September *Charity* formed part of the screening element of the UN force that carried out the amphibious landings at Inchon. She took up a

HMS Charity *sailing from Malta on 14 August 1946. Awning stanchions are rigged forward and awnings are in place aft. The ship to starboard is a 'Town' class cruiser.* *(Steve Bush Collection)*

position off Fankochi Point before dawn on 15 September 1950 to block any enemy approach to the amphibious operating area from the north. *HMCS Sioux* carried out a similar function to the south and the aircraft carrier *Triumph* operated with *Ceylon, Cockade, Consort* and *HMA Ships Warramunga* and *Bataan* in support of the landings. On 17 September *Charity* engaged and silenced two enemy guns ashore which had fired at a South Korean warship. Her fire was supported by a spotting aircraft from *Triumph*. On 22 September *Charity* carried out a bombardment of enemy troops in trenches and gun emplacements ashore with *Kenya* off Fankochi Point. Spotting aircraft remarked on the effectiveness of the shoot. She was ordered to search for a ditched USN pilot on 24 September and found herself in a mined area north west of Choppeki Point. She managed to withdraw unharmed and the pilot was eventually found by a USN destroyer.

In October 1950 *Charity* continued to operate off the west coast with other Commonwealth destroyers and the aircraft carrier *Theseus* which had replaced *Triumph* and by November, despite some ominous signs, it appeared that the war was nearly over. The scale of naval operations was, therefore, reduced and *Charity* was one of several destroyers that returned to Hong Kong for a maintenance period. The Chinese intervention, with no warning from the Intelligence Services, changed that perception and showed that the war was far from over. In December 1950 *Charity* rejoined the Commonwealth Task Force in the Inchon area in weather that included frequent snow showers and winds up to 60 knots. She operated as part of *Theseus*' screen while the carrier continued to fly effectively in the marginal conditions, operations that won the Boyd Trophy for her air group. The force returned to Sasebo in late December 1950.

During the Chinese offensive in January 1951 *Charity* took up apposition off Inchon, which had to be evacuated, and continued to play an important part in blockade operations off the west coast. There was always concern that the war might esca-late with a possible Soviet overt or covert intervention with submarines a particular worry. To maintain currency in anti-submarine tactics *Cossack, Consort, Charity* and *Cockade* took part in hunter/killer exercises organised by the USN off Okinawa in July 1951. These were largely successful and maintained skills that would, otherwise, have faded but fortunately they were not needed. In August *Charity* formed part of the screen for *Glory*, the latest British aircraft carrier on station. On 25 August she detached to join *Ceylon* in a bombardment of the Amgak peninsula after which she covered a landing by a Royal Marines raiding party at Sogon-ni and bombarded targets on the Amgak peninsula again before proceeding to patrol off the mouth of the Yalu River. During September 1951 the Chinese managed to re-open the railway between Tanchon and Songjin using a clever technique of erecting temporary bridges by night and removing them by day. Lookouts in *Charity* actually saw this happening and she carried out a series of successful bombardments using both spotters and strike aircraft to support her. She came under return fire herself on 10 September but by 13 September she had rendered the railway line unusable once more.

In October *HMAS Sydney* took over from *HMS Glory* as the Commonwealth aircraft carrier on station and *Charity* joined her task group together with the RN, RAN and RCN ships *Cossack, Concord, Amethyst, Anzac, Tobruk* and *Cayuga*. While she returned to Sasebo for logistic support and rest periods, *Sydney* was replaced on station by the *USS Badoeng Strait*. In January 1952 'Bingdong' Strait, as she was familiarly known, was on patrol escorted by *Charity*, the Dutch destroyer *Van Galen* and the *USS Hanson*; a representative UN team. Back on station to relieve her subsequently, *Sydney* was escorted by the *USS Radford* and *HMCS Sioux*. *Charity* was patrolling off the Amgak peninsula again in February 1952 when USN minesweepers came under fire from guns ashore. No damage was suffered and *Charity* engaged and silenced the guns.

HMS Charity carrying out a jackstay transfer with an aircraft carrier during operations in rough weather off the west coast of Korea. *(Steve Bush Collection)*

A number of Commonwealth warships operated off the east coast of Korea for short spells and *Charity* did so between 11 and 29 September 1952. In October 1952 the First Sea Lord Admiral Roderick McGrigor toured the war zone and intended to visit Commonwealth warships, including *Charity*, anchored off Chodo. Unfortunately bad weather caused the visits to be cancelled but he was able to witness bombardments of known enemy positions ashore. In early August *Charity* operated as part of the aircraft carrier *Ocean's* screen together with three USN destroyers. Later in the month she was screened by *Charity, HMCS Nootka, HNethMS Piet Hein* and the *USS Marsh* giving a

good indication of how closely integrated the allied fleets had become. In October when *Glory* relieved *Ocean, Charity* remained in the carrier screening group making her one of the very few destroyers to have screened all the Commonwealth aircraft carriers off Korea at some stage.

She rotated these duties with further periods off the north-east coast of Korea, carrying out a patrol in February and March 1953 which her commanding officer described as "intensely disappointing with no enemy activity and not a shot fired in anger". The Korean railway ran close to the east coast and trains were frequently engaged by warships when they came into view. A 'Trainbusters

Club' was established in July 1952 (although it did not include ships that had destroyed trains before that date) with certificates signed by CTF 95 being awarded for every successful destruction of an enemy train. *Charity's* sister-ship *HMCS Crusader* scored the most out of eighteen allied destroyers with 4 trains to her credit. *USS Endicott* came second with 3 and *Charity* came equal third with 2. Eleven ships, including *Piet Hein* scored 1. By late March she had returned to screening duties with *Glory* together with *HMCS Athabaskan* and two American destroyers. The carrier's strike operations were limited in April when the cease fire negotiators in Panmunjon agreed to a release of sick and wounded prisoners and the UN decided to limit offensive activity rather than risk upsetting progress. By then *Charity* had been joined by her

sister-ship *Consort* and *HMAS Anzac* in the screen.

The armistice that ended the Korean War was finally signed at Panmunjon on 27 July 1953. Vice Admiral Sir Charles Lambe KCB CVO the C-in-C Far East Station was visiting the war zone at the time and transferred his flag to *Birmingham* and then *Tyne* off the west coast. On 28 July he transferred his flag to *Charity* for passage to Kure in Japan where he held talks with the US authorities. She had served throughout the war and steamed 126,000 miles, more than any other Commonwealth warship during the conflict, consuming 29,000 tons of furnace fuel oil.

After the war she remained with the Far East Fleet but was considered to be obsolescent as her armament and equipment were still much as they were when she was completed. To remedy this she

HMS Charity *returning to the UK flying her paying-off pennant in October 1954. 'Squid' anti-submarine mortars had replaced 'X' mounting during a modernisation completed in Singapore Dockyard earlier in the year.*
(National Museum of the Royal Navy)

underwent an interim modernisation in Singapore Dockyard between 31 August 1953 and 16 January 1954. This involved the removal of 'X' mounting, its replacement with two 'Squid' mortars and their associated magazine/handling room and improvements to her sonar outfit after which she returned to 8 DS. In July 1954 she re-joined the Mediterranean Fleet, re-joining the 1st Destroyer Squadron with her sister-ships *Chequers, Chevron* and *Chaplet* before returning to the UK in October. In 1955 she was re-fitted in Rosyth Dockyard and remained there until December 1957 when she was towed to Portsmouth to form part of the high-readiness reserve fleet based there.

On 16 June 1958 it was announced that she had been sold to the US Navy under the 'Military Assistance Programme' for transfer to the Pakistan Navy. She was refitted but not modernised by J Samuel White & Co in Cowes, Isle of Wight, after which she was transferred to US ownership (on paper) and then to Pakistan in fact as *PNS Shah Jahan*, leaving the UK on 10 January 1959. Her new name translates as 'Emperor of the World' and, initially she retained her RN pennant number D 29; in 1963 the Pakistan Navy adopted a new system of pennant numbers and she became 164. In the first years after its formation the Pakistan Navy retained the Commonwealth system of numbering operational units and *Shah Jahan* formed part of the 25th Destroyer Squadron.

In September 1965 war broke out between India and Pakistan and *Shah Jahan* joined a task force comprising the cruiser *Babur* and the destroyers *Khaibar, Badr, Alamgir Tippu Sultan* and *Jahangir* which sailed from Karachi for Operation 'SOM-NATH', a bombardment of Dwarka intended to draw Indian naval units over the submarine Ghazi, destroy radar installations ashore and divert Indian Air Force attention away from southern Pakistan The ships opened fire at ranges of between 5 and 6 miles and fired 50 rounds each in the space of about 4 minutes. The action was aggressive but the results did not fully match expectations and both sides subsequently claimed a degree of success.

War broke out again in 1971 and the Indian Navy planned to open hostilities with an attack on shipping in Karachi by Osa class missile-armed fast attack vessels which had recently been acquired from Russia. The Pakistan Navy suspected that such an attack might be imminent and sailed the cruiser *Babur* and three destroyers to escort shipping off Karachi. *Khaibar* and *Shah Jahan* were ordered to form an outer patrol line on 4 December by which time the Indian force was already at sea heading towards Pakistan. *Khaibar* detected radio signals to the south east at 1905 and anomalous propagation conditions allowed shore radar stations to detect fast moving contacts at 2020 and 2040 but a warning was not passed to *Khaibar*. At just after 2300 she was hit by two 'Styx' missiles which had been fired at a range of 20 miles by the Indian missile boats *Nipat* and *Nirghat*. She sank within minutes. A subsequent missile hit the minesweeper *Muhafiz* as it attempted to rescue survivors and literally blew it out of the water. The Indian attack vessel *Veer* joined the action at this stage and fired missiles at radar contacts 32 miles south west of Karachi. One of them proved to be the Liberian freighter *Venus Challenger* which was hit and blew up, sinking rapidly with all hands and the other may have been *Shah Jahan*. The Indian Navy subsequently claimed to have sunk *Shah Jahan* but in fact she neither saw nor heard the missiles which destroyed the unarmed merchant ship and returned safely to Karachi. She was lucky to have escaped.

Shah Jahan continued in service for a number of years without further modernisation. She had served two navies faithfully and seen considerably more active service than most of her sister ships but by the late 1970s was obsolescent. She was not finally withdrawn from service, however, until 1982 when she was thirty-seven years old. She was broken up for scrap in Pakistan.

Chapter 11

HMS Chequers

HMS Chequers *carrying out sea trials in the Clyde on 28 September 1945, a day after her completion by Scotts of Greenock.* *(Syd Goodman Collection)*

The order for *Chequers* was placed with Scotts of Greenock and she was laid down on 4 May 1943, launched on 30 October 1944 and completed just too late for war service on 28 September 1945. After her sea trials and a period of defect rectification she worked up at Portland from 22 October 1945 and in Malta from 21 November to become the leader of the 14th Destroyer Flotilla. The Flotilla was re-numbered as the 1st DF in August 1946 as part of a post-war re-organisation of destroyer units.

Chequers was involved in patrol duties off Palestine from 1946 as part of the RN force tasked with intercepting ships carrying Jewish immigrants into the British mandated territory. On 27 March 1946 she was guided to intercept the 430 ton *Asya* by an RAF Warwick aircraft. The vessel was boarded and found to have 748 illegal immigrants on board in addition to the Master and a crew of 9 Turks and 3 Greeks; about half the immigrants proved to be pregnant females. The ship was arrested and taken to Haifa where the Army took charge of the ship and its passengers. Her next arrest was the *Alma*, formerly *Fenice*, which was also located by aircraft following an intelligence lead. *Chequers* intercepted the vessel 140 miles north of Haifa on 18 October 1946 and shadowed her through the night. The actual arrest was carried out 12 miles off Haifa by *Chaplet, Moon* and *Rowena* who found 513 men, 261 women and 40 children on board; after a spell in Haifa all were taken to Cyprus and held in camps since their numbers exceeded the agreed immigrant quota allowed into Palestine.

During July 1947 a succession of British warships

An overhead view of Chequers *carrying out sea trials on 28 September 1945 shows how her armament was arranged. For their size, the 'Ch' class were well-armed and flexible warships.* (Syd Goodman Collection)

shadowed *Exodus*, the former *President Warfield* on her voyage from France through the Mediterranean to Palestine. Captain D1 sailed in *Chequers* on the morning of 17 July 1947 with *Chieftain, Charity* and *Cardigan Bay* in company to intercept and, if necessary, board and arrest the 1,814 illegal immigrants on board. D1 had been provided with drawings of the ship and, together with observations from the shadowing destroyers, these proved crucial in planning the difficult boarding operations that proved to be necessary. The ship was eventually boarded and arrested in the most difficult circumstances by parties put on board by *Chieftain, Childers* and *Charity*. Violent resistance led to tear gas and eventually firearms having to be used and

there were 3 fatalities among the passengers and crew and several casualties among the boarding parties. When the ship was finally stopped, *Chequers* went alongside to transfer her medical officer and SBA to give aid.

During her periods away from the coast of Palestine *Chequers* carried out more normal peace-time duties and 'showed the flag' in a number of visits to Mediterranean ports including Villefranche and Genoa early in 1947 and Istanbul, Sevastopol and Limassol later in the year. While the Palestine Patrol continued, however, she had to return frequently to the Eastern Mediterranean. On 27 September 1947 she arrested the former USN *LCT 256*, renamed *Ferida*, with 446 illegals on board in

a combined effort with *Talybont*. On 28 December she intercepted a vessel thought to be acting suspiciously by an air patrol which proved to be the Turkish sailing ship *Karagu* with 881 illegals on board; *Chequers* shadowed her as the vessel closed the coast but the actual boarding and arrest was carried out by *Mermaid* and *Volage*. For every successful interception there were other attempts that came to nothing due to faulty intelligence and in some cases the migrant ships were persuaded to turn back. The Palestine Patrol was a difficult and distasteful task carried out with skill and objectivity by the many RN ships involved.

When the Palestine Patrol ended in 1948 *Chequers* returned to peacetime duties with the Mediterranean Fleet and carried out visits to St Tropez in 1948 and Navarino, Cannes and La

Spezia in 1949. She underwent dockings in Malta during May 1948, February 1949 and again in October 1949. On 15 October 1949 HRH the Duke of Edinburgh joined her as First Lieutenant, serving in her for nearly a year before leaving in September 1950 to take command of *Magpie* which was also part of the Mediterranean Fleet and based in Malta. In July 1951 she deployed to the Persian Gulf with *Chevron*, *Chivalrous* and *Chieftain* during a period of tension between Britain and Iran over the latter's nationalisation of oil production facilities. The over-crowded, poorly air-conditioned accommodation spaces were especially unpleasant in a leader with its larger ship's company and there was relief when the deployment ended in September and the ships returned to the Mediterranean.

In March 1952 *Chequers* entered Malta Dockyard

HMS Chequers as leader of the 1st Destroyer Squadron in Malta during March 1953. She completed a modernisation a year earlier and by now had double Mark 6 'Squid' anti-submarine mortars in 'X' position; a twin Mark 5 Bofors forward of the torpedo tubes and single Mark 7 Bofors aft of the funnel and on the bridge wings. Her Mark 6 director retained the optical range-finder, however. Note the 25 foot motor cutter being lowered.

(Syd Goodman Collection)

HMS Chequers *in November 1952 immediately after the completion of her modernisation. She retained her original open bridge structure.*
(Syd Goodman Collection)

for a partial modernisation which was completed in August. In this 'X' mounting was removed and replaced by a double Mark 6 'Squid' mortar installation with its associated magazine and handling room. The sonar outfit was upgraded to provide the target information required for the mortars but otherwise she remained largely as she had been built seven years earlier. In May 1954 she formed part of the escort for the new Royal Yacht *Britannia* with the HM The Queen and HRH the Duke of Edinburgh embarked for the passage between Malta and Gibraltar, one of the last legs of their world tour. After serving in the Mediterranean Fleet for nearly nine years, *Chequers* was due for a more extensive modernisation refit and left Malta for the last time in September 1954. After a period spent de-storing, she was taken in hand for the work in Chatham Dockyard on 20 September but the work was given a low priority and a shortage of skilled workers delayed progress still further with the result that the modernisation was not completed until September 1957. By then the notorious

'Duncan Sandys Defence Review' of 1957 was having an effect and there was a shortage of naval manpower. *Chequers* was not re-commissioned but placed in operational reserve at Chatham, kept nominally at about a month's notice for steam by a small maintenance party who ran and tested her systems from time to time.

In October 1959 she was towed to Portsmouth where she joined the reserve fleet at 'G' Moorings on the south side of Whale Island. With the number of new anti-submarine and general purpose frigates joining the fleet it was subsequently decided that *Chequers* was surplus to requirements and she was placed on the Disposal List on 24 September 1962. With so many destroyers in both Britain and the USA up for sale at the time, there was no foreign interest in her despite her relatively short operational life and the fact she was in good condition after a significant modernisation. Approval was given to scrap her on 18 September 1964; she was sold to John Cashmore Ltd on 19 July 1966 and towed to their yard on the next day for demolition.

Chapter 12

HMS CHEVIOT

HMS Cheviot in the Clyde shortly after her completion in December 1945. Her Admiralty Standard paint scheme is rather scruffy and her funnel marks her as a 'half-leader' in the 14th Destroyer Flotilla. Like her sister-ships, she has a boat under a canvas cover positioned to hide the absence of the forward set of torpedo tubes.

(Steve Bush Collection)

HMS *Cheviot* was laid down on 27 April 1943 at the Linthouse, Glasgow shipyard of Alexander Stephen & Co. She was launched on 2 May 1944 and completed on 11 December 1945, commissioning in the builder's yard on the same day. After sea trials and a work-up at Portland she joined her sister-ships in the 14th Destroyer Flotilla as part of the Mediterranean Fleet. After successive rationalisations of the RN destroyer force, the unit became the 1st Destroyer Flotilla in 1946 and the 1st Destroyer Squadron in 1952. She was refitted in Malta during the first two months of 1947 and, like other ships of her class was involved in patrol duties off Palestine interspersed with less stressful peacetime operations. On 17 July 1947 she sailed from Malta with the

Mediterranean Fleet for its first post-war summer cruise, showing the flag in the Levant but in early August *Cheviot* detached to carry out a patrol off Palestine.

On 13 August 1947 the immigrant ship *Guardian* was boarded and stopped by the frigate *St Bride's Bay* with 2,623 illegal immigrants onboard. A tug attempted to tow her into Haifa but the tow rope parted leaving the elderly ship in a dangerous position with the migrants, crew and boarding party still on board only a few hundred yards off a lee shore in Acre Bay with deteriorating weather. *Cheviot* moved in to pass a tow from her forecastle but the attempt proved to be unsuccessful. Minutes later the minesweeper *Octavia* managed to pass an 8-inch manilla successfully in only three minutes and

HMS Cheviot *sailing down the Clyde in December 1945. The wire 'cage' at the top of her foremast is an FH4 High-Frequency Direction Finder or HF/DF and the small mainmast forward of 'X' mounting carries a Type 291 air-warning radar aerial. Considering that she is only days out of the builder's yard with no urgency for her completion her paintwork aft is in surprisingly poor condition.* (Steve Bush Collection)

when secured she hauled the ship to safety in sheltered water, averting what could have been a humanitarian disaster. Ten days later on 23 April *Cheviot* intercepted and arrested the Turkish steamer *Galata* with 773 illegals on board. Tear gas was used but there was still considerable opposition to the boarding and a number of sailors suffered cuts and bruises. *Cheviot* was one of a number of warships that shadowed and then arrested *Exodus/President Warfield* in July 1947 in one of the most highly publicised incidents during the period during which the Palestine Patrol was in operation.

The next incident involving *Cheviot* was the interception and shadowing of the two immigrant ships *Paducah* and *Northland* when they emerged from the Dardanelles. The former was arrested by *Chaplet* and *Cheviot* with 1,385 illegals on board on 2 October 1947. The other vessel with 2,664 ille-

gals was arrested later on the same day. *Cheviot*'s last arrest was the wooden motor vessel *Cicilio* with 678 illegals on board. In this case the passengers actively assisted the boarding party and the ship was towed into Haifa without difficulty. After returning to peacetime duties *Cheviot* remained with 1 DF in the Mediterranean Fleet and underwent dockings in Malta in 1948 and Gibraltar in 1949 and 1950. During 1949 she passed through the Suez Canal to visit Aqaba in Jordan and acted as allied guard-ship in Trieste for a while, being relieved by a USN destroyer. On 16 May 1950 her ship's company moved into *Chevron* and *Chevron's* took over *Cheviot* as part of a series of measures that reduced the size of 1 DF by 3 ships. Loch class frigates made up the number to improve the Mediterranean Fleet's anti-submarine capability.

She was given an interim modernisation in Malta Dockyard, to improve her anti-submarine capabili-

HMS Cheviot *leading other ships of the Far East Fleet and the Commonwealth Strategic Reserve in line astern. The aircraft carrier fourth in the line is* HMAS Melbourne.   *(Crown Copyright/MoD)*

ty, between August 1952 and January 1953 during which two 'Squid' anti-submarine mortars and their associated handling room replaced the Mark 5 gun mounting in 'X' position and associated improvements were made to the sonar outfit. In September 1954 she returned to the UK and was reduced to reserve in Chatham.

She subsequently sailed to Singapore with a reduced ship's company where she underwent a refit in the Dockyard and modifications were carried out that would allow her to become leader of the 8th Destroyer Squadron, replacing *Cossack*. She re-commissioned on 25 August 1956 with some of *Cossack's* ship's company augmented by others flown out from the UK. She spent the next 4 years in the Far East Fleet, visiting places as far apart as East Africa, Korea, Japan, Ceylon and Christmas Island in mid-Pacific. In between exercises and patrols off the coast of Malaya she spent time in the major RN bases at Singapore and Hong Kong, earning a reputation as a good sporting ship; her pulling crew won the 'Cock of the Fleet Trophy' on more than one occasion. She re-commissioned on station for a second time on 5 May 1958 with a new ship's company flown out from the UK. Later in the year she carried out a further refit in Singapore and was in Hong Kong for Christmas.

The Malayan Emergency continued until 1960 and *Cheviot* was one of a number of destroyers and frigates that carried out patrols in Malay waters to prevent guns and other contraband being smuggled ashore for use by the communist insurgents. She also spent time as guard-ship in Trincomalee, protecting British interests when there were riots ashore. 1959 was a particularly busy year for *Cheviot* and she acted as plane-guard for the aircraft carrier *Albion* during exercises which included *Ceylon, Cavalier, Chichester* and *HMA Ships Queenborough* and *Quiberon*. While refuelling at sea from the *RFA Olna*, *Cheviot* was hit by a large wave which washed one of her sailors overboard; he was subsequently rescued, unconscious, by *Chichester*. Later in the year she escorted HM The Queen in the Royal Yacht *Britannia* from Singapore to Australia, visiting Albany and Fremantle.

She was replaced as leader of 8 DS by the modernised *Carysfort* in September 1959 after which she returned to the UK. The number of destroyers in the operational fleets was being reduced following the 1957 Defence Review and her after arrival in Portsmouth, *Cheviot* was de-stored and reduced into reserve in October 1959. This was not quite the end of her useful life in the RN, however, for in December it was decided to move her to Rosyth to replace *Talybont* as a harbour training ship for artificer apprentices, attached to *HMS Caledonia*. *Cheviot* was employed on these duties for two years before being replaced by *Saintes* in 1962 after which she was left in an un-maintained state awaiting a decision about her disposal. Approval was given to scrap her on 18 October 1962 and four days later she was towed from Rosyth to Inverkeithing to be broken up by Thomas Ward & Co. Demolition was complete by the end of 1963.

Chapter 13

HMS CHEVRON

HMS Chevron *in the Clyde carrying out sea trials in 1945. Like her sister-ships, she has a boat positioned to disguise the absence of the forward torpedo tubes. The visible reduction by half of what was still considered to be the destroyers' main armament obviously caused concern at the time.* (Crown Copyright/MoD 1945)

HMS *Chevron* was built by Alexander Stephen & Co at their Linthouse, Govan yard; laid down on 18 March 1943, launched on 23 February 1944 and completed on 23 August 1945, the first of the 'Ch' class to be completed by just one day. She carried out an initial work up in Scapa Flow and then to Malta where she was declared to be operational in early 1946. She was allocated to the 14th Destroyer Flotilla in the Mediterranean Fleet and remained with the same unit for ten years. It was re-designated 1 DF in 1946 and 1 DS in 1952 in line with changing Admiralty policy on the identification of destroyer units. Together with other ships of the Mediterranean Fleet she formed part of the RN patrol off Palestine between 1946 and 1948 that tried to prevent illegal Jewish migration under the

terms of a UN mandate prior to the creation of the State of Israel. She made her first arrest during the night of 25/26 March 1946 when she intercepted and escorted into Haifa the 144 ton motorised sailing ship, the *Charles Orde Wingate* alias *Kismet Adalia* with 248 illegal immigrants on board. Although the arrest went well, there was subsequent violence between Jewish reception groups in Haifa and the security forces resulting in the vessel being taken from its Turkish owners by a District Court.

In May 1946 *Chevron* brought a draft of Palestinian Royal Navy ratings from Alexandria to Haifa. After they had disembarked it was found that one of them had left a kit bag full of gun cotton fitted with a detonator on board. When members of the draft were stopped and searched ashore detonators were found hidden in clothing and a Sick Berth

HMS Chevron *moored in Malta with awnings spread. A number of 'wind-scoops' have been fitted in scuttles and escape hatches have been opened to get air into the messdecks; the summer heat, especially when reflected off buildings as well, could be oppressive.* (T. Ferrers-Walker Collection)

Attendant, who was returning from the minesweeper *Sphinx*, was arrested and charged with conspiring to cause explosions in HM Ships.

Some of the immigrant ships foundered before they got close enough to the Palestinian coast to be arrested. Such a one was the *Athini*, alias *Rafiah* built in 1898 and of only 273 tons which had 784 illegals on board. It grounded on rocks off Sirina Island north east of Crete on 9 December 1946 and sank. Most of the crew and passengers managed to struggle ashore but several, including 3 children were drowned. Some of the illegals had a radio and they managed to get it ashore where they had just enough battery power to send a message to the Mossad in Palestine. In turn they asked the British High Commissioner for help and RAF aircraft were sent to drop food and medical supplies by parachute

on what was described as 'this desolate isle' by the High Commissioner. *Chevron* was ordered to close the island 'at best speed' but bad weather restricted her to 23 knots. On arrival after dark on 9 December she found the Greek Hunt class destroyer *Themistocles* on the scene with a British doctor from Rhodes. Despite high seas and driving rain *Chevron* landed a party of sailors with tea and food for the survivors at daybreak on 10 December and the Algerine class minesweeper *Providence* arrived to help. The long and difficult task of embarking the survivors by boat commenced at once but there were frequent spells when the conditions were too bad and it had to stop. The provisions taken ashore and the culinary skills of the boarding party who prepared them proved to be of vital importance. Embarkation was finally completed at 0300 on 11

December after which *Chevron* and *Providence* sailed for Suda Bay in Crete where the passengers were transferred to HMS LST3016 with a guard provided by *Stevenstone* which then escorted the LST to Cyprus where the passengers were landed.

Chevron and *Chieftain* gave cover on 28 February 1947 when boarding parties from the minesweepers *Welfare* and *Rowena* boarded and arrested the *Ulua* with 1,409 illegal immigrants on board. The ship was a former US Coastguard cutter of 898 tons that had collected migrants from all over Europe and was attempting to confuse the British authorities with a carefully worked-out cover plan. When this failed the first attempts at boarding were fiercely resisted but eventually *Rowena* got 27 men across who began to achieve order by firing over the heads of the crowd. Eventually 84 personnel were taken on board, three of whom were seriously injured, but they failed to take the wheelhouse and *Ulua* ran aground near the Army barracks at Mount Carmel where the illegal immigrants were arrested.

On 8 March *Chevron* and *Chieftain* intercepted the *Abril*, alias *Ben Hecht* flying the flag of Honduras, which was making 16 knots towards Tel Aviv where the Hebrew Committee for National Liberation planned to run her aground so that the illegals could land over the beach to evade arrest. She was too fast for minesweepers to board and so *Chivalrous* and the frigate *St Brides Bay* joined the group. The vessel refused to stop as she neared the coast and boarding parties of 32 from *Chieftain*, 30 from *Chevron* and 20 from *Chivalrous* were put across to arrest her and take her to Haifa where her passengers were transferred peacefully to transports and taken to Cyprus. An officer from *Chevron* took down the Honduran flag and kept it but many years later presented it to the Immigration and Naval Museum in Haifa. *Chevron* formed part of the escort for a convoy of ships that carried Jewish refugees from the South of France to Gibraltar in August 1947 on the first part of a journey to displaced person camps in Germany. The cruiser *Phoebe* and the frigate *St Brides Bay* made up the rest of the escort; ships from the local squadrons at

the three Home Ports took over the escort task after Gibraltar.

In between patrols off Palestine there was scope for Fleet activity and on 17 July 1947 the Mediterranean Fleet sailed from Malta for the Levant on its first post-war Summer Cruise. Participating ships included *Liverpool*, the flagship, *Triumph, Ocean, Phoebe, Mauritius, Leander, Woolwich, Surprise, Chequers, Chaplet, Cheviot, Chieftain, Charity, Chevron, Venus, Virago, Haydon, Talybont, Stevenstone, Brissenden, Mermaid, Bigbury Bay, Whitesand Bay, Protector* and *Dieppe*.

On 28 December 1947 *Chevron* and *Volage* intercepted a vessel with 'Haganah Ship 29 November 1947' painted on her wheelhouse. When she crossed into territorial waters *Chevron* came alongside and put across an unopposed boarding party that arrested her. She was towed into Haifa where Police from *ML 1126* arrested the crew and illegal immigrants. A day later the 4,500 ton banana ships *Pan Crescent* and *Pan York* emerged from the Dardanelles, each with over 7,000 illegal immigrants on board. The Royal Navy persuaded them to head straight for Famagusta in Cyprus but there were concerns that there were insufficient troops to guard such a large number and so troops from the 6th Airborne Division in Palestine were sent in a transport ship escorted by *Chevron*. When the Pans anchored off Famagusta, *Chevron* moored near them to guard against attempted sabotage by militants among the passengers.

In 1948 as the British Mandate neared its end and the date set for the creation of the new state of Israel by the United Nations approached, fighting broke out between Jewish and Palestinian groups ashore and Jewish forces carried out a mortar attack on the Arab quarter of Haifa. Thousands of Arabs tried to flee in boats but were attacked as they did so and 40, 42 and 45 Royal Marines Commandos were landed to set up a barrier between the two sides. This proved difficult as the bitter fighting intensified. Amidst this deteriorating situation, attempts were still made to intercept illegal immigrants and

HMS Chevron *alongside following her collision with* Comet *in 1949, showing the extensive damage to her bows.*
(T. Ferrers-Walker Collection)

Chevron arrested the *San Michelle*, alias *Mishmar Haemeck* with 785 illegals on board on 24 April 1948 after which she towed the vessel to Cyprus. The British Mandate formally ended on 15 May 1948 when the High Commissioner left Palestine in the cruiser *Euryalus*. She joined a task force comprising the aircraft carrier *Ocean* with *Chevron*, *Childers*, *Volage*, *Pelican* and *Widemouth Bay*. The British Army and the Royal Marines Commandos withdrew into an enclave around Haifa which gradually contracted while their equipment, stores and ammunition were shipped out with air cover provided by the aircraft carrier *Triumph*. The last British forces left on 30 June 1948.

With the end of the Palestinian Patrol the Mediterranean Fleet returned to peacetime fleet routines and the destroyer flotillas practised manoeuvres which included night torpedo attacks.

In 1949 *Chevron* collided with the destroyer *Comet* during night exercises and suffered extensive damage to her bow. Repairs were carried out in Malta Dockyard between early June and August. Annual refits and boiler cleaning had been carried out in Malta and Gibraltar during her time in the Mediterranean. In 1950 her ship's company was exchanged with that of *Cheviot*.

In April 1951 the Iranian Government nationalised a British-owned oil refinery at Abadan and there were riots when the largely British staff closed it down. The cruiser *Mauritius* was sent to the area to protect British interests in June and she was relieved by *Euryalus* in July. Later in the same month *Chequers*, *Chevron*, *Chivalrous* and *Chieftain* were deployed from the Mediterranean and took over the task. They were relieved by Battle class destroyers of the 3rd Destroyer Flotilla

and returned to the Mediterranean in September, their crews having found the high temperatures particularly trying in their cramped, non-air-conditioned hulls. The British nationals were withdrawn from Abadan in *Euryalus* in October.

In 1953 *Chevron* paid off in Malta and underwent an interim modernisation, re-commissioning there on 8 January 1954 for further service. She returned to the UK in April 1955 and spent a year with the Home Fleet. During this time she took part in a historic visit to Leningrad (St Petersburg) on 12 October 1955 in company with the flagship *Triumph* and *Apollo, Decoy, Diana* and *Chieftain*. A reciprocal visit by the cruisers *Sverdlov* and *Aleksandr Suvarov* and four destroyers to Portsmouth was carried out by the Soviet Navy at the same time.

Following the Egyptian nationalisation of the Suez Canal in 1956 she rejoined 1 DS in the Mediterranean as part of large-scale reinforcement of the Fleet. By October the Squadron comprised *Chieftain, Chaplet* and *Chevron* and formed part of the large Anglo-French Fleet ordered to carry out Operation 'MUSKETEER'. On 6 November the amphibious assault began with the minesweepers *Darlaston* and *Letterston* sweeping a channel into Port Said followed in by the LCT *Sallyport*, which had been fitted out as a headquarters ship. Next astern came *Chevron* flying a large blue flag which identified her as carrying the Naval Officer in Charge Port Said and his staff. She secured stern-on to the central mole at 0938 after which volunteers from her ship's company manned harbour launches and 2 tugs to help bring LSTs and LCTs into improvised beaching grounds near the Casino Palace Hotel when the original sites chosen were found to be obstructed by block-ships. Once clearance divers found the harbour to be clear of mines,

HMS Chevron *returning to the UK in April 1955 after service the Mediterranean as leader of the 1st Destroyer Squadron.* *(T. Ferrers-Walker Collection)*

troopships were brought alongside and the NOIC, complete with his blue flag, moved ashore to continue his task. She was still in Port Said on 11 November but subsequently sailed to rejoin Task Force 345 in the Eastern Mediterranean.

Chevron remained with 1 DS until May 1957 when she was relieved by *Lagos*, subsequently returning to the UK to be de-stored at Portsmouth before commencing an extended refit at Rosyth on 22 July 1957. A shortage of skilled manpower at the yard and a lack of urgency after the reduction announced in the 1957 Defence Review slowed the work on her and the refit was not completed until 20 October 1959 when she re-commissioned briefly for sea trials. On 4 December 1959 she paid off into operational reserve at Rosyth, kept 'alive' for a number of years by use as an accommodation ship forming part of *HMS Caledonia*, the artificers' training establishment at Rosyth. With a number of new Type 12 frigates joining the operational fleet and the recognition of her diminishing state of readiness she was placed on the Disposal List in June 1963. No overseas interest was expressed in her and approval was given to scrap her on 18 September 1964 but given her short-term usefulness as an accommodation ship, formal offers for her purchase were not requested until October 1969. Once this step was taken the end came quickly and she was sold to T W Ward on 18 November 1969. She was towed to their yard at Inverkeithing a month later and broken up for scrap.

Chapter 14

HMS Chieftain

HMS Chieftain *in March 1946 shortly after completion marked as a 'half-leader,' by her black funnel band, in the 14th Destroyer Flotilla.* *(Crown Copyright/MoD 1946)*

HMS *Chieftain* was laid down on 27 June 1943 at Scott's shipyard in Greenock and launched on 26 February 1945. She was commissioned on 22 February 1946 but not completed until 7 March. Perhaps surprisingly in view of her name, she was not completed as a leader. Her initial close-range armament comprised a Mark 4 Bofors 'Hazemeyer' amidships, two single Bofors abaft the funnel and single Oerlikons in the bridge wings but this was modified to the standard twin Mark 5 Bofors and four single Bofors in the other positions as opportunity arose during normal refits. After work up she joined the 14th Destroyer Flotilla in the Mediterranean Fleet and, like a number of her sister-ships, stayed with the unit after it was re-numbered as 1 DF in 1946 and 1 DS in 1952. After a short refit in Malta at the end of 1946 she joined

the other ships of her Flotilla in patrol duties off Palestine from February 1947.

On 8 February 1947 she encountered the barquentine *Merica* after dark with no prior warning from intelligence sources which had thought the vessel was headed from Marseille to Cuba. The minesweeper *Welfare* joined and boarded the vessel at 0244 on 9 February; despite violent opposition which only calmed when warning shots were fired, *Merica* was arrested and towed into Haifa. Her 657 illegal immigrants were subsequently shipped to camps in Famagusta. On 27 February *Chieftain* was guided to intercept the 880 ton former US Coastguard cutter *Ulua* by RAF reconnaissance aircraft and began to shadow her. The vessel had over 1,400 people on board in cramped conditions, half of whom had been embarked from rubber rafts off

HMS Chieftain *under way soon after her completion. The depth charge arrangements aft, including the davits used to hoist them into the racks, are clearly visible.* (Crown Copyright/MoD 1946)

Taranto, where she claimed to be headed for Alexandria. A day later *Chevron, St Austell Bay, Welfare* and *Rowena* joined and the minesweepers attempted to board. Some men got across but met fierce opposition and jumped overboard after being badly beaten; they were picked up by *Chieftain* and the police-manned *ML 1145*. Subsequent boardings were successful after firing warning shots but failed to capture the wheelhouse or take complete control of the ship. *Ulua* eventually drifted ashore and grounded near Mount Carmel; nine immigrants swam to the beach where they were arrested by the Army.

On 8 March 1947 intelligence sources identified the 750 ton *Abril*, alias *Ben Hecht*, with 650 illegals on board at sea trying to enter Palestine territorial waters to a beach near Tel Aviv where her passengers would attempt to evade capture. She was intercepted by *Chieftain, Chevron, Chivalrous* and *St Bride's Bay* and was found to be too fast to be boarded by minesweepers. *Chieftain* went along-

side and put 32 men on board while forcing the ship round onto a westerly heading so that she could not be beached. *Chevron* and *Chivalrous* added another 50 boarders between them. Unlike in other vessels, no resistance was offered in *Abril* and the American crew offered the boarding party soup and fudge! The only casualty was a photographer from 'Life' magazine working on a human-interest story who was accidentally kicked while taking pictures of the boarding party jumping onto the deck. This patrol was followed by a refit in Malta which lasted from 31 March to 12 May 1947.

On 17 July 1947 Captain D1 was sailed in *Chequers* with *Chieftain* and *Charity* to support *Ajax, Cheviot, Childers* and a number of other warships in boarding and arresting *President Warfield*, alias *Exodus 1947*. D1 decided to board her from destroyers putting across the largest possible number of men as quickly as possible. A number of men were transferred by boat from *Ajax* to *Childers* and *Chieftain* so that both had boarding parties of 50

men. It was accepted that some structural damage might be caused when the destroyers were brought close alongside the *Warfield*. The arrest took place after 0200 on 18 July with *Childers* alongside to port, *Chieftain* alongside to starboard and both as close as possible to the wheelhouse. *Cardigan Bay* was stationed astern to pick up men who fell into the sea. *Warfield* manoeuvred violently and it took both destroyers several attempts to get alongside and only a few boarders made it across. *Chequers* and *Charity* had to board as well but after nearly 3 hours only 40 men had got across and were meeting stiff resistance. All four destroyers suffered buckled plates and some consequent flooding so *Ajax* closed in at 16 knots to come close alongside and use her armoured sides to force *Warfield* away from the beach. Seeing that further resistance would not avail the Haganah leader on *President Warfield* surrendered at 0540 and the ship was arrested. In addition to passengers injured in the fighting, many on board were found to be sick and medical staff from

the British warships were sent on board to help treat them. One sailor from *Chieftain* suffered a broken shoulder blade and a number of others had cuts and bruises. Later on that day *Warfield* was brought successfully into Haifa and the illegal immigrants taken into custody. The damage caused during the boarding was rectified during repair work in Malta Dockyard between 31 July and 2 November 1947.

Chieftain's last act in this series of incidents took place on 12 May 1948 when she intercepted the *Borea* with 243 illegal immigrants on board. *Chieftain*'s captain suggested that *Borea's* master remained outside territorial waters until 15 May when the British mandate ended and he could then do as he pleased. Surprisingly he elected instead to divert to Cyprus. With the end of the Palestine Patrol commitment, *Chieftain* returned to peacetime duties with 1 DS. She was re-fitted again in Malta during 1949.

In 1951 *Chieftain* deployed to the Persian Gulf with *Chequers, Chevron* and *Cheviot* to reinforce

HMS Chieftain at sea in June 1955 shortly after her conversion to a minelayer. She now has two 'Squids' in 'X' position but unusually retains 'Y' mounting in place. It would have to be removed to reduce topweight before any mines could be loaded onto their rails. (National Museum of the Royal Navy)

British capability in the region after Iran nationalised British-owned oilfields. She returned to the Mediterranean in October but on 13 December 1952 a deliberate fire was started in her tiller flat. The culprit was never identified and, after repairs in Malta, she returned to Devonport Dockyard in July 1953 and was reduced to operational reserve in August after de-storing. In May 1954 she was towed to Portsmouth and modernised to the same standard as *Chaplet* as a minelayer after which she re-commissioned on 13 June 1955. She carried out a work-up with the Home Fleet before rejoining 1 DS in the Mediterranean Fleet on 12 December 1955.

The 1st Destroyer Squadron, comprising *Chieftain*, *Chaplet* and *Chevron* concentrated as part of Task Force 345 to prepare for Operation 'MUSKETEER' the Anglo-French landings at Port Said in the autumn of 1956. *Chieftain* formed part of the escort for convoy MES 2 from Malta to the operational area in the first week of November during which time she was refuelled at sea by *Wave Laird* and *Brown Ranger*. On 6 November during the amphibious landings at Port Said she was ordered to silence any Egyptian guns on the breakwater that tried to interfere with the landings but did not need to open fire. Shore bombardment by larger ships was ruled out to avoid the risk of civilian casualties. At 0630 *Chieftain* was ordered to act as Inward Traffic Control Ship, a task she carried out successfully until the assault phase was over and more normal harbour control arrangements could be put into effect by the harbour-master. She returned to the UK after the Suez intervention and re-joined the Home Fleet for a spell. On 24 April 1957 she re-commissioned for service in the Nore Local Squadron with a reduced ship's company, replacing *Obdurate*. On 29 June 1957 she carried HM Queen Elizabeth The Queen Mother to Dunkirk where she unveiled a War Memorial.

Her time at the Nore was short and on 29 October 1957 it was announced that, as part of the economies after the notorious Defence Review that year, she would not be refitted but would, instead, be reduced to extended reserve at Chatham with no maintenance. She was replaced in the Local Squadron by *Paladin* and, after de-storing, she was laid up on 19 December 1957. In April 1958 she was placed on the Sales List but there was no overseas interest in her and on 21 March 1960 approval was given for her to be scrapped. She was sold to T Young at Sunderland and towed out of Chatham by the tug *Samsonia* on 13 March 1961. Her demolition was completed within a year.

Chapter 15

HMS Childers

HMS Childers *in the Clyde shortly after her completion. She has Type 291 air-warning radar on her small main-mast but no close-range weapons have been fitted in the 'bandstand' aft of the funnel. (Crown Copyright/MoD 1946)*

The contract for *HMS Childers* was originally placed with Vickers at their Barrow shipyard but it was transferred to Denny Brothers of Dumbarton due to the intense pressure of work at Vickers. She was laid down on 27 November 1943, some moths later than most of her sister-ships and was, in consequence, among the last of her class to complete. She was launched on 27 February 1945 and completed on 19 December 1945. After a period working up, she joined her sister-ships in 14 DF, subsequently 1 DF in the Mediterranean Fleet, based on Malta. She left the UK for what proved to be the last time in January 1946 and, after a further work-up off Malta served on Palestine Patrol duties. In August the policy of deporting illegal immigrants who had hoped to reach Palestine to camps in Cyprus was introduced and Captain D1 warned that ships could expect violent opposition from passengers in the ships that they tried to arrest.

Childers intercepted *Fede* after a sighting report by an RAF aircraft on 2 September 1946 and attempted to stop her as she crossed the 3-mile limit into Palestinian territorial waters. Shots across her bows had no effect and firing over her was not possible because of the number of fishing boats nearby. *Childers* then put her bow alongside *Fede* and started to put a boarding party across but she turned sharply away before they could all jump across and 'toughs' with iron bars attacked the party and took their Lanchester sub-machine guns. A second run alongside got more men across until eventually the vessel was stopped. A towing wire was attached between *Childers'* fo'c'sle and *Fede's* stern and she was towed further out to sea to prevent passengers from attempting to swim for the shore. Eventually *Chivalrous* joined and put more men on board and the combined parties forced the passengers below and took over the ship. She was towed into Haifa

HMS Childers *boarding the illegal immigrant ship* Sette Fratelli, *February 1948. There were 300 illegal immigrants aboard the ship that was camouflaged as the* Abdul Hamid. *Note the protective netting and scaffolding over the forecastle and bridge together with the ad-hoc fendering along the hull* (Yad Vashem Photo Archive)

where her 985 passengers were transferred to *Empire Heywood* and taken immediately to Cyprus. It had taken 6 officers and 70 sailors from the two destroyers to arrest *Fede* as earlier days of passive resistance were clearly over. Repairs to the damage caused as she went close alongside *Fede* were carried out in Malta in January 1947 and Gibraltar in April.

Childers was one of the force assembled to intercept *President Warfield*, alias *Exodus 1947*, in July 1947. On 15 July she relieved *Cheviot* shadowing the vessel, kept her under close observation and was able to signal details of her anti-boarder preparations to *Ajax* and D1. When joined by *Chequers, Chieftain, Charity* and *Cardigan Bay, Childers'* brief was to put a boarding party enlarged by men from *Ajax* onto *Warfield* by coming alongside to

port while *Chieftain* did the same to starboard. At 0200 on 18 July the attempt to arrest the ship began but her violent manoeuvring made things extremely difficult and several attempts had to be made to get boarders across. Like *Chieftain* she was damaged and after three periods alongside she was replaced by *Charity* and *Chieftain* replaced by *Chequers*. At 0500 *Ajax* prepared to come alongside but resistance collapsed and *President Warfield* was arrested and taken into Haifa. Medical staff were put onto the captured vessel to help treat sick passengers found in the awful conditions onboard.

Several days later *Childers, Verulam* and *Rowena* joined *Espiegle* which had been shadowing the *Bruna* on the last stage of her voyage from France with 684 illegals on board. Faced with overwhelming force the vessel's master agreed to go to Haifa

but in view of the risk of deception the two destroyers put 4 officers and 59 men on board on 28 July 1947. The crew still managed to sabotage their engine and she had to be towed into Haifa by *Rowena*. *Childers* was subsequently docked in Malta for repairs to the damage caused in the *Warfield* boarding in August 1947.

Childers formed part of the screening force that looked for the *Paducah* and *Northland* in October 1947 but was not involved in their arrest. She intercepted and shadowed the *Pan Crescent* on part of her journey to the eastern Mediterranean but, again, was not involved in the arrest. On 31 January 1948 *Childers* closed and investigated a two-masted sailing vessel bearing the name *Sylvia Starita*. She appeared to be innocent with few people on the upper deck but when the destroyer made a second,

closer pass and sounded her siren, a tarpaulin was hauled back and immigrants poured onto the deck. A notice was displayed which identified her as the Haganah ship *Heroes of Ezion*. Advised to proceed to Famagusta they refused but said they would agree to be boarded at the 3-mile limit. When they eventually took over the ship, the boarding party, many of whom were veterans of the *President Warfield* boarding, found the engine to be defective and she was towed into Haifa. On 19 February she boarded and arrested the *Abdul Hamid* with 704 people on board, again with no resistance. This time the vessel was able to enter Haifa under her own power.

When the British Mandate for Palestine finally ended on 15 May 1948, *Childers* joined *Ocean, Euryalus, Chevron, Volage, Pelican* and *Widemouth*

HMS Childers *entering Malta during 1953 after her passage from Gibraltar where she had been laid up in reserve. The close-range weapons are covered and there are few hands to man the upper deck. 'X' mounting has been removed to prepare her for the planned modernisation and the vacant space has been filled with motor cars for delivery to Malta. More vehicles fill the vacant forward torpedo tube space.* (National Museum of the Royal Navy)

Bay in the Task Force that carried the British High Commissioner away from Palestine. She was refitted in Gibraltar in August 1949 and again in December 1949. In 1950, however, it was decided to reduce the size of 1 DF by 3 ships and replace their number with Loch class frigates in order to strengthen the Mediterranean Fleet's anti-submarine effectiveness. *Childers* was reduced to reserve in Malta on 15 September 1950, retained in the Mediterranean so that she could be re-commissioned quickly to expand 1 DF again should the need arise in an emergency. She was used as an accommodation ship for the maintenance group responsible for the upkeep of the local reserve fleet who kept her 'alive' to a certain extent but her armament and all upper deck fittings were cocooned during this period and she used shore power to ventilate the accommodation spaces. In May 1951 she was towed to join the reserve fleet at Gibraltar and remained there until March 1953 when she was returned to high-readiness reserve in Malta. In August 1955 she was taken in hand by Malta Dockyard to commence an extended refit and interim modernisation which was completed in June 1956. 'X' turret was removed and replaced by two 'Squid' anti-submarine mortars and their asso-ciated bomb handling room and her sonar was upgraded. For a brief period after that she was re-commissioned with a reduced ship's company for post-refit trials, operating as a tender to the repair ship *Ranpura*. On completion of the trials she went back into operational reserve again, still at Malta.

In January 1959 she was moved back to Gibraltar where she was retained at 7 days' notice for steam. She was never re-commissioned, however, and despite her excellent physical condition and remarkably short period of operational service, she was declared to be surplus to requirements, downgraded to un-maintained extended reserve and placed on the Disposals List on 17 June 1960, remaining at Gibraltar. On 16 August 1963 she was sold to Letti at La Spezia and towed from Gibraltar by the tug *Noordzee* to La Spezia where she was broken up for scrap from September. During the 1950s the RN maintained a number of ships in operational reserve in naval bases throughout the world which allowed rapid expansion in an emergency and the ability to replace units damaged on active service. It was a necessary function but, as was the case with *Childers*, not all of them saw further service.

Chapter 16

HMS CHIVALROUS
(PNS TAIMUR from 1954)

HMS Chivalrous, *still in her original configuration, sailing from Malta in 1946.*

(National Museum of the Royal Navy)

The contract for *Chivalrous*, like that for her sister-ship *Childers*, was transferred from the overworked Vickers yard at Barrow-in-Furness to William Denny's Dumbarton yard and she subsequently completed later than most of her sisters. She was laid down on the same day as *Childers*, 27 November 1943, but launched much later on 22 June 1945. She was not completed until 13 May 1946, the excessive build-time due mainly to shortages of equipment such as the Mark 6 director and manpower shortages at the shipyard. After working up she joined the 14th Destroyer Flotilla in the Mediterranean with her sister-ships.

She soon became involved in operations off Palestine and on 22 October she escorted a transport full of illegal immigrants that had been arrested off Haifa in the *Alma* on their journey to Cyprus. Her first arrest was the 733 ton *San Dimitrio*, alias *Latrun*, with 1,279 people on board which she intercepted on 30 October 1946 after her initial detection by air reconnaissance. As passengers came on deck to watch the destroyer she listed dangerously and, concerned that the ship might capsize, *Chivalrous* moved clear and tracked her from a distance. She was joined by the minesweepers *Octavia* and *Providence* and, despite fears about *San Dimitrio's* safety, ordered them to board and arrest the vessel as she crossed into territorial waters. The illegal immigrants attacked the boarding parties with broken bottles and metal objects with shouts of 'Gestapo' and 'Nazis' and used women and children to block the entrance to the wheelhouse but violence was quickly subdued and the vessel ordered into Haifa. Arrest brought all the passengers on deck and the ship lolled dangerously before she was brought alongside. She listed

toward the jetty by 30 degrees as police took the passengers ashore. All were then taken to camps in Cyprus.

On 8 March 1947 *Chivalrous* assisted *Chevron* and *Chieftain* in arresting the 753 ton *Abril*, alias *Ben Hecht*, putting a boarding party of 20 men on board. On 28 July 1947 she intercepted the caique *Luciano M*, alias *Shivat Zion*, with 398 people on board. She was supported by *Widemouth Bay* and *Providence* with the latter carrying out the boarding and arrest as the ship entered territorial waters. There was no opposition and the passengers were found to include about a hundred young children and babies that were covered in sores and skin diseases and who appeared to be in very poor general health.

By this stage naval operations concerned with illegal immigration into Palestine by sea had spread throughout the Mediterranean. In addition to the ships working off the Palestinian coast, others shadowed ships that intelligence reported as being potential law-breakers. After a short refit in Malta during July, *Chivalrous* was used to shadow the suspect vessel *Pan York* in the western Mediterranean in September 1947 as the ship made for Marseilles. Once the ship sailed again the shadowing task was transferred to *Volage, Bigbury Bay* and *Surprise* in turn. In December 1947 she shadowed the *Giovani Maria* from Algeria until handing over to *Verulam* to make the unopposed arrest once she entered territorial waters. Several days later she stood by as a boarding party from *Chevron* arrested a vessel identified as the '*Haganah Ship 29 November 1947*' as it entered territorial waters. It was subsequently towed into Haifa after an apparent machinery break-down. *Chivalrous*' final contribution to the Palestinian Patrol was to join *Mauritius, Chequers* and *Volage* in intercepting *Pan York* which was persuaded to proceed directly to Famagusta where she disembarked over 7,000 passengers. She subsequently reverted to less demanding peacetime tasks and was refitted at Gibraltar between September and November 1948.

Sometimes she deployed through the Suez Canal into the Red Sea as in July 1949 when she was guard ship in Aqaba. She was guard ship again in February 1950, after which she was refitted in Malta until May. In June 1951 she deployed to Abadan in Iran together with *Chequers, Chevron* and *Chieftain* to defend British interests until September when they were relieved by ships of 3 DS. After the reduction in the number of destroyers in the Mediterranean Fleet she was prepared for reduction to reserve status at Gibraltar in February 1953 and subsequently moved to Devonport where, in March, she was laid up in the reserve fleet on the River Tamar. Her inactive time was not to be long however and in 1953 the Admiralty agreed to lend the ship to Pakistan for a period of 3 years in order to help the new Commonwealth navy's expansion plans. She was refitted and brought up to the anti-submarine standard of her sister-ships with twin 'Squid' mortars in 'X' position, improved sonar and other minor changes at Crichton's Shipyard in Liverpool between September 1953 and June 1954; the work being paid for by the Government of Pakistan.

On 14 June 1954 she re-commissioned briefly as HMS *Chivalrous* with a reduced complement for post refit sea trials. On their successful completion, she was taken over by the Pakistan Navy and re-commissioned as *PNS Taimur* on 29 June 1954. After her first 3 years in Pakistan, the period of loan was extended to terminate in June 1961 but it transpired that she would not serve that long. Shortly before midnight on 3 June 1958 she was severely damaged in Karachi harbour when she was hit by the American tanker *Californian*, thankfully without casualties. An initial survey, quoted by the British High Commissioner stated that she could be repaired in Pakistan in about 5 weeks and returned to service provided that her gearing was found to be undamaged. Subsequent investigation revealed that she was in a worse state than had at first been thought with the result that the Pakistani Government decided that it was not worth the cost of repairing her. She was returned to RN control in December 1958, sold for scrap and subsequently broken up locally by 1961.

The 'Co' Class
The 13th Emergency Flotilla

With one important exception, the eight ships of the 13th Emergency Flotilla, the 'Co's, were repeats of the 'Ch' class with the same Mark 6 director and RPC for the main armament. The same reduced torpedo and depth charge outfits were accepted to compensate for the added topweight. They were ordered on 24 July 1942, the same day as the 'Ch' class and would today probably be considered as a different 'batch' of the same class.

The exception was the modified, all-welded hull and the first ship completed, *Contest*, was the first all-welded destroyer to be completed for the Royal Navy. Her builders, J Samuel White had suffered extensive damage when their shipyard at Cowes on the Isle of Wight had been bombed by German aircraft and had taken the opportunity to replace the damaged buildings with fabricating shops designed specifically for this new form of construction. It was a bold and forward-looking step to take at the height of a difficult wartime construction programme and led to a number of changes, not least the re-training of riveters as welders. Eventually 160 were employed on *Contest*, 50 of them women. To allow the new construction technique the hull had to be re-designed so that it could be made in sections up to 10 tons in weight and less than 40 feet long. Plating had to be re-configured to allow flush butt joints rather than the overlaps needed for riveting. Sections were built upside down to allow

'down-hand' welding and then craned onto the slipway for assembly with the midships bottom shell first with the boiler, engine and machinery seatings produced in the fabrication shops and dropped into place. As far as possible the midships sections were structurally complete and partially fitted out under cover before being craned onto the slipway. Welded construction was already used widely by American shipbuilders and these techniques were soon adopted for all British warship construction.

Completion was slowed by the late delivery of fire control equipment and none of these ships saw service in the Second World War; *Concord* was not completed until the end of 1946. *Cockade, Contest, Cossack, Comet* and *Constance* were completed with a close-range armament comprising a twin 'Hazemeyer' Bofors mounting amidships with 20mm Oerlikon mountings abaft the funnel and in the bridge wings. The remaining three completed with a twin Mark 5 Bofors amidships and single Mark 7 Bofors abaft the funnel and in the bridge wings. The five earlier ships were brought up to this standard during refits.

Once commissioned the entire class was deployed to the Far East where it formed the 8th Destroyer Squadron and gave valuable service during the Korean War.

Data is the same as the 'Ch' class with minor variations between ships.

Chapter 17

HMS COCKADE

HMS Cockade *anchored in the Clyde in September 1945 shortly after her completion. (Crown Copyright/MoD 1945)*

HMS *Cockade* was laid down by Yarrow at their Scotstoun yard on 11 March 1943, launched on 7 March 1944 by Viscountess Weir and completed on 29 September 1945. She left Greenock on 11 October and began her work-up at Portland two days later. She subsequently took passage to Malta where she used the warmer Mediterranean weather to complete her work-up to operational efficiency between December 1945 and February 1946. Once declared operational she deployed through the Suez Canal to join the British Pacific Fleet as part of the 8th Destroyer Flotilla. She visited Australia and New Zealand in 1947 and took part in a number of exercises with Commonwealth and allied warships. In November 1947, during a post-war manpower shortfall in the Royal Navy, she returned to the UK and served as an air target ship in the Plymouth Local Flotilla

with a reduced ship's company. However, in 1949 her sister-ship *Comet* collided with *Chevron* during a darkened night-encounter exercise in the Mediterranean and had to return to the UK for repairs. *Comet's* ship's company transferred to *Cockade* and prepared to deploy in her to the Far East but she suffered an engine defect that delayed her departure. She finally sailed on 26 November 1949 and worked up off Malta to prepare for service in the Far East Fleet.

Cockade arrived in Singapore to join the 8th Destroyer Flotilla in the Far East Fleet in early 1950 and deployed with *Triumph, Jamaica, Kenya, Cossack, Constance* and *Comus* in the spring for exercises with the USN in the areas off Subic Bay and later Japan. On one occasion she was acting as plane-guard for *Triumph* when a Seafire crashed on deck, causing one of the flight-deck handlers to fall

HMS Cockade *leaving the UK to work up in Malta prior to re-joining the Far East Fleet. In 1948 her pennant number changed from R 34 to D 34 under the new NATO system..* *(National Museum of the Royal Navy)*

into the sea; *Cockade* rescued him and passed him back to the carrier by jackstay transfer. The timing and location of the manoeuvres meant that the British task force was close to Korean waters when war broke out in June 1950 and *Cockade* began her first war deployment in company with the cruiser *Kenya*. She remained with her to form a task unit within the West Coast Support Group with orders to enforce a blockade of the coast held by North Koreans; prevent infiltration by sea on coasts held by South Koreans and to attack North Korean targets that presented themselves at sea and on land. Shortly after arrival in Korean waters, *Cockade* spotted floating mines nearby and destroyed them with gunfire. Her first action occurred on 2 August 1950 when she joined *Cossack* to bombard North Korean forces in the port of Mukpo with the aim of creating a diversion behind the enemy troops advancing on the UN perimeter at Pusan and denying them the use of the port. Spotting was provided by aircraft from *Triumph* and fire opened at

0820. It continued for two hours during which over 1,000 rounds of 4.5-inch ammunition were expended by the 2 destroyers in an operation that was judged to have been well planned and executed by the Flag Officer Second-in-Command (FO2) Far East Station who commanded Commonwealth naval forces in the area. On 9 August the Dutch destroyer *Evertsen* (formerly *HMS Scourge*) ran aground on the south-west coast of Korea while returning from a patrol off Pusan and was badly damaged. *Cockade* went to her aid and, once she was re-floated, towed her to safety.

In September the landing at Inchon by the 1st US Marine Division changed the course of the war. FO2's Commonwealth force was re-organised to supply air and bombardment units as well as a seaward screen of destroyers. *Cockade* joined *Charity*, *Concord* and *HMA Ships Warramunga* and *Bataan* to form a screen which remained to the west of Inchon to guard against interference by hostile ships or submarines. In October UN forces carried

out a further amphibious landing at Wonsan and *Cockade* was one of a number of British, Australian, Canadian and New Zealand warships that reinforced the USN shore bombardment group. In the event the landing was delayed by the need to clear an extensive minefield laid by the North Koreans and Wonsan was captured by South Korean troops advancing overland. By November it appeared that the war was almost over and *Cockade* ended her first deployment to return to more routine duties with the Far East Fleet.

The massive Chinese intervention in early 1951 was to prolong the war for another two-and-a-half years and *Cockade* returned for a second deployment in March 1951. On 10 March 1951 *Cockade* sailed from Inchon with the new C-in-C Far East Station who had been meeting USN authorities ashore to co-ordinate action. In the afternoon he transferred to the aircraft carrier *Theseus* to witness flying operations and *Cockade* took up a position in

her screen. On 16 March *Belfast, Cossack* and *Cockade* bombarded beaches where communist troops were digging trenches and on 7 April 1951, while acting as air search and rescue ship in the Yalu Gulf, *Cockade* was ordered to search for the crew of a crashed US bomber. This involved moving close inshore among shoals in thick weather and searching in co-operation with a USAF amphibious aircraft which was able to land and pick up the one survivor that was located; the rest of the crew were never found. Fortuitously she was able to rescue another US airman who had been shot down in January, concealed by friendly Koreans and brought out to the ship in a junk when she was seen to be close inshore.

In June *Cockade* joined *Constance* and 2 USN destroyers to act screen for the aircraft carrier *Glory*. Her aircraft were heavily involved in armed reconnaissance, strikes against enemy transport and spotting for shore bombardments at this time and

This photograph of Cockade *in March 1952 shows some of the bitter winter conditions endured by Commonwealth warships off Korea. It was taken from the frigate* Mounts Bay; *note the loaded Mark 7 Bofors in the foreground.*
(Ken Kelly Collection)

HMS Cockade *photographed refuelling at sea from a cruiser during the Korean War. The cruiser's crane is supporting the weight of the hose and a generous bight is maintained so that it is not pulled taught as both ships move.*
(Syd Goodman Collection)

she was launching more than 50 sorties every day. In July *Cossack, Consort, Charity* and *Cockade* left the Korean coast to participate in USN 'hunter-killer' anti-submarine exercises off Okinawa intended to improve allied capability in case Soviet submarines were deployed in support of North Korea. She left the war zone for a brief spell in August but was back again in October for her third deployment. In late November she relieved *Cossack* covering operations by South Korean special forces to capture islands in the Yalu Gulf. On

30 November 1951 the enemy struck with complete surprise at Tae Wha Do Island and *Cockade* closed it to open fire on Junks carrying enemy troops close inshore, sinking several of them, but came under fire herself from shore batteries at Ka Do. She suffered a hit on 'Y' mounting which killed one rating and communication with the forces ashore was soon lost with the result that she was unable to bring down supporting fire for them. At daylight, *Cockade* withdrew south after the island had fallen to the enemy.

She left Korean waters for a brief spell after December 1951 but returned for a fourth tour January 1952 when she formed part of the screen for the aircraft carrier *HMAS Sydney* which had relieved *Glory* for a spell. In late January she was detached to search for the pilot of a Sea Fury who failed to return from a mission but no trace was found despite a wide area search. Later in the month *Cockade* supported minesweeping operations in the Haeju estuary, bombarding any enemy positions that were detected on small islands to the north.

Cockade left Korea again in March 1952 and was taken in hand by Singapore Dockyard from April for an interim modernisation which included the removal of 'X' mounting and the installation of two Mark 6 'Squid' mortars, their associated bomb handling room and modifications to the sonar outfit. The work finished in August and she re-commissioned and worked up prior to returning to Korea

for her fifth tour of duty in December. For the second time in her career she took a new C-in-C Far East Station to sea while he was on an inspection visit, this time on 22 December. When the aircraft carrier *Glory* returned to the station, *Cockade* joined her screen, continuing with the task into February. Her fifth tour was a short one, ending in February 1953 but she was back for her sixth and last in April and this lasted until the end of hostilities. On 2 May 1953 she was one of a number of Commonwealth destroyers that patrolled the Songjin area when she saw several enemy junks drawn up on a beach north of Yang Do; she destroyed one and damaged 2 others with gunfire. On 6 May she closed the coast to shoot at railway repair parties seen south of Songjin, scattering them and destroying 3 box-cars. An enemy shore battery opened fire on her but *Cockade* was two miles offshore, close to a fog bank into which she promptly withdrew. She was under fire for about 3½ minutes

HMS Cockade *refuelling at sea from the cruiser* Newcastle *so this photograph must have been taken between December 1952 and February 1953 when both ships were in the Korean War Zone.* *(Syd Goodman Collection)*

during which time 45 to 50 rounds straddled her but none of them hit.   In May *Ocean* relieved *Glory* and *Cockade* remained with the carrier screen, the other ships in it at this time being *Cossack*, *HMCS Crusader* and 2 USN destroyers. She remained with the carrier task group until the armistice that ended the fighting in July 1953. *Cockade* had served on six deployments to the Korean theatre of operations throughout the war and steamed 105,500 miles between 1950 and 1953, consuming 28,250 tons of fuel oil in the process. These were the third highest totals for a British warship in the conflict, exceeded only by *Charity* and *Comus*.

After the end of hostilities she remained with 8 DS, re-commissioning in Singapore in 1956. After working up she joined *Newcastle* and *Consort* to escort the Royal Yacht *Britannia* which was carrying the Duke of Edinburgh on a tour of the Pacific. The group visited Australia, New Zealand, the Gilbert and Ellis Islands, Fiji, Manus and Nauru. In 1957 she carried out patrols off the west coast of Malaya to prevent weapons being smuggled to the insurgents ashore and visited Korea and Tokyo to 'show the flag' in support of British interests. In the autumn of 1957 she gave assistance to the civil population of Ceylon during severe floods. She finally left Hong Kong flying her paying-off pennant to return to the UK on 19 December 1957, arriving in Devonport on 27 January 1958. It was nearly the end of her career and, after de-storing, she was placed on the Sales List on 19 February and laid up in the River Tamar in extended reserve in April.

It proved not quite to be the end of her useful life, however, and she was transferred to dockyard control and brought alongside for use as an accommodation ship for the ship's company of the new Tribal class frigate *Tartar* as they began to gather at Devonport after her launch in September 1960. Approval was given for her to be scrapped, however, and when she was no longer needed as an accommodation ship she was sold to John Cashmore & Co. *Cockade* arrived at their breaker's yard at Newport for demolition on 13 July 1964.

Chapter 18

HMS COMET

HMS Comet *photographed in September 1945 during her break between guard-ship duties at Wilhelmshaven. As in the 'Ch' class a small canvas-covered boat has been positioned to fill the space left when the forward torpedo tubes were removed to reduce topweight.* *(Crown Copright/MoD 1945)*

HMS *Comet* was the second 'Co' to be built by Yarrow at their Scotstoun yard. She was laid down on 14 June 1943, launched on 22 June 1944 and completed remarkably quickly on 6 June 1945, the first of her class to do so. She worked up from 13 June and then spent a short period at Greenock having defects discovered during her sea-trials rectified. In August 1945 she was guard-ship at Wilhelmshaven for a while in support of the occupation forces and, after a break in September, returned to the same task in October. She then sailed for the Far East to join 8 DF in the British Pacific Fleet and, after short stops in Singapore and Hong Kong, she anchored off Tokyo in February 1946 in support of the British Commonwealth Occupation Force. Thus she had

the unusual distinction of having participated in the occupation forces of both Germany and Japan.

In August 1946 she visited Fremantle in Western Australia and during February and March 1947 she escorted the despatch vessel Alert and the cruiser *Belfast* on a visit to Kure by the Commander-in-Chief British Pacific Fleet, after which she was refitted in Hong Kong Dockyard. On 15 September 1947 she ran aground on the Kwirse Reef off southern Japan and suffered significant damage; both propellers were damaged, one shaft was bent and several fuel tanks were open to the sea. Immediate repairs were carried out in Hong Kong; these took until January 1948 when she sailed back to the UK for more permanent rectification work in Devonport. These were combined with an exten-

HMS Comet *in Malta on 28 April 1954 after her conversion to a minelayer. Additionally, double 'Squids' have replaced 'X' mounting and both 'Y' mounting and the torpedo tubes have been removed to reduce topweight. Rails, each for up to 25 mines, run along either side of the iron deck with sloping 'shelves' on each quarter from which the mines were rolled into the sea.* (Author's Collection)

sive refit which lasted until May 1949 when she re-commissioned with a reduced ship's company for service as a target ship for aircraft, working with the light fleet carrier *Warrior* in the Mediterranean Fleet. In May 1949 she re-commissioned fully and began to work up for a planned return to 8 DF in what was now the Far East Fleet.

However, while carrying out night encounter exercises without light off Malta on 30 May 1949, *Chevron* collided with her causing extensive damage to her starboard side abreast the bridge. Flooding was contained by damage control parties and temporary repairs were carried out in Malta in June, after which she sailed back to the UK and reduced to reserve in Devonport in August. She was taken into dockyard hands for permanent repairs in September. These were completed in January 1950 when she returned to reserve, moored in the River Tamar. The collision and subsequent

period in reserve meant that she was one of only two 'Co' class destroyers that did not see service with 8 DS in the Korean War. In June 1953 she was modernised and fitted out as a minelayer with mine rails aft, 'Y' mounting removed to save top weight and 'X' mounting removed and replaced by two 'Squid' mountings and their handling room. All torpedo armament was removed to save topweight and her close-range armament was brought up to the latest standard with a twin Mark 5 Bofors and four single Mark 7 Bofors.

She re-commissioned for service with the Mediterranean Fleet on 18 March 1954 and served with it until late 1955. In October 1954 Britain and Egypt signed an agreement that British forces would withdraw from the Suez Canal Zone by June 1956; a period of tension followed during which there were fears that British shipping in the canal might be attacked. *Comet* was one of a number of

HMS Comet *seen from astern with a load of mines on her rails.*   *(Syd Goodman Collection)*

destroyers that escorted groups of ships through the canal during this period. She was also used to patrol around the coast of Cyprus to stop 'gun-runners' landing arms for EOKA terrorists on the island who sought union with Greece and the withdrawal of British troops. After a further refit, she re-commissioned again on 28 August 1956 for service with 6 DS with *Cavendish* and *Contest*. The squadron was assigned to the Home Fleet but deployed to the eastern Mediterranean for Operation 'MUSKE-TEER' the Anglo-French landings at Port Said in early November 1956. She was one of a large number of British warships in Port Said on 11

November but this commission proved to be relatively short-lived and she returned to Devonport to de-store in December 1957. On 29 January 1958 she reduced to extended reserve, laid up in the River Tamar and was placed on the Sales List. There was no overseas interest in her as a running warship and the Admiralty authorised her disposal by scrapping in September 1961. A rather unlucky ship that had not seen a great deal of service, she was sold to West of Scotland Shipbreakers at Troon on 22 October 1962. Demolition was complete by the end of 1963.

Chapter 19

HMS COMUS

HMS Comus *photographed off the south coast of the UK on 22 July 1946, a fortnight after her completion. She has Oerlikons on the bridge wings but an otherwise all-Bofors close-range armament.* (Crown Copyright/MoD 1946)

HMS *Comus* was laid down at Thornycroft's Woolston shipyard near Southampton on 21 August 1943 and launched on 14 March 1945. With the end of the war in August there was no longer any urgency for her completion and both the delivery of fire-control equipment and work on the ship itself proceeded slowly. She eventually commissioned in the shipyard on 25 June 1946 and was finally signed off as complete 8 July 1946. She was allocated to the 8th Destroyer Flotilla in the British Pacific Fleet but post-war manning problems prevented her from leaving the UK until early 1947. She arrived in the BPF in April and subsequently spent her whole ten-year operational career in the Far East. During 1947 she visited Inchon in Korea, a port that was to be familiar later under very different circumstances. In July she visited

Sasebo in Japan, another port that was to become familiar as a forward base for Commonwealth warships during the Korean War. She lost a man overboard on 14 July in rough weather but, fortunately, managed to recover him. *Comus* was one of the ships present at Sasebo in 1948 for the BPF's last regatta, in September of that year it was renamed the Far East Fleet and its headquarters moved from Hong Kong to Singapore. She was refitted in Hong Kong in February 1948 and in Singapore in April 1949. She deployed to Japanese waters in February with *Triumph, Jamaica, Kenya, Concord* and *Constance* for exercises with the USN but was due a further refit in June 1950 when the Korean War broke out.

Immediate refit plans were postponed and *Comus* joined the aircraft carrier *Triumph* to act as plane-

A fine view of Comus *in 1947; the 27 foot whaler is rigged as a sea-boat with the boat-rope taken right forward. Note that the boat's tiller is lashed so that it will turn to port, away from the hull, on entering the water as it is pulled forward by the boat-rope.* (Steve Bush Collection)

guard; the two ships were allocated to the US 7th Fleet on 5 July so that *Triumph* and the American aircraft carrier *Valley Forge* could operate together. After their first strikes against North Korean targets on 3 July, the carriers had moved to Okinawa to counter potential further Communist aggression and on 16 July the carrier task force sailed to cover an American amphibious landing at Pohang on 18 July. When this was accomplished without opposition the carriers were released to strike at targets in North Korea. *Valley Forge* flew strike missions with her Skyraider and Corsair aircraft while *Triumph* flew combat air patrols (CAP) and anti-submarine patrols for the task force with her Seafires and Fireflies. On 21 July *Triumph* developed a problem with her starboard stern gland and she detached to Sasebo with *Comus* for repairs. By 24 July they were back in action with *Triumph*

resuming CAP and anti-submarine patrols, flying an average of 42 sorties a day with *Comus* on her starboard quarter while she was at flying stations. *Triumph's* time with the 7th Fleet ended on 30 July when more USN carriers arrived. She detached to Kure in Japan for a ten-day self-maintenance period with *Comus* after which both ships joined the Commonwealth task force blockading the Korean west coast.

Triumph and *Comus* joined the west coast task force at Sasebo on 10 August and sailed two days later, using the carrier-borne aircraft for a series of searches and strikes that strengthened the blockade; FO2 was embarked in the carrier until 16 August. On the night of 20/21 August 1950 *Comus* was detached to join Consort to give covering fire, if necessary, for the *USS Horace A Bass*, an amphibious ship that was to land a reconnaissance party on

a west coast beach. The landing proved to be successful and covering fire was not required. On 23 August 1950 *Comus* was steaming about 85 miles west of Kunsan when she was attacked by 2 North Korean Il-10 'Sturmovik' bombers which dived on her singly from astern. The first dropped 4 bombs that hit the ship on the port side, killing one sailor and wounding another and leaving a hole 4 feet by 8 feet on the waterline which flooded the forward boiler room. The second aircraft's aim was less accurate; it dropped its bombs ahead of the ship and all missed completely. *Comus* was able to make for Kure under her own power, escorted by *Consort* with a CAP of USMC fighters. Fears that this marked the beginning of a communist attempt to break the blockade led FO2 to order his ships off the west coast to concentrate in order to increase their anti-aircraft firepower and *Triumph* to maintain a CAP over them in daylight hours for the

immediate future. In the event, the attack proved to be an isolated incident and no further air attacks on Commonwealth warships took place.

The repairs marked the end of *Comus'* first deployment off Korea; in November 1951, when they were complete, sand was found in her steering motor. Sabotage by some person unknown was suspected but never proved and it did not delay her return to the war zone. *Comus'* second deployment to Korea began in January 1951, after the Chinese offensive when she formed part of the screen, with *Cossack, Consort* and *Constance*, for the aircraft carrier *Theseus* which had replaced *Triumph* on station. On 26 January a Sea Fury crashed into the sea while on CAP over the fleet; *Comus* was ordered to search for the pilot but found only two small pieces of wreckage. Occasionally British warships deployed to the east coast to share the task of bombarding road and rail communications with USN

HMS Comus *refuelling at sea from an aircraft carrier during the Korean War.* (Syd Goodman Collection)

HMS Comus *steaming at high speed in a choppy sea.* *(Syd Goodman Collection)*

warships. Railways ran close to the steep shoreline in the east but were much further inland on the marshy, flat west coast. Between March and April 1951 *Concord, Comus, Alacrity, Black Swan* and the repaired Dutch *Evertsen* were employed in this role. For most of the time, however, *Comus* continued to operate with *Theseus'* screen which later included the RCN tribal class destroyers *Cayuga, Nootka* and *Athabaskan*. In April *Comus* joined a number of other warships in the search for a communist Mig-15 fighter which was reported to have come down on mud flats near Simni. Despite an extensive hunt, no trace of it was found and the task force assembled for its recovery was dispersed.

Between 8 and 13 May *Comus* joined the US Ships *Floyd B Parker, John R Craig* and *Tacoma* off Wonsan for day and night bombardments of enemy positions ashore. These were hampered by fog but it was believed that they had stopped movement by rail for a time. Her second war patrol ended in June and she withdrew to more routine Far East Fleet duties in Hong Kong. On 4 July 1951 she was sailed to go to the assistance of the *SS Peterstar* which had run aground on the Pratas Reef. She stood by her for a number of days and her ship's company eventually received a substantial award after the vessel was salvaged. *Comus* subsequently carried out a short refit before returning to operations off Korea.

Comus returned for her third patrol in September 1951 as part of the maintenance carrier *Unicorn's* screen with *Cossack*. On 24 September *Comus* covered a raid by South Korean special forces on the Amgak peninsula; it was successful and the raiders withdrew with 9 prisoners including a North Korean colonel and his mistress. The withdrawal took place under fire and *Comus* opened fire to cover the South Koreans who were also supported by air strikes from *Glory*, the new aircraft carrier on station. *Comus* covered another raid in the Pungehon area on 29 September but this time there was no opposition and, thus, no need for her to open fire. Later that day, however, enemy troops were observed to be concentrating near the special

forces' headquarters and *Comus* closed the area with *Black Swan* to bombard them. Subsequently one or other of the warships remained close at hand until the threat was deemed to have receded. In early October *Comus* was in Sasebo with other Commonwealth warships when the C-in-C Far East Station visited his units deployed in the war zone.

On 10 October *Comus* sailed as plane-guard for the aircraft carrier *Sydney* on her second patrol; both formed part of large-scale attacks on transport from the east coast aimed at cutting enemy road and rail communications to the south. Among other tasks, *Comus* rotated with other ships in the Han estuary to bombard enemy troop locations near the coast. She spent 9 days from 29 October 1951 in the Han on a task previously carried out by frigates. The tidal stream proved to have much more effect on her than it had on the frigates for some unexplained reason but she found a sheltered anchorage near Songmo Do (or Spoon Island). Her heavier armament did considerable damage to enemy installations when she fired over a hill using spotters in boats clear of the anchorage to observe her fall of shot. On 7 November 1951 FO2 transferred from *Sydney* to *Comus* by jackstay and sailed in her back to Sasebo. *Comus'* third tour of duty in the war zone ended shortly afterwards and she returned to Hong Kong for a maintenance period over Christmas.

Comus began her fourth war patrol in May 1952 with the familiar task of plane-guard for the duty carrier, by that stage *Ocean*, and on blockade duties off the west coast of Korea. She continued to form part of the screen when *Glory* relieved *Ocean* later in the year, sharing the task with *Consort* and the *USS Taylor*. This patrol ended in September 1952 for a brief maintenance period but she returned for her fifth and final tour of duty in November. She operated on bombardment duties off the east coast between 3 and 20 January 1953 but was unfortunately not credited with the destruction of a train during this period and was not inducted into the 'Trainbusters Club' like her sister-ships *Charity* and *HMCS Crusader.* For the remainder of January and

part of February she formed part of *Glory's* screen before leaving Korean waters for the last time. In late February she paid off into dockyard hands at Singapore and was given the standard interim modernisation. This was completed in August 1953 and she re-commissioned for further service with 8 DS.

The remaining four years of her operational life were spent on patrols off the Malayan coast to prevent movement by terrorists during the emergency, visits to ports 'showing the flag' and participation in exercises. In early 1955 she joined the cruiser *Newcastle* to bombard about 60 terrorists known to be hiding in the Selangor swamps during a series of concerted actions that also included attacks by Lincoln bombers and shore-based artillery. After re-commissioning on 14 July 1955 she went to the aid of the *SS Helikon* which was being attacked by a pirate vessel off Foochow, about 400 miles south of Shanghai. The vessel made off as *Comus* arrived and trained her main armament on it; *Helikon* pro-

ceeded on her lawful business.

On 13 February 1957 the ship's company from *Comus* moved to *Cossack* and re-commissioned her in Singapore. *Comus* was steamed back to the UK by the ship's company from the frigate *Modeste*, which had completed its time in the Far East. She arrived in Portsmouth on 9 May 1957 after ten years away from the UK, de-stored and was immediately placed in reserve. Following the 1957 Defence Review there was a surplus of destroyers and it was decided not to modernise her or carry out a further refit. Her end came quickly and the Admiralty announced its approval to scrap her on 7 March 1958, after which she was stripped of any useful equipment. *Comus* was sold to the British Iron and Steel Corporation on 10 November 1958 and arrived at John Cashmore's Newport yard for demolition on 13 November. She had enjoyed a short but eventful career.

Chapter 20

HMS Concord

HMS Concord *photographed under way carrying out sea trials shortly after her completion in December 1946.*
(Crown Copyright/MoD 1946)

Originally to have been named *Corso* and launched as such on 14 May 1945, she was renamed *Concord* in June 1946. In the era after the Anglo-French supersonic airliner and the agreed French spelling of its name, the spelling of this ship's name appears unusual but it is the correct English spelling of the word and is the better for it. She was ordered from Thornycroft at their Woolston, Southampton yard and was the last unit of the 'Co' class to be laid down on 18 November 1943. She was also to be the last 'Co' to be completed, on 20 December 1946. She was finished with single Oerlikons in the bridge wings but these were soon replaced by single Bofors to give her the standard close-range armament of one twin Mark 5 and four single Mark 7 Bofors. After an initial work-up, she joined the Portsmouth local flotilla for

the first months of 1947 during a difficult period for manpower planners to cope with in the years immediately after the post-war demobilisation. She sailed for a further work-up in Malta in April 1947 and then deployed to join the British Pacific Fleet calling at Port Said, Aden, Trincomalee, Singapore and finally Hong Kong where she joined the 8th Destroyer Flotilla with which she spent her entire operational career.

On 31 July 1949 the frigate *Amethyst* managed to escape from the position in which she had been trapped in the River Yangtse by communist gun batteries and headed for the open sea. Just as dawn broke she met *Concord* which had been sent into the river to engage the Woosung forts if they opposed *Amethyst's* passage. This was the moment when *Amethyst's* commanding officer sent his

famous signal 'have rejoined the fleet south of Woosung, God save the King'. On 12 February 1950 *Concord* went to the aid of *SS Wing Hing* which was aground on Chillang Point, 70 miles to the east of Hong Kong and rescued her crew.

In the initial stages of the Korean War, *Concord* was assigned to the screening force for the aircraft carrier *Triumph* together with *Charity, Cockade* and the RAN destroyers *Warramunga* and *Bataan*. She was not with the group as it covered the landing by the 1st US Marine Division at Inchon on 15 September 1950 but later formed part of the blockade patrol off north-west Korea with the cruiser *Ceylon* and *Charity*. Subsequently *Kenya* relieved *Ceylon* and the 3 ships operated off Fankochi Point, north of Inchon. *Concord*'s particular task at this time was to support the work of 3 small South Korean vessels which gathered intelligence close inshore with particular success. In October *Concord* remained with the west coast blockade force which now comprised the aircraft carrier *Theseus*, the cruisers *Jamaica* and *Kenya*, the RN destroyers *Constance* and *Charity* in addition to herself together with the RCN destroyers *Cayuga* and *Sioux* and the RAN destroyer *Bataan*. By November 1950 it appeared that the United Nations offensive into North Korea had all but ended the conflict and a number of Commonwealth warships departed the war zone; *Concord* returned to Hong Kong. On 27 November, however, the communist Chinese army struck with complete surprise and began to drive the UN forces south. British ships were ordered to rejoin the UN forces off Korea, among them the cruiser *Kenya* which resumed the blockade with *Concord*. The redeployment of British forces was complete only four days after the UN commander asked for their return. In December *Concord* joined *Theseus*' screen with *Cossack* and the Dutch *Evertsen* for operations off Chinnampo to cover the evacuation of UN forces. Once this was over *Concord* remained with the carrier screen together with *Cossack* and *Constance* but had to return to Sasebo on 16 December with condenser problems. She remained with the carrier

screen until she completed her first period in the Korean war zone in January 1951, after which she returned to Hong Kong for a short maintenance period.

She returned for a second, short tour of duty in April 1951 and took her place in the rotation of ships in the 'gun-line' off Wonsan, alternating with *Comus, Alacrity, Black Swan* and the Dutch *Evertsen*. Their targets included anything that moved on specified sections of road and railway, interdiction against previously registered targets at night and counter-battery fire when needed. On 28 April she moved to the west coast and joined the *USS Toledo* in silencing an enemy battery near Inchon. *Concord* continued to give gunfire support into May as UN forces checked the communist advance and eventually stabilised the front on the Imjin line. Once Inchon had been re-taken *Concord* gave support to minesweepers which spent four days clearing the sea approaches under difficult conditions. On completion of this task she joined *Glory*'s screen having been relieved in the support role by *Constance*. At the end of May she returned to Hong Kong.

Concord returned for her third war patrol in August 1951 and joined *Glory*'s screen. On 19 August the fleet was warned of the impending typhoon 'Marge' and *Glory*'s task group concentrated in an area where it had sea-room to ride out the storm. By 20 August winds reached Force 10 with a heavy, confused sea and 30 foot swell. Things moderated slightly and the group put into the shelter of Buckner Bay in Okinawa where the destroyers were able to refuel. There could be no flying operations until 24 August when the *USS Sicily* was due to relieve *Glory* for a spell so it was decided to sail *Glory* direct for Kure escorted by *Charity* and *Concord*. Whilst on passage, *Concord* lost a man overboard but managed to launch her sea-boat and recover him in only 9 minutes; an outstanding feat of seamanship in the prevailing rough conditions.

On 30 August 1951 a raid was carried out against enemy troops reported at Choni-dong. Opposition was expected to be light and the landing force com-

prised 2 platoons of Royal Marines and one of stokers from the cruiser *Ceylon*. Gunfire support was provided by *Ceylon*, *Concord* and *HMNZS Rotoiti* and the assault was to be made by one platoon at a time in landing craft embarked in the cruiser at Sasebo for the purpose. At dawn the 3 warships fired a heavy, 12 minute bombardment which lifted as the first party landed. As they moved across the beach, heavy and accurate mortar and machine-gun fire was opened on it from the flanks. Fire was returned and the shore bombardment resumed while the party withdrew with 15 casualties, one of them serious. The bombardment continued for some time and later aircraft from *Sicily* reported an enemy supply dump near the beach and signs of

heavy enemy casualties. FO2 decided as a result of this experience not to repeat the raid unless intelligence could guarantee more accurate information about the target.

In September *Concord* rejoined *Glory's* screen with the Canadian *Sioux* and *Cayuga* for a series of strikes in the Wonsan area. At the end of September *Glory* sailed for a refit in Australia and was relieved off Korea by *HMAS Sydney*, retaining *Concord* in the screening group. From 21 October 1951 *Concord* moved to join the 'gun-line' off the east coast of Korea, operating first off Hungnam and then Songjin. Her interdiction task brought her close inshore and off Hungnam she came under heavy and accurate fire at times, being straddled at

A port quarter image of Concord *in 1947 that gives a good view of the single bank of torpedo tubes and the depth charge arrangements aft. The mainmast with its Type 291 air-warning radar is mounted forward of the twin Bofors, further forward than in most other ships fitted with the equipment.* (Crown Copyright/MoD 1947)

HMS Concord *photographed at speed before 1952 when her limited modernisation began in Singapore Dockyard. She already had an all-Bofors close-range armament.* (Syd Goodman Collection)

15,000 yards from the enemy guns and near-missed at 12,000. She departed for Hong Kong on 3 November after a busy and effective three months in the war zone; her place being taken by *Constance*. She was able to spend Christmas 1951 in Hong Kong for a welcome break from operations.

Concord's fourth war patrol began in January 1952 with operations in support of South Korean island garrisons off the west coast. On 31 January enemy junks were seen approaching Ho Do from the east; *HMCS Sioux* drove them off while *Concord* silenced a shore-battery that had supported them. In early March she embarked FO2 for a visit to Nagasaki where he held discussions with the Governor and on 16 March *Concord* prevented an enemy attempt to cross mud-flats and attack Yong Mae Do and other Commonwealth destroyers kept them clear on subsequent days. Between 9 and 27 April *Concord* operated on the 'gun-line' off the east coast on interdiction tasks. These frequently brought her close inshore and she was engaged by shore batteries whenever she came into range. On 23 April 1952 she was hit on 'Y' mounting by a 76mm shell which killed 2 men and wounded 4 others. She subsequently returned to Hong Kong for repairs and a maintenance period.

In July 1952 she returned to Korea for another short spell and was deployed off Cho Do on 12 August as the enemy massed forces for an assault. *Concord*'s gunfire broke up the attacks before they could be launched, however, with her gunfire being directed by a fire-control party on the island. Enemy guns on either side of the Haeju Gulf continued to be a nuisance, firing over 100 rounds at UN positions on 21 August but they were then neutralised by *Concord* and the *USS Strong*. After a brief spell in *Glory's* screen, *Concord* left Korea at the end of August for Singapore Dockyard where she underwent an interim modernisation between September 1952 and January 1953. After re-commissioning she worked up in the Singapore areas and then returned to Hong Kong. Her last deployment to Korea lasted from May 1953 to July when

the armistice ended hostilities.

She remained with 8 DS and re-commissioned in August 1953 for further service with the Far East Fleet. In late August she went to the assistance of *ML 1323* which suffered damage and casualties when shelled by communist guns in the Pearl River estuary and Christmas was celebrated during a visit to Kure. During 1953 her whaler's crew had won the fleet pulling competition and she came second in the fleet athletics competition, no mean feat for a relatively small warship. Much of her time was spent taking part in exercises and 'showing the flag' but she also took part in patrols off the coast of Malaya intended to prevent guns and ammunition being smuggled to communist insurgents ashore. On 29 April 1954 SS *Inchulva* was stopped by a Chinese Nationalist warship off the Chinese coast. When *Concord* and *HMNZS Pukaki* came to her assistance she was released in less than 10 minutes.

In early 1956 she formed part of the RN force that kept shipping clear of the British atomic bomb tests carried out at Montebello, Operation 'MOSAIC'. While she was steaming to her allotted position she was damaged by storm force winds and high seas and had to proceed to Fremantle for emergency repairs. Her task was taken over by *Consort* and more permanent repairs were subsequently carried out in the dry-dock at Hong Kong.

Concord re-commissioned for the last time on 20 June 1956 at Hong Kong and spent the next year on patrol off Malaya and visiting over 30 ports. One such was Nelson on the north shore of the South Island of New Zealand where the ship's company marched through the streets and the Mayor took the salute.

After ten years away from the UK, *Concord* left the Far East Fleet in October 1957. She arrived in Portsmouth on 5 November and paid off immediately into un-maintained reserve with no future in prospect after the reduction in the size of the fleet announced in the 1957 Defence Review. She was de-stored and placed on the Sales List on 8 January 1958 but in September she had a reprieve when it was decided that *Concord* and *Cheviot* would be

HMS Concord *outboard of* Chevron *and the cruiser* Swiftsure *in Thomas Ward's scrap yard at Inverkeithing pho-tographed days before work started to dismantle them in 1962.* *(T. Ferrers-Walker)*

removed from the Sales List and allocated to the apprentice training school *HMS Caledonia* at Rosyth to be used for mechanical engineering instruction. This involved flashing up the boilers and running machinery so, to an extent, the ships were kept 'alive'. The role lasted until 4 July 1962 when she was placed into extended reserve at Rosyth and replaced by *Saintes* in the training task. The Admiralty gave approval for her to be scrapped on 18 October 1962 and her sale was announced immediately. Five days later she was towed from Rosyth to Thomas Ward's scrap yard at Inverkeithing where work started almost at once on her demolition. A year later it was complete.

Chapter 21

HMS CONSORT

HMS Consort *carrying out post-completion sea trials in the Clyde during March 1946 shortly after her completion.*
(Crown Copyright/MoD 1946)

Ordered from Alex Stephens & Co's Govan shipyard, *Consort* was laid down on 26 May 1943 and launched on 19 October 1944. She commissioned at Govan on 7 March 1946 a few days before her final completion was signed off on 19 March.   After sea trials she sailed to Devonport Dockyard where she was fitted with an all-Bofors close-range armament prior to an intended deployment to the British Pacific Fleet. A shortage of manpower delayed her work up in Malta but she eventually deployed to join the 8th Destroyer Flotilla in the British Pacific Fleet at the end of 1946. Her duties included time with the RN occupation force in Japanese waters with visits to Kure and Sasebo. She also carried out patrols in Malayan coastal waters to prevent gun-running and illegal support for the communist insurgents that were

beginning to cause trouble in what was to become known as the Malayan Emergency. She was refitted in Hong Kong in November 1947 and Singapore in January 1949.

In April 1949 *Consort* was the British guard-ship in the Chinese Nationalist capital at Nanking, 200 miles from the sea up the Yangtse River and *Amethyst* set off up the river to relieve her. On hearing that *Amethyst* had been engaged by communist shore-batteries and driven ashore with damage and casualties at Rose Island about 100 miles downstream, *Concord* left Nanking and steamed down river at 26 knots, flooding the river banks with her wake. Early on she came under small arms fire but silenced it with a salvo from three of her four 4.5-inch guns; like many RN ships at the time she was suffering from a shortage of manpower and only

HMS Consort *photographed in the Clyde during 1946. Note the scrambling net in the stowed position by 'X' mounting.*
(Crown Copyright/MoD 1946)

had sufficient men to man 'A', 'B' and 'X' mountings and half the close-range armament at any one time. *Concord* closed *Amethyst* at about 1400 on 20 April and engaged the communist batteries, knocking out some of the guns but receiving hits herself; after her first pass she turned back toward *Amethyst* and slowed to 8 knots trying deliberately to silence the enemy guns and pass a tow rope to the stricken frigate. Several of the communist guns were taken out but anti-tank guns were brought into action by troops waiting to assault the Nationalists across the river and *Consort* began to take casualties and suffer damage. The wheelhouse was hit, killing the coxswain and she had to go to emergency steering aft; both 'A' and 'B' guns were put out of action. The engine telegraphs were lost when the bridge

was hit and a hit on the gun director support cut the main firing circuits, forcing 'X' gun into local control. The survivors from 'A' and 'B' mountings moved aft and brought 'Y' mounting into action with local control.

At this stage *Amethyst* signalled that any attempt to tow her off would not be possible under fire and, with deep regret, *Consort* had to leave her and withdraw down river at high speed. Within minutes she was under fire again but her after guns knocked out six of the communist guns ashore. *Consort* was hit four times in just over a minute and 6 of the 8 men killed on board died in this final stage of the action. In the brief engagement *Consort* had fired 240 rounds of 4.5-inch ammunition and 25% of her close-range ammunition. She subsequently berthed

in Shanghai and made immediate repairs with the help of men from other ships. Her dead were buried with full naval honours at Hungjoa Cemetery. More permanent repairs were carried out in Hong Kong in April and May 1949 after which she undertook a Malayan coastal patrol. In May 1949 her ship's company took over the former British escort destroyer *Mendip* in Hong Kong after it was returned from loan with the name *Lin Fu*, to the defeated Chinese nationalist forces. She re-commissioned on 9 June 1949 and served in Singapore while *Consort* was refitted there, eventually paying-off on 12 September 1949 when *Consort* re-commissioned for further service. A steaming party subsequently took *Mendip* to Alexandria where she was sold to the Egyptian Navy and renamed first *Mohamed Ali* and then *Ibrahim El Awal*. This colourful ship was later captured by, and then served with the Israeli Navy as the *Haifa*.

On 25 June 1950 when the Korean War broke out, *Consort* was at Ominato in Japan with *Cossack* as part of a number of visits to Japanese ports by ships of the new Far East Fleet following exercises with the USN. She was thus ideally placed when FO2 ordered his fleet to concentrate at Kure. She formed part of the aircraft carrier *Triumph's* screen with *Cossack* when she joined the *USS Valley Forge* on 2 July for concerted attacks against North Korean positions. On 5 July *Triumph* joined the US 7th Fleet off the Korean east coast temporarily and both *Consort* and *Cossack* left her to join *Belfast* in Sasebo. This group was to alternate with two other cruiser/destroyer groups to enforce the blockade, prevent communist infiltration behind UN lines and provide naval gunfire support to influence the land battle where and when it was required. FO2 sailed from Sasebo in *Belfast* with *Cossack* and *Consort* on 9 July to establish the blockade that was to last

HMS Consort *photographed after the completion of her modernisation which had been carried out in Singapore Dockyard between October 1951 and February 1952.* (Syd Goodman Collection)

without break for a further three years.

On the night of 20/21 August *Consort* and *Comus* stood by to give covering fire for a reconnaissance party that was to be landed from the *USS Horace A Bass* onto a west coast beach. The landing was a success and covering fire was not required but *Consort* subsequently moved to the Kunsan area where she engaged military targets ashore while a Seafire from *Triumph*, which had now joined the Commonwealth task force, spotted the fall of shot and made corrections. On 23 August *Consort* escorted the damaged *Comus* to Kure for repairs after she was damaged by air attack. During the landings by the 1st US Marine Division at Inchon on 15 September, *Consort* operated with *Triumph's* screen to the west of the target in company with *Ceylon, Cockade* and the Australian *Warramunga* and *Bataan*.

When the UN offensive in the north appeared to have been successful, *Consort* withdrew to Hong Kong together with several other RN ships but after the communist offensive in November, she hastened back to operate with *Theseus'* screen alongside *Cossack, Constance* and *Concord* while the aircraft carrier flew large numbers of offensive sorties, often in foul weather. In January 1951 FO2 decided that in view of the considerable distance his carrier aircraft had to cover between the operating area at sea and the targets inland he would station a destroyer, known as a 'bird-dog' detached from the carrier screen to operate close inshore south of the Inchon Gulf while flying was in progress. *Consort* initiated the new duty on 14 January 1951. In February *Consort* remained with the screen, now reinforced by the repaired *Comus*. Later in February *Consort* formed part of the covering force for feint landings at Inchon which had fallen to the communists. In the event no landings took place and the port was re-taken by UN land forces.

On 5 March 1951 *Kenya* and *Consort* bombarded enemy positions in the Chinnampo-Choppeki area to create the illusion that UN forces were planning to land there. *Kenya* fired 169 rounds of 6 inch and *Consort* 145 rounds of 4.5-inch shell. After this

diversion she rejoined the carrier screen with the Canadian ships *Huron, Nootka* and *Athabaskan*. In early April an experiment was carried out operating 2 carriers together; *Theseus* and the *USS Bataan* operated between 9 and 15 April screened by *Consort*, the Australian *Bataan* (confusingly), the Canadian *Athabaskan* and *Huron* and the American *English* and *Sperry*; a fair representation of the UN fleet off Korea. Despite the 9 knot discrepancy between the carriers' top speeds all went well but *Theseus'* air group suffered an unusually high number of operational losses. On completion of the trial *Theseus* was due to leave the station and *Consort* was detached from her screen to meet *Glory*, her replacement, as she arrived. At the end of April *Consort* herself returned to Hong Kong for a maintenance period at the end of a long period of operations in the war zone.

She returned for a second patrol in June 1951 and initially rejoined the carrier screen. In July she joined *Cossack, Charity* and *Cockade* to take part in USN 'hunter-killer' anti-submarine exercises off Okinawa designed to strengthen the UN fleet's ability to counter communist submarines if the war escalated. In August communist troops gathered at the southern approach to Chinnampo and two enemy 120mm guns fired at the island from the Amgak peninsula 5 miles to the east. The guns were engaged in turn by the Dutch *Van Galen*, the Australian *Warramunga*, the Canadian *Cayuga* and *Consort, Kenya* and *Ceylon*. Between them they neutralised the opposition. On 17 August *Consort* detached to the gun-line on the east coast. She found few targets and had no 'excitement' but when *Cossack* relieved her on 24 August she was immediately straddled by shore batteries. In early September 1951 *Consort* left the war zone and proceeded to Singapore where she paid off into dockyard hands to undergo an interim modernisation between 20 October 1951 and 26 February 1952. On its completion she re-commissioned and worked up in the Singapore areas before returning to Hong Kong. She returned to operations off Korea for third time in May 1952.

HMS Consort *at sea in April 1952 after the completion of her modernisation in Singapore Dockyard.*
(Syd Goodman Collection)

On 15 June 1952 the UK Defence Secretary, Field Marshal Lord Alexander of Tunis accompanied by Mr Selwyn Lloyd the Minister of State visited British warships assembled in Inchon which included *Ocean, Belfast, Ceylon, Consort* and *Amethyst*. He addressed representatives of ships companies on *Ocean's* flight deck but his words were not well received as he spoke entirely about the troops ashore and made no mention of RN activities at sea. *Consort's* third patrol was a short one and she returned to Hong Kong in August. On 25 September 1952 the British-flagged ferry *Takshing* sailing from Hong Kong to Macao was fired on by Chinese communist gunboats 5 miles west of Lantau Island at 0200 and taken to the mouth of the

Pearl River where 2 passengers were taken off. *Consort* and *Mounts Bay* went to her aid at 0700 and escorted her back to Hong Kong. As they did so they were fired on by communist guns at Lap Sap Mei and fire was returned by both warships. She was back off Korea in November 1952 and joined the screen on 10 November for *Glory's* first patrol of her third deployment in the Korean war zone. Other ships in the screen were *Comus* and the *USS Taylor*. On Christmas Eve she joined *Cossack* and *Constance* in engaging and silencing enemy guns that had fired about 500 rounds at the islands of Choda and Sok To the day before. In February 1953 she returned to Hong Kong for a maintenance period, returning to Korea for her fifth and last

deployment between March and May 1953.

Between 14 March 1953 and 12 April *Consort* was on the 'gun-line off the east coast but was not rewarded with any targets for her guns. On 6 April, however, she captured an enemy sampan which she presented to the Republic of Korea garrison in Yang Do. By late April she was back in *Glory's* screen with *Charity*, the Australian *Anzac* and the American *Southerland, Cowell* and *Thomas*. In late April she carried out a jackstay transfer to *Glory* in fog in a remarkable display of seamanship. Visibility was estimated at 2 cables (400 yards) and *Consort* was given position information as she closed by *Glory's* Type 974 pilotage radar using tactical VHF radio to pass ranges and bearings. *Consort* saw *Glory* visually at 2½ cables but she herself was not visible from the carrier's higher bridge until she was less than 2 cables distant. *Consort* remained with *Glory* until May 1953 when she left the war zone for the last time and returned to Hong Kong.

Consort remained with 8 DS after the Korean War, re-commissioning at Hong Kong in 1955 with a new ship's company brought out from the UK. She took part in a number of SEATO exercises and visited ports in Japan, Korea and the USN base at Subic Bay in the Philippines for joint exercises. In August 1956 she joined *Newcastle* and *Cockade* to form the escort for the Royal Yacht *Britannia* in which the Duke of Edinburgh was touring Commonwealth states in the Pacific. Visits were made to Australia, New Zealand, the Gilbert and Ellis Islands, Fiji, Manus and Nauru. On completion of this duty she carried out a long refit in Singapore Dockyard and then prepared to return to the UK; unusually she sailed east-about across the Pacific. After passing through the Panama Canal she arrived at Bermuda on 8 February 1957.

She finally returned to Devonport after a decade in the Far East and the Admiralty decided that she was not worth further modernisation. She was placed on the Sales List on 4 March 1957 but placed into extended reserve in the River Tamar in May. In September there were discussions with the Imperial Iranian Navy about a possible sale of *Consort* and *Comus* but these came to nothing. On 21 March 1960 Admiralty approval was given to remove her from the sales List and she was brought into the dockyard for final de-storing and the removal of equipment that could be re-used in other warships, after which she returned to the trots in the river. On 14 March 1961 she was sold to the Prince of Wales Dry Dock Company at Swansea and towed to their yard to be broken up for scrap. Work on her was complete by 1962.

Chapter 22

HMS CONSTANCE

HMS Constance *off the Tyne in December 1945. Her appearance and weapons appear standard for the class and the mainmast with its Type 291 radar is in the more common place just forward of 'X' mounting.*

(Crown Copyright/MoD 1945)

HMS *Constance* was built by Vickers Armstrong at their Walker Naval Yard on the Tyne, laid down on 18 March 1943 and launched on 22 August 1944. She was commissioned on 4 December 1945 and finally completed and handed over to the Royal Navy on 31 December 1945. She carried out an initial work-up at Portland in January 1946 and proceeded to Malta in February where she was brought fully up to operational standard. In March she collided with the destroyer Marne and had to undergo repairs in Malta Dockyard. After their completion, she sailed to join the British Pacific Fleet and her sister-ships in the 8th Destroyer Flotilla.

The Far East was an unstable area in 1946 and ships of the BPF carried out a number of visits aimed to restore Britain's pre-war status in the region and demonstrate her resolve to maintain peace. Among other places she visited a number of Japanese ports to support the US and Commonwealth occupation forces, Penang, Manilla and Nanking, the Chinese Nationalist capital. In 1947 she diverted to Manilla in the Philippines to provide an RN guard of honour at the funeral of the late President Hoxa. 8 DF was normally based in Hong Kong but made frequent operational visits to Singapore. In December 1947 the former Japanese destroyer *Sumire* which had been donated to the BPF as part the Japanese war reparation to the UK, was taken out to sea off Hong Kong and used as a target. *Constance* was one of a number of warships that sank her with gunfire.

The civil war in China between the communists and nationalists caused considerable international concern and ships of the BPF carried out a number of duties as guard-ships protecting British and Commonwealth interests. In 1948 the BPF was re-named as the Far East Fleet and *Constance* repre-sented the 'new' fleet at Shanghai. On 7 December 1948 she sailed up the River Yangtse to relieve the frigate *Amethyst* as guard-ship in Nanking. She was relieved in turn by the frigate *Alacrity* and sailed downriver on 19 December carrying the Czechoslovakian Ambassador to Shanghai. In April 1949 after *Amethyst* was attacked and ground-ed on her way up the Yangtse, *Constance* was ordered to join *London* and *Consort* in Shanghai. Several members of her ship's company were trans-ferred to replace men killed and wounded in the other ships when they had attempted to move up river to support *Amethyst*. She remained with the force concentrated off the mouth of the Yangtse until July when *Amethyst* escaped to rejoin the fleet.

Constance had refitted annually in Hong Kong and underwent a full docking between December 1949 and February 1950, after which she deployed to Japanese waters with the fleet for exercises with the USN but subsequently returned to Hong Kong and did not become involved in the Korean War until October 1950, after the Inchon landings. Her initial duty was to form part of the screen for the aircraft carrier *Theseus* together with *Concord*, *Charity*, the Canadian *Cayuga* and *Sioux* and the Australian *Bataan*. On 21 October *Theseus, Sioux* and *Constance* returned to Sasebo after a particu-larly successful series of air strikes in the Haeju region. On 10 November she was stationed off Chinnampo to direct and control traffic into and out of the port through a minefield that had been par-tially cleared by the USN; it was finally cleared on 20 November.

With UN forces moving into North Korea, naval operations began to reduce in scale from mid November 1950 but the unexpected Chinese assault at the end of the month changed the situation dra-matically. *Constance* was in Hong Kong when it

happened together with *Theseus, Kenya, Charity, Concord, Mounts Bay* and *Whitesand Bay*. They returned quickly to the war zone and were soon back in action. By 4 December, only four days after the recall to the war zone, the redeployment of British and Commonwealth warships was com-plete; *Constance* was delayed by weather and was the last ship to resume station with *Theseus'* screen. The immediate concern was the withdrawal of UN forces from Chinnampo after which *Theseus* oper-ated west of Inchon screened by *Cossack, Constance* and *Concord*. In December 1950 the car-rier task force encountered snow and winds of up to 60 knots which prevented flying for a while but when they abated strikes and reconnaissance sorties were resumed. USN carriers were all heavily com-mitted off the east coast and *Theseus* spent practi-cally the whole of December flying intensely with-out relief; by the end of the month she deserved a break and she returned to Kure with her destroyer screen, her place being taken by the *USS Badoeng Strait*.

In January *Constance* was at sea with *Theseus, Cossack* and *Concord* again for a further period of intense flying, much of it in support of the US 25th Division ashore. On 3 February *Theseus, Cossack* and *Constance* returned to Kure for a further period of rest. *Constance* had a change of activity on 27 February when she joined a bombardment group comprising *Belfast, Cossack*, the Australian *Bataan* and the American *Hank* as part of a feint landing demonstration intended to draw enemy attention away from the east. By the time the operation fin-ished on 4 March 1951 *Constance* had fired 522 rounds of 4.5 inch ammunition at enemy positions and the feint had drawn a communist division away from the UN offensive near Wonsan. After this operation *Constance* returned to Hong Kong for a maintenance period.

She was back in the war zone in May 1951, oper-ating with the cruiser *Kenya* off Inchon to provide support for the Commonwealth Division ashore. Attention was also paid with success to intercepting enemy junks that tried to ferry supplies close

inshore along the coast. In June *Constance* joined *Cockade* and the American *Hawkins* and *Fiske* in the screen supporting *Glory* which had taken over from *Theseus*. She continued to serve in operations off the west coast until July 1951 when she returned to Hong Kong again for a further assisted maintenance period.

In November 1951 *Constance* returned to the war zone for a third time and relieved *Concord* on the gun-line off the east coast near Hungnam. Later in the month she joined *HMAS Sydney*, the latest carrier on station, and a number of other ships off the east coast for a series of strikes against shore batteries near Hungnam which had recently shown themselves to be a nuisance. A lot of material damage was done to the enemy and *Sydney* returned to the west coast with *Constance*. In December she joined other ships in coastal operations to protect islands near Sok To, many of which changed hands several times in fierce fighting. The communist battery at Amgak fired in support of the communist

forces and was promptly silenced by *Ceylon* but not before *Constance* was hit by a single 105mm shell that blew a hole two feet in diameter in her side and damaged her sonar room. It proved possible to make repairs locally and she remained with the force off the west coast, alternately forming part of the carrier screen by day and patrolling off Pengyong at night. She was able to spend Christmas 1951 at Sasebo before returning to operations off the west coast islands in January 1952. She carried out a sweep looking for enemy junks carrying ammunition from China to the North Korean People's Army on 12 January; bombarded Kumsuri north of Yuk To on 20 January and Ka Do on 23 January. On 26 January she was, herself, fired on by a battery on Wolsa-ri and hit by splinters. She was able to continue in action, however, and rejoined Sydney's screen in February with *Cockade*, the Canadian *Sioux* and American *Hanson*. Her third war patrol ended in February 1952.

HMS Constance *making her way up the English Channel to Chatham where she was to pay off in October 1954 after only eight years' service. Unlike her sister-ships she was never modernised but 'X' mounting has been removed. Her iron deck is loaded with crates for passage to the UK.* (Syd Goodman Collection)

She returned for her fourth and last war deployment at the end of May 1952 and achieved a considerable measure of success from the outset when she intercepted enemy junks on four separate occasions and sank them in the Yalu Gulf. Useful intelligence was taken from some of the prisoners taken from them. She operated on the gun-line off the east coast to replace *HMCS Nootka* on 8 June but her spell of duty was cut short when she ran in to anchor off the southern side of Yang do on 10 June and unfortunately ran aground, causing damage to her hull, sonar dome, propellers and shafts. Her place was taken by *HMAS Bataan* and she proceeded slowly to Kure where repairs in the Haruma dockyard took until 26 July. She was back off the west coast of Korea in October, however, during a period of relative quiet. She was one a several ships anchored off Choda on 14 October 1952 that were visited by the First Sea Lord. He was to have visited *Constance* but his programme was limited by bad weather.

Constance returned to the east coast gun-line on 17 November and remained there until relieved by *HMAS Anzac* on 20 December 1952. On 23 December she successfully bombarded enemy guns in the Choda area together with *Cossack* and *Consort*. This was to be her last wartime activity, however, and she left Korea for Hong Kong. She had steamed for 109,000 miles during the conflict. During 1953 she patrolled in support of British shipping in the Strait of Formosa where there was an uneasy truce between the communist and nationalist Chinese but fighting could break out again without warning.

Constance re-commissioned for the last time on 6 December 1953. She left 8 DS in June 1954 and steamed to the Mediterranean where she joined 3 DS until October when she returned to the UK. She arrived at Chatham after eight years away on 15 October 1954. Unlike her sister-ships, time had never been found to modernise her and she still had her original outfit of sonar and depth charges. Considered to be obsolescent, she was immediately de-stored and reduced to reserve at Chatham. After that the end came quickly for *Constance*; she was placed in un-maintained reserve on the Disposal List in April 1955 and then sold to the British Iron and Steel Corporation on 10 October 1955 while still less than ten years old; the first of the 'Co' class to be scrapped. She was towed from Chatham on 5 March 1956 and arrived at Inverkeithing on 8 March to be broken up. Her career had been short but full of incident and she had played a significant part in the wide range of activities undertaken by the RN in the immediate post-war years.

Chapter 23

HMS CONTEST

HMS Contest *was the first all-welded destroyer to be completed for the Royal Navy. This bow view shows the smooth effect of the butt-welded plates that make up her hull, contrasting with the overlapping plates of her riveted sisters. The white edging to her pennant number is rather unusual.* (Syd Goodman Collection)

The first all-welded destroyer to be completed for the Royal Navy, *Contest* was built by J Samuel White at their Cowes yard which had been extensively re-built after bombing and specifically set up for welding. The design had to be modified for the new form of construction and she was not laid down until 1 November 1943, later than all but one of her sister-ships. She was launched on 16 December 1944 and the greater speed with which ships could be assembled in pre-fabricated sections that were partially fitted out was reflected in her completion date of 9 November 1945; eleven months against an average of over a year for her class.

She commissioned on 29 October 1945 and, after sea-trials, worked up in Portland and Malta. She joined the 8th Destroyer Flotilla in Hong Kong in

February 1946 and operated with the British Pacific Fleet for two years. During this period, she visited Shanghai with *Cossack* and carried the British Ambassador to Nationalist China up the River Yangtse to the embassy in Nanking. She took part in a simulated attack on Singapore to test its defences in late 1947 in company with the aircraft carrier *Glory* and the destroyer *Finisterre*. Unusually she returned to the UK for a refit in Portsmouth from May 1948, probably due to a fleet-wide shortage of manpower but also, possibly, to evaluate the condition of her hull and make comparisons with the more 'traditional' riveted hulls of her sister ships. In September 1948 she re-commissioned with a reduced ship's company, most of whom came from *HMS Nonsuch*, a former German destroyer which had been commissioned for com-

HMS Contest *sailing from Portsmouth in November 1948. She has her new NATO pennant number D 48 painted on the hull. When the new system was introduced earlier in 1948 most ships were able to keep their original numbers but substituted 'D' flag superior for 'R'.* Contest *was an exception since D 12 had already been allocated and she had to change from R 12 to D 48.*
(National Museum of the Royal Navy)

parative trials by the Royal Navy.

She joined the Portsmouth Local Flotilla and was used as an air target training ship. In June 1949 her role changed to that of a gunnery training ship and she was used for live-firings by courses of officers and ratings. In March 1950 she was re-classified yet again, this time as a submarine target ship, acting as a 'clockwork mouse' for submarine commanding officers to practice attacks and escort evasion tactics. In April 1951 the submarine *Affray* failed to surface as expected about 20 miles southeast of Start Point. 'Subsmash' procedure was instigated by the Admiralty and *Contest* joined 25 other ships of four nations in the search for her. She was eventually located on the sea bed 67 miles southwest of St Catherine's Lighthouse by underwater camera equipment operated by the diving trials ship *Reclaim*. On 31 January 1953 *Contest* went to the aid of the Stranraer to Larne ferry *Princess Victoria*

which foundered in a storm with heavy loss of life. Two men from *Contest* were awarded George Medals for their gallantry in jumping into mountainous seas to rescue a survivor who had reached the limit of his endurance and could no longer cling to a life-raft.

Contest was present at the Coronation Review of the Fleet by Her Majesty Queen Elizabeth II on 15 June 1953; she was anchored in Line D between the depot ship *Forth* and the destroyer *Savage*. She remained with the Portsmouth Flotilla and continued on training duties with a reduced ship's company until November 1953 when she reduced to reserve in Portsmouth.

In July 1954 she was taken in hand by Portsmouth Dockyard for modernisation and conversion to a minelayer, similar to *Chaplet*. Two 'Squid' mortars and their associated handling room were fitted in the former 'X' position; 'Y' mounting and the tor-

pedo tubes were removed and it was also found necessary to remove one 27 foot whaler and its davits to reduce topweight to within acceptable limits when mines were carried. Work was completed in August 1955 and she re-commissioned to replace *Crossbow* in 6 DS with the aim of increasing the number of destroyer minelayers available to the fleet. She remained with 6 DS for the remainder of her operational career and one her final tasks was a patrol off Iceland during the first Cod War between 25 April and 9 May 1959. In June 1959, however, her ship's company transferred to *Scorpion* and

HMS Contest *manoeuvring at speed after her conversion to a minelayer. The helicopter in the distance is a Westland Dragonfly and the blurred rotor blade at top left shows that this photograph was taken from a second helicopter.*
(Syd Goodman Collection)

HMS Contest *off Portsmouth in August 1955 shortly after the completion of her modernisation and conversion to a minelayer. The mine rails and launch chutes on the quarter show up well in this image. By then she was serving with the 6th Destroyer Squadron and, unusually for a minelayer, has 'Y' mounting in place.*

(Syd Goodman Collection)

Contest was reduced to un-maintained reserve.

Her demise came quickly after that and in August 1959 she was placed under the administration of the Senior Officer Reserve Fleet at Chatham and laid up without maintenance. On 2 February 1960 she was sold for scrap and dismantled at Grays in Essex. She had only seen six years operational service, none of it in the operational areas where her sisters had served. Her early withdrawal from the Far East, extensive use on second-line duties and the haste with which she was finally withdrawn from 6 DS and scrapped, despite recent modernisation as a minelayer led some analysts to speculate that she had an underlying problem which could not, economically be put right but it was more likely due to shortages of manpower and the dramatic reduction in the number of destroyers retained in service after the 1957 Defence Review.

Chapter 24

HMS COSSACK

HMS Cossack *running builder's trials before her completion in September 1945. Under the rust-streaks on her hull she is painted in the Admiralty Standard camouflage scheme and she has the standard close-range armament.*
(Crown Copyright/MoD 1945)

The 'Co' class gave the Admiralty Ships' Name and Badge Committee the opportunity to perpetuate the famous name *Cossack* after the previous Tribal class destroyer *Cossack* had been sunk on 27 October 1941, west of Gibraltar by a torpedo fired by *U-563*. She had a fine war record which included the rescue, in Norwegian waters, of British seamen from the German auxiliary *Altmark* in 1940. The new *Cossack* was ordered from Vickers Armstrong and laid down at their Walker Naval Yard on the Tyne on 18 March 1943. She was launched on 10 May 1944 and completed on 4 September 1945, one of 2 ships in the class built as Leaders; the other was *Constance*. Her work up started at Portland a month later and ended in Malta in December 1945. She was then allocated to the

8th Destroyer Flotilla in the British Pacific Fleet and joined it appropriately enough in Tokyo where she carried out several coastal patrols as part of the Commonwealth Occupation Forces. Docking and repairs were carried out in Hong Kong on several occasions.

Cossack spent Christmas 1946 in Hong Kong and subsequently supported the Commonwealth occupation forces in Japan with a number of port visits. In March 1947 she visited Sasebo followed by Fukuoka in April. In May, while on patrol off Amoy north-west of Hong Kong, she rescued the *SS Ethel Moller* which had been seized by Chinese Nationalist troops. The vessel was escorted back to Hong Kong and *Cossack*'s ship's company subsequently received salvage money for their work.

HMS Cossack *at speed in the South China Sea. The glassy calm sea surface shows that there is no natural wind and a number of 'wind-scoops' have been fitted in scuttles to take advantage of the ship's motion to ventilate the mess decks. Temperatures inside these cramped, poorly air-conditioned ships could be unpleasant.* (Steve Bush Collection)

During early 1950 *Cossack* carried out three patrols in support of British interests in the River Yangtse and in April she visited Japanese waters with other units of the recently named Far East Fleet for exercises with the USN. On 25 June 1950 when the communist North Korean People's Army attacked the south, *Cossack* was visiting Ominato in Japan with the cruiser *Jamaica* and the aircraft carrier *Triumph*.

The senior British officer, FO2 Far East Station

ordered his ships to concentrate and the British Government ordered the fleet to join UN forces under American command to resist the unprovoked aggression. Once concentrated, *Cossack* and *Consort* formed the screen for *Triumph* which joined the *USS Valley Forge* to launch strikes against targets in North Korea. On 5 July *Triumph* joined the USN carrier task force and *Cossack* returned to Sasebo with *Belfast* and *Consort*. On 8 July 1950 FO2 began blockade operations off the west coast using three cruiser/destroyer groups that alternated on task and in harbour for replenishment; *Cossack* continued to operate with *Belfast* and *Consort*. *Cossack* detached to Pusan, the only port left in allied hands, to pick up South Korean naval liaison teams who were then distributed among all the Commonwealth warships and helped greatly with communications. Later, when more USN air-

craft carriers arrived off the east coast, *Triumph* joined the Commonwealth ships in the west coast support force. On 13 July the *Belfast* force searched for the crew of a USAF B-29 that had been shot down off Poromu in the estuary of the Seoul River. Nothing was found but 3 survivors were subsequently located by the *Jamaica* group that relieved them.

On 17 July 1950 *Belfast* and *Cossack* deployed to the east coast off the Pusan perimeter to provide gunfire support for UN troops and a day later *Cossack* bombarded a North Korean naval base at Sukcho just north of the 38th parallel. On 2 August *Cossack* and *Cockade* carried out a prolonged bombardment off Mokpo to create a diversion in the rear of enemy forces advancing on Pusan and to destroy port installations that would be useful to the enemy. Spotting was provided by Seafires from *Triumph*

HMS Cossack *in rougher sea conditions that require the scuttles to be firmly closed.*

(Crown Copyright/MoD 1945)

HMS Cossack *entering Grand Harbour, Malta on 26 November 1959 on her way back to the UK after fourteen years deployed in the Far East.*
(Author's Collection)

and over 1,000 rounds of 4.5-inch ammunition were fired in two hours. At short notice *Belfast*, *Cossack* and *Charity* moved to the shallow waters off Inchon on 5 August from Sasebo and *Kenya* joined them from patrol to carry out an urgent bombardment requested by the UN command. The destroyers stood slightly to seaward to protect the cruisers against artillery fire from the many islands nearby and the cruisers successfully bombarded enemy positions in and around Inchon. As the force left the area, a report was received from the USN that 300 enemy junks had been sighted to the west of Inchon; *Kenya* and *Cossack* searched the area but found nothing. On 10 August *Cossack* left Korea to return to Hong Kong and then proceed to Singapore for a refit.

Cossack was back in the war zone by November when the communist Chinese offensive caught the UN completely unawares. On 29 November 1950 she was in Kure with *Ceylon, Cardigan Bay, HMAS Bataan*, the Dutch *Evertsen* and HMNZS *Rotoiti*.

She sailed at once to join *Theseus* and *Concord* which were returning to the west coast from Hong Kong and subsequently formed part of the screen during an intensive period of carrier strike operations. By December the carrier task force comprised *Theseus, Cossack, Consort, Constance* and *Concord* and the group operated to its limit in stormy winter conditions to support the fighting ashore. At the end of December they took a break to relax for a few days in Kure before returning to operations in January; *Theseus'* place was taken in her absence by the *USS Badoeng Strait*. *Cossack* continued to operate as part of the carrier screen into February 1951.

In late February 1951 the UN command instructed ships off the west coast to carry out a feint landing south of the Taedong estuary to draw enemy attention away from operations in the east near Wonsan. *Cossack* joined a bombardment group centred on *Belfast* that also included *Constance*, the Australian *Bataan* and the American *Hank*.

Between 1 and 4 March *Cossack* fired 530 rounds of 4.5-inch ammunition at enemy positions ashore and the successful feint drew a whole Chinese army division away from the fighting in the east. A further bombardment was carried out on 16 March by *Belfast*, *Cossack* and *Cockade* against enemy troops that were seen digging trenches close to beaches on the west coast. Between 18 and 30 July 1951 *Cossack* joined *Consort, Charity* and *Cockade* to carry out anti-submarine 'hunter-killer' exercises with the USN off Okinawa. These were intended to strengthen the allied navies' ability to counter Soviet submarines if, as appeared likely at the time, they became involved in the conflict. *Cossack* returned to blockade duties off the west coast in August and carried out occasional bombardments in the Amgak area in mid-September. Later in the month she joined *Belfast* again to bombard enemy positions on the Chorusan peninsula, the furthest north that enemy positions had been attacked by ships' gunfire on the west coast. In late August she moved to the east coast gun-line and was straddled by an enemy shore battery on the day she arrived. She later covered the establishment of a South Korean Marine garrison on Yang Do, south of Songjin and carried out a number of bombardments. On 20 September, having returned to the west coast, intelligence reported that communist forces had ejected friendly forces from the island of Wolto, west of the Chorusan peninsula. *Cossack* closed the area at speed and bombarded enemy positions on the island and the adjacent mainland to good effect.

On 22 September 1951 *Cossack* joined *Comus* to escort the maintenance carrier Unicorn to a position near Pengyong Do where 2 of *Glory's* aircraft that had carried out forced-landings were recovered for repair. At the beginning of October the new C-in-C Far East visited Commonwealth ships in Kure in his despatch vessel *Alert*. Those present included *Glory* which was about to leave for a refit in Australia; *Sydney* that had arrived to relieve her; *Unicorn, Cossack, Concord, Amethyst, Charity, HMA Ships Anzac* and *Tobruk, HMCS Cayuga*, the *RFA Brown Ranger* and the Hospital Ship *Maine*.

In October *Cossack* patrolled the Yalu Gulf and on 9 October 1951 she covered a landing by allied forces on the island of Sinmi do. They met stiff resistance after an initially successful landing and the gunfire support given by *Cossack* proved to be invaluable in achieving success against heavy odds. Once the landing force had overcome the opposition, *Cossack* departed for Sasebo on 12 October. She had spent longer in the war zone than any other British destroyer up to that time and on 17 October 1951 she left Korea to refit and re-commission in Hong Kong.

Cossack returned to the Korean war zone in February 1952 and relieved *Morecambe Bay* on the east coast 'gun-line' on 26 March. She earned an immediately high reputation for herself by destroying 3 trains and causing damage to 4 others in three consecutive nights before returning to the west coast on 9 April. This was the first of two short deployments to Korea in mid 1952 which were followed by a longer period of operations from September 1952. In October she embarked the First Sea Lord in Iwakuni for passage to Kure as part of his tour of Commonwealth forces in the Far East. On 24 December 1952 she joined *Consort* and *Constance* to silence enemy shore batteries near Choda that had ended a period of quiescence to fire about 500 rounds at UN positions on Sok To the day before. Christmas Day was spent at sea in the operational area and this period of operations ended in January 1953 and she arrived back in Hong Kong for a refit on 12 January 1953.

The refit ended on 21 February 1953 and *Cossack* re-commissioned for further war service. She returned to Korea, after working up, in early May 1953 and joined *Glory's* screen with *HMCS Crusader* and the American *Southerland* and *Thomas*. By 21 May *Ocean* had relieved *Glory* and she sailed for operations with *Cossack, Cockade, HMCS Crusader* and the American *Higbee* and *Taylor* forming her screen at various times. She returned to the gun-line off the east coast between 8 and 21 June 1953 but was unable to repeat her earlier success through lack of targets. By then the

('C' Class Destroyers)

HMS Cossack *entering Devonport Dockyard in December 1959 flying her paying-off pennant. The Admiralty gave* *approval to scrap her only two months later.* *(Steve Bush Collection)*

armistice negotiators were about to agree terms that would end the fighting and much of *Cossack*'s time was spent helping to organise the evacuation South Korean forces from Yang Do which was north of the cease-fire line. *Cossack*'s last war patrol involved screening *Ocean* between 15 and 23 July together with *Cockade*. When the armistice was signed *Cossack* was in Japanese waters, one of a small number of Commonwealth warships that had served, albeit with some breaks for maintenance, throughout the Korean War.

She was taken in hand by Singapore Dockyard for an interim modernisation on 23 November 1953 and the work lasted until 1 March 1954 when she re-commissioned for furthers service with 8 DS.

Cossack had spent her entire operational life in 8 DF/DS in the Far East and was one of the last of her class to leave. She returned to the UK after an absence of 14 years and reduced to reserve at Devonport on 10 December 1959. Like her sisters, she was considered to be obsolescent and with the reduction in the number of destroyers required by the contracting RN was not considered to be worth modernising. Admiralty approval to scrap her was given on 29 January 1960 after which she was laid up in the trots in the River Tamar and left to deteriorate. On 28 February 1961 she was sold to the British Iron and Steel Company and towed to Troon where she arrived on 1 March and was broken up immediately.

The 'Cr' Class
The 14th Emergency Flotilla

The Fourteenth Emergency Flotilla comprising 8 ships of the 'Cr' class was ordered on 12 September 1942. The whole class was originally to have been transferred to the Royal Canadian Navy for Pacific operations and were, thus, not fitted out for arctic operations like the earlier classes. In the event, only the two leaders, both built by John Brown, were transferred.

They were repeats of the 'Co' class and suffered the same limitations in topweight caused by the incorporation of the Mark 6 director and remote power control for the four 4.5 inch mountings. Like the earlier class they were completed with only one set of torpedo tubes and a reduced outfit of depth charges and throwers. They were all standardised with a close-range armament comprising a twin Mark 5 Bofors and four single Mark 7s soon after completion. They all had welded hulls.

Only 2 ships, *Creole* and *Crispin*, served for any length of time with the Royal Navy, both in a training role for which they underwent modification.

They were subsequently modernised with American 'offshore' funds and sold to Pakistan, becoming the longest serving ships of the 'C' group. Two ships, *Crescent* and *Crusader*, were commissioned directly into the RCN in 1946 and the remaining 4 only ever commissioned for post-completion sea trials in the RN before being sold to Norway between 1945 and 1947. The 2 Canadian ships underwent considerable modification, one of them becoming the only one of the 32 'C' class vessels to be converted into a Type 15 fast anti-submarine frigate. The 4 Norwegian vessels were never modernised and served their entire careers pretty much as originally completed. By NATO standards they were considered obsolescent as anti-submarine units from the mid 1950s but their gunnery system gave them some value as patrol vessels suitable for surface action.

Details are similar to the 'Ch' and 'Co' classes with minor variations between ships.

Chapter 25

HMS CREOLE
(PNS ALAMGIR from 1957)

An immaculate Creole *photographed shortly after her completion in October 1946 with the light on her starboard side showing the smooth, butt-welded plates to advantage. The 'Cr's had Oerlikons fitted on the bridge wings but an otherwise all-Bofors close-range armament. The mainmast with its Type 291 radar is mounted just forward of the Simple-Type –Director for the Mark 5 twin Bofors.* (Crown Copyright/MoD 1946)

HMS *Creole* was ordered from J Samuel White's shipyard at Cowes on the Isle of Wight and laid down on 3 March 1944. She was launched on 22 November 1945 by which time there was no great urgency for her to enter service and was not completed until 14 October 1946. She was to be one of only 2 'Cr' class destroyers to serve for any length of time with the RN and after working up joined the 4th Escort Group based at Londonderry in Northern Ireland. The unit formed part of the Joint Anti-Submarine School (JASS) and had responsibility for maintaining high standards and practices in anti-submarine warfare in the RN. It frequently exercised with ships of the RCN and other allied navies to exchange ideas. In 1948 4th ES was renamed as the 3rd Training Flotilla but

remained based at Londonderry. Also in 1948 her 'B' 4.5-inch gun mounting was removed and replaced by a deck house that contained direction-finding and communications equipment that effectively formed an extension of her operations room and improved her anti-submarine command and control capabilities.

1949 proved to be an unlucky year for *Creole*. On 26 January she collided with *SS Poole Fisher* and suffered some damage to the ship's side aft. On 28 February she grounded in the River Foyle on her way into Londonderry and damaged the sonar dome. On a brighter note, *Creole* escorted the liner *Empress of Scotland* to Canada in 1951 when it carried Princess Elizabeth across the Atlantic for a Royal Tour. She continued on her training duties

HMS Creole *under way in October 1948.* *(Crown Copyright/MoD 1948)*

for a further four years without incident but on 4 May 1953 she went to the aid of the submarine *Alaric* that had grounded on a wreck and was, herself, damaged when she towed her off. On 15 June 1953 *Creole* was present at the Coronation Review of the Fleet at Spithead by Her Majesty Queen Elizabeth II. She was anchored in Lane D between *Myngs* and her sister-ship *Crispin*. The Review marked the effective end of her short RN career and, still not repaired from the damage in May, she was de-stored and paid off into un-maintained reserve in August 1953 at Portsmouth. On 26 January 1955 she was placed on the Sales List although her material state had deteriorated somewhat.

In November 1955 *Creole* was offered to the Pakistani Navy as part of a package that included the cruiser *Diadem*, *Creole* her sister-ship *Crispin* and the Battle class destroyers *Gabbard* and *Cadiz*. *Creole* was brought out of reserve and given an interim modernisation by J S Thornycroft in 1956-57, the cost being borne by the Mutual Defence Agreement funding. It followed the same lines as the work carried out on RN ships of the 'Ch' and

'Co' classes to produce a vessel that was viable at the time of purchase but which would soon become obsolete as newer warships with improved anti-submarine systems joined the larger navies over the next decade. She was commissioned by a Pakistan Navy ship's company in the UK and re-named *Alamgir*. After a work-up in the UK she sailed for Pakistan and was to serve in a largely unaltered state for a further two decades despite a gradually deteriorating structural and mechanical state. She saw war service in September 1965 when she formed part of a task force centred on the cruiser *Babur* with the destroyers *Khaibar, Badr, Shah Jehan* and *Jahangir* deployed to bombard Dwarka in north-west India. She fired 50 rounds at Dwarka in the space of four minutes at a range of six miles in an attack that was deemed to be successful. *Alamgir* also saw duties patrolling off the coast of Pakistan during the war that broke out in 1971. Her weapons systems became gradually more difficult to maintain, however, and she was withdrawn from service and broken up for scrap locally in 1982 having played a major role in the early expansion of the Pakistani Navy.

Chapter 26

HMCS CRESCENT

HMCS Crescent during her shake-down in UK waters in October 1945. She has been re-painted in Admiralty light grey overall and now has the red maple-leaf emblem on the funnel but still retains her RN pennant number, R 16, on the hull.
(Steve Bush Collection)

The Canadian Government contributed ships and men to the British Pacific Fleet in 1944 but wanted to form its own Canadian Pacific Fleet to gain experience and to form the nucleus of a post-war RCN based on aircraft carrier battle groups. In January 1945 the Royal Navy agreed to transfer the light fleet carrier *Warrior* and all 8 ships of the 'Cr' class to the Royal Canadian Navy on long term loan to facilitate this. The transfer would have helped both Britain and Canada as, by 1945, the RN had more ships under construction than it could man and their operation by a Commonwealth Navy would get them into action against the Japanese more quickly. In the event, the war ended earlier than expected and only two 'Cr' class destroyers, *Crescent* and *Crusader*, were handed over to the RCN.

Crescent was laid down in John Brown's Clydebank yard on 16 September 1943 and launched on 20 July 1944. She was commissioned into the RCN on 10 September 1945 and formally handed over when completed on 21 September. Her original pennant number R16 was changed to 226 in Canadian service. After a shake-down period in UK waters, she sailed for Esquimalt on the Canadian Pacific Coast, arriving in November 1945. She was used mostly for training duties. Initially she had been transferred on a long-term loan to the RCN but her loan was made permanent in 1951.

In January 1949 she deployed to Shanghai to make a contribution to the support of Commonwealth interests in the region. She was not directly involved in the outbreak of the Korean War

HMCS Crescent *off Halifax, Nova Scotia, in 1951. She now has her Canadian hull number, 226, and is painted in the contemporary RCN dark hull, light upper works scheme. Her armament remains much as it was when she was completed.* (Steve Bush Collection)

but her initial presence in the Far East allowed more British destroyers to deploy leaving a viable force in Chinese waters to defend Commonwealth ships carrying out their lawful trade. In December 1950 she arrived in Halifax and was subsequently used for training duties with the Atlantic Fleet. In 1951 the loan agreement under which she had been operated by the RCN was changed into a permanent transfer of ownership. Her time with the Atlantic Fleet ended in January 1953 and she returned to the Pacific Fleet based at Esquimalt.

Crescent was the only one of the 32 'C' class destroyers to be converted into a fast anti-submarine frigate based on the British Type 15 design, the work being carried out in Esquimalt Dockyard in 1956. There were a number of differences, however, and she was arguably a better ship for them. The twin 4-inch Mark 19 gun was mounted forward of

the bridge on the forecastle and a twin USN-designed 3-inch 50 calibre mounting, similar to those fitted in *HMS Victorious*, was fitted aft. Single 40mm Bofors were mounted abreast the foremast. Two Mark 10 'Limbo' anti-submarine mortars were fitted aft, a considerable improvement on the earlier 'Squid' with more than double the range and larger projectiles. She was fitted with British Type 170 Sonar which was linked to the mortars and effectively provided fire-control for them together with the Type 177 medium-range sonar. The bridge structure was slightly larger than the equivalent in British Type 15s, making room for a larger operations room beneath it. She became the senior officer's ship for the Canadian 2nd Escort Squadron from 1956 and underwent a long refit in 1958 after which she carried out a three-month cruise to ports in the Far East. She returned to the

HMCS Crescent *after conversion to a Type 15 fast anti-submarine frigate in 1956. Note the twin 4-inch mounting on the forecastle and the darker paint applied to the original destroyer part of the hull.* (Dave Shirlaw)

HMCS Crescent *after 1960 when fitted with the prototype Type 199 variable depth sonar aft.* (Dave Shirlaw)

Atlantic in March 1959 and in 1960 she was modified with a prototype Canadian-designed variable-depth sonar (VDS) unit fitted right aft, a shield was fitted on the 3-inch mounting and three fixed torpedo tubes were fitted on the upper-deck for Mark 43 anti-submarine torpedoes. To compensate for the additional weight of the VDS the after 'Limbo' mortar was removed. The VDS had been removed from her sister-ship *Crusader* which had acted as a trials-ship for the equipment until 1960. *Crescent* continued with VDS trials through the first half of 1961 but later in the year the prototype equipment was removed and replaced by production standard equipment designated Type 199 which went into operational service with both the RCN and RN.

Crescent was used for a variety of training and operational tasks off the Canadian east coast and in the Caribbean until January 1965 when she was reduced to reserve in Halifax. In 1967 she was re-commissioned by a steaming party who sailed her to Esquimalt where she reduced to reserve again. This proved to be the end of her career, however, and she was placed on the disposals list on 1 April 1970. She was eventually sold to the Chi Shun Hua Steel Company of Taiwan and towed from Esquimalt on 21 April 1971 with the Tribal class destroyer *Algonquin* for the breakers' yard in Taiwan.

Chapter 27

HMS Crispin
(PNS JAHANGIR from 1958)

An immaculate Crispin *at anchor shortly after completion in June 1946. Her close-range armament comprised a twin Mark 5 Bofors; two single Mark 7 Bofors and hand-worked Oerlikons on the bridge wings.*

(Crown Copyright/MoD 1946)

The name originally chosen for the ship by the Admiralty Ship's Name and Badge Committee was *Cracher* and she was ordered as such from J Samuel White at Cowes and laid down on 1 February 1944; launched on 23 June 1945 and subsequently re-named *Crispin*. Despite the lack of urgency that followed the end of hostilities, she was completed just over a year later on 10 July 1946 and commissioned as *HMS Crispin* on 28 June 1946. After sea-trials and work-up, she replaced the destroyer *Fame* in 4th Escort Flotilla based first at Rosyth and then at Londonderry. The Flotilla was used to provide training in anti-submarine warfare as the sea-going element of the Joint Anti-Submarine School and also evaluated new tactics and equipment. There were breaks from the routine, however and in September 1948 *Crispin* paid a visit to the Irish Naval Service at Dun Laoghaire together with *Loch Fada* and *Loch Arkaig*. In 1950 the squadron was re-named as the 3rd Training Flotilla, a title more in keeping with its role.

Crispin spent her whole active career in the Royal Navy with this unit and became increasingly specialised. 'B' mounting was removed and replaced by a deck house that contained direction-finding equipment and additional communications equipment which formed an extension of her operations room but she was never modernised liked her sisters in the 'Ca', 'Ch' and 'Co' classes. In January 1953 she took part in the search for survivors for the Stranraer to Larne ferry *Princess Victoria* which had foundered with heavy loss of life. Unfortunately all she found in her search was a single lifebelt.

She participated in the Coronation Review of the Fleet by Her Majesty Queen Elizabeth II on 15 June 1953 at Spithead; she was anchored in Line 'D' in between her sister-ship *Creole* and the Type 16 frigate *Tenacious*. In January 1955 she sailed to Portsmouth, paid off and on 26 January reduced to low-readiness reserve without maintenance. She was placed on the Sales List and in November 1955 she was sold to Pakistan, the funds for her refur-

HMS Crispin *anchored at Spithead for the Coronation Review of the Fleet in June 1953. Note the 'Red Hand of Ulster' on the funnel and the communications deck-house just visible in 'B' position. She was another destroyer that could not just substitute 'D' for 'R' in the pennant number change in 1948. D 68 had already been allocated so she changed from R 68 to D 168.* (Syd Goodman Collection)

bishment being provided by the United States Mutual Defence Assistance Scheme as part of a deal that included the cruiser *Diadem, Crispin*, her sister-ship *Creole* and the Battle class destroyers *Gabbard* and *Cadiz*. *Crispin* was refitted and modernised by J S Thornycroft at Woolston and commissioned by the Pakistan Navy at Southampton on 18 March 1958 when she was re-named *PNS Jahangir*.

She saw war service with Pakistan and bombard-ed Dwarka on the night of 7 September 1965 during the First Indo-Pakistan War, together with *Babur, Khaibar, Badr, Shah Jehan* and *Alamgir*. The shoot lasted 4 minutes and *Jahangir* fired 50 rounds of 4.5-inch shell. She saw further service while still based at Karachi during the Second Indo-Pakistan War in 1971. *Jahangir* outlived the majority of her contemporaries and was not finally broken up until 1982 in Pakistan.

Chapter 28

HMS CROMWELL
(HNoMS BERGEN from 1946)

Launched as Cretan *and inexplicably re-named* Cromwell *shortly before completion, this ship never served operationally with the Royal Navy but was commissioned briefly for post-build acceptance trials in September 1946 before she was handed over to a Norwegian ship's company in October. She is painted in Admiralty light grey and has no pennant number or other marking.*
(Steve Bush Collection)

The Admiralty Ships Name and Badge Committee originally allocated the name *Cretan* to this ship which was ordered as such from Scotts of Greenock on 24 November 1943 and launched on 6 August 1945. Surprisingly she was then re-named *Cromwell*; a name that Winston Churchill had tried to bestow on a battleship when he was first Lord of the Admiralty in 1912 but King George V had emphatically refused to accept it. The decision to revive the name in 1946 is, therefore, somewhat surprising. The renamed destroyer was destined never to serve operationally with the Royal Navy and was not completed until 16 September 1946, by which time she was considered surplus to RN requirements after the end of the war and was purchased by Norway which wished to create a new navy of modern ships. She was commis-

sioned by a Royal Navy steaming crew on 6 September for post-build sea acceptance trials which found the ship fit for service. She was then transferred to a Royal Norwegian Navy crew who commissioned her as *HNorMS Bergen* on 25 October 1946. Three other ships of the 'Cr' class, *Crown, Croziers* and *Crystal* were also purchased for the Royal Norwegian Navy but not all at the same time. A work-up was carried out at Portland using RN expertise to train the crew in their new equipment, after which she took on stores and ammunition at Chatham She sailed for her new home at Bergen, arriving on 30 November 1946. At first she was given the pennant number J 03 by the Norwegian Navy since the Norwegian word for destroyer begins with a 'j'. After Norway joined NATO, however, the pennant number was changed

to D 304 in the NATO range to align with allied standards and practices.

Her first task was to ferry over 100 merchant seamen to New York where they manned a number of Liberty ships and tankers that had been purchased by Norway to replace her war losses. The passage was a rough one and *Bergen* was hit by an enormous wave which caused considerable damage and shorted electrical installations in the director which caused a fire.

Bergen took part in a number of NATO exercises and was a hard working ship although her equipment fit remained unchanged and she was largely obsolescent by the end of her career. In addition to her fleet roles she was used to patrol Norwegian waters in support of the fishing industry and other activities of national importance. She 'showed the flag' and was a frequent visitor to a number of European ports. Considered to be a good sea-boat, her simple machinery was reliable and she proved an ideal warship with which to build up what was, in effect, a new Royal Norwegian Navy after most of its previous ships had been destroyed during the German invasion of 1940.

In 1965 she was fitted with an early version of the Norwegian-designed Terne rocket-fired depth charge system mounted on a new structure forward of 'X' mounting that took the place of the torpedo-tubes. The weapons system was developed with the aid of USN and NATO mutual defence funding and, given the short time *Bergen* had left in service, this example may have been a prototype installation. It consisted of a six-barrelled launcher which was covered by curved shutters when not in use which could fire depth charges with 264lb warheads out to distances between 400 and 920 yards against targets tracked by sonar. Six further salvoes were held in the magazine under the launcher and automatic reloading took only 30 seconds. Depth limits were 50 to 700 feet and the weapons was roughly equivalent to the RN Mortar Mark 10, 'Limbo' although with lighter charges.

She and her 3 sister-ships rotated the duty of serving as a training ship for officer-cadets from the Royal Norwegian Navy Academy. She was formally withdrawn from service on 1 January 1967 and six months later was sold to Staubo and Son A/S of Oslo and towed to Grimstad to be broken up for scrap.

HNoMS Bergen *passing RAF Mountbatten as she moves into Plymouth Sound with the Norwegian ship's company that had just taken her over manning the upper deck. Completed to the same weapons standard as her RN contemporaries, she served for nearly twenty-one years in the Royal Norwegian Navy with little alteration.*

(Steve Bush Collection)

Chapter 29

HMS CROWN
(HNoMS OSLO from 1947)

Crown was completed on 17 May 1947 as the last of 32 'C' class destroyers and the very last to be built under the emergency war destroyer programme. She never served with the Royal Navy at all but was taken over from the builders by a Norwegian ship's company and commissioned as HNoMS Oslo. She is seen here with her new Norwegian pennant number J 02 painted on the hull. (World Ship Society)

Laid down by Scotts of Greenock as *Crown* on 16 January 1944 and launched on 12 February 1945, this ship was to have been transferred to the RCN together with the rest of the 'Cr' class but the war ended before she was complete and she was destined never to fly the white ensign. Fitting out continued without any sense of urgency until she was purchased by the Norwegian Government on 2 August 1946. She was eventually completed on 17 May 1947 as the last of the 32 'C' class destroyers and was commissioned directly into the Royal Norwegian Navy on the same day as *HNoMS Oslo*. She carried out sea trials and a work-up in UK waters with RN assistance and then sailed

from Sheerness Dockyard for Norway on 28 May 1947, arriving at Horten on 30 May. The original flag superior in her pennant number was 'J', the first letter of the word destroyer in Norwegian but her pennant number was subsequently changed to D 303 in order to conform to NATO standards.

She saw active service with the Norwegian fleet for 15 years, taking part in a number of NATO exercises and 'good-will' cruises to foreign ports. Like her sister-ships she was used for a period as a training ship for officer cadets. She never underwent any modernisation and remained throughout her service career very much as she had been on completion. By the early 1960s anti-submarine warfare

had become one of NATO's primary missions and *Oslo* was regarded as obsolescent with very little capability in that discipline; she was withdrawn from active service on 2 April 1962 and laid up in reserve. The name was subsequently given to the first of a new class of frigates and the former *Crown* became known as '*D303 Ex-Oslo*' whilst laid up. She was put up for disposal and then sold to be broken up for scrap in 1966.

Chapter 30

HMS CROZIERS
(HNoMS TRONDHEIM from 1946)

HMS Croziers *as she originally appeared at Scotstoun in Admiralty Standard camouflage in November 1945. She saw no operational service with the Royal Navy.* (Author's Collection)

HMS *Croziers* was ordered from Yarrow and laid down at their Scotstoun yard on 26 October 1943. She was launched on 19 September 1944 and was originally to have been transferred on loan to the RCN but when the war ended the offer was not taken up and she was commissioned temporarily into the RN. She commissioned on 12 November 1945 as *HMS Croziers* at Scotstoun and was handed over to the RN on her formal completion date, 30 November 1945. On completion of sea trials, however, the Admiralty decided that she was surplus to requirements and she was reduced to reserve, albeit at a high state of readiness, from March 1946. In April 1946 *LCT 4001* collided with her and caused a gash nine feet long in the side below deck level between frames 46 and 47.

In July 1946 she was purchased by the Norwegian Government, renamed *Trondheim* in October and commissioned into the Royal Norwegian Navy in November, after the completion of docking, repairs and a short refit in Chatham Dockyard. She carried out a work up to operational efficiency in the UK and then sailed for Norway on 21 December 1946, arriving in Bergen a day later. She was refitted at Horten between March 1949 and January 1951, subsequently seeing another decade of service. She took part in a number of NATO exercises, visited foreign ports and shared the task of training cruises for midshipmen from the Royal Norwegian Naval Academy with her sister-ships.

She underwent no modernisation and by 1960 she was considered to be obsolescent, especially in the anti-submarine role upon which NATO was con-

centrating. She was removed form the active list in May 1961 and subsequently sold for scrap in Belgium during the same year.

HMS Croziers *in September 1946 after being brought out of reserve for sale to the Royal Norwegian Navy. Her guns are still covered or cocooned and she has no motor boat on her starboard davit. In this ship the mainmast is installed aft of the torpedo tubes.*   (Syd Goodman Collection)

Chapter 31

HMCS Crusader

HMCS Crusader *carrying out sea trials shortly after her completion.* *(Syd Goodman Collection)*

HMCS *Crusader* was ordered from John Brown at Clydebank and laid down on 15 November 1943. She was launched on 5 October 1944 and plans to transfer her on loan to the RCN went ahead as she was fitted out. She was commissioned into the RCN on 15 November 1945 and formally handed over on the day of her completion on 26 November, one of only two out of the eight 'Cr' class destroyers to be transferred. The loan agreement ended in 1951 when she was transferred permanently to Canadian ownership as a gift. She carried out a work-up at Portland with RN assistance in December 1945 and sailed for her new home, stopping for a brief refuelling visit to Jamaica between 31 December 1945 and 4 January

1946. She arrived at Esquimalt in British Columbia on 21 January having transited the Panama Canal. The RCN, like the RN, was suffering from a post-war manpower crisis in 1946, however, and lacked the men to retain *Crusader* in commission. She paid off into reserve, therefore, and was to be inactive for the next four years.

She remained in reserve on the west coast until January 1951 when she was refitted and commissioned for service as a training ship based on Esquimalt in May 1951. In March 1952 she was refitted again, this time to equip her for war service and she sailed for Korea in May, arriving in June. Her first action came on the night of 14/15 August 1952 when she joined *HMNZS Rotoiti* to cover a

raid from the sea by 120 South Korean irregulars on Ongjin, behind enemy lines. It proved to be successful and the men returned after five hours with prisoners having inflicted casualties on the enemy and destroyed a field gun. She operated on the 'gun-line' off the east coast of Korea between 14 and 29 October with some success and again between 20 January and 9 February 1953. By then her score had grown to 4 communist trains destroyed and by the end of the war she headed the list of ships in the 'Trainbusters Club'.

When not off the east coast she joined the screen in *Glory's* battle-group and played a significant part in west coast blockade activities. By April *Glory's* screen comprised *Cossack, HMCS Crusader* and the American *Southerland* and *Thomas* at various stages. In May 1953 *Ocean* took over as the Commonwealth carrier on station and *Crusader*

remained with the screening group which also comprised *Cossack, Cockade* and the American *Higbee* and *Taylor*. In early June *Crusader* carried out shore bombardments in the Choda area with British, Dutch and USN ships; after that she spent a brief period with the carrier screen before returning to Esquimalt on 1 July 1953.

Crusader refitted in Esquimalt Dockyard between July and September 1953 and then returned to Korean waters between November 1953 and August 1954 as part of a series of UN patrols intended to ensure that the cease-fire agreement was being upheld by the communist regime in North Korea. She returned to Esquimalt in September 1954 and refitted between November 1954 and February 1955. She then transferred to the Canadian east coast to become the flagship of the Flag Officer Atlantic and take part in a number

HMCS Crusader *in reserve at Esquimalt on the Canadian west coast in October 1946. Her hull is painted in the contemporary RCN dark grey which has suffered rather while in reserve. Upper works are light grey and work is being carried out on the 4.5 inch mountings. She has a red maple-leaf on the funnel but still retains her RN pennant number, R 20, on the hull. When re-commissioned she was allocated the RCN hull number 228.*

(Syd Goodman Collection)

HMCS Crusader *under way off the Canadian west coast.* *(Dave Shirlaw)*

of national and NATO exercises. She took part in a series of anti-submarine exercises and trials in the West Indies between January and June 1957 with a break in September when she joined the search for survivors from the German barque *Pamir* which sank with the loss of all but 6 hands during a hurricane 600 miles west of the Azores. In August 1958, after a visit to the Joint Anti-Submarine School at Londonderry, she joined the British sonar-trials frigate *Brocklesby* to search for a Royal Dutch Airline Super Constellation aircraft that had gone missing approximately 130 miles north-west of Ireland. Wreckage and human remains were located and subsequently landed in Galway.

In November 1958 *Crusader* was modified to act as a trials ship for the new Canadian Type 199 vari-

able-depth sonar (VDS) equipment. This involved the removal of 'Y' mounting to fit a large winch on the quarterdeck. The sonar body was lowered into the water from this, on the end of a cable paid out from a drum which allowed it to be towed some distance astern at variable depths. Trials were carried out with the 3rd Canadian Escort Squadron and proved successful. The equipment subsequently went into service with both the Canadian and Royal navies.

On 15 January 1960 *Crusader* paid off into Dockyard hands at the Point Edward Naval Base at Sydney, Nova Scotia to prepare for a refit which was subsequently cancelled as an economy measure. She was laid up in un-maintained reserve after useful equipment was removed. The prototype

HMCS Crusader *after 1958 with the prototype variable-depth sonar equipment fitted in place of 'Y' mounting. Surprisingly she was never fitted with Squid ASW mortars and retained 'X' mounting throughout her career. Note the modified funnel cap.* *(Dave Shirlaw)*

VDS was fitted to her sister-ship *Crescent* for further trials. Navy Board approval to scrap her was given in October 1962 and on 31 October she was allocated to the Crown Assets Disposal Corporation. In August 1963 she was sold to Metal Processors Ltd and broken up for scrap.

Chapter 32

HMS CRYSTAL
(HNoMS STAVANGER from 1946)

HMS Crystal *carrying out acceptance trials in the Clyde during February 1946. She only saw a few weeks service with the Royal Navy and paid off into reserve in May before her sale to Norway in July 1946. (Steve Bush Collection)*

HMS *Crystal* was built by Yarrow at Scotstoun, laid down on 13 January 1944 and launched on 12 February 1945. Plans for her transfer to the RCN were not completed when the war ended and she was commissioned into the Royal Navy on 28 January 1946. She was formerly handed over and accepted on her nominal completion date 6 February 1946. After sea trials she steamed to Portland where she worked up and then to Chatham where she reduced to high-readiness reserve in May 1946. In July 1946 she was sold to the Norwegian Government at the same time as her sister-ship *Croziers*. She was commissioned into the Royal Norwegian Navy on 16 October 1946 as *HNoMS Stavanger*. Unfortunately she ran aground off Chatham on 6 November whilst carrying out trials. There was no serious damage and she sailed with *Trondheim* to Horten on 21 December 1946.

She carried out a docking period in Stavanger in 1948 and suffered a serious accident when the blocks supporting her hull collapsed and she fell to the dock floor. New propellers and shafts had to be bought from the UK and the 'A' brackets straightened and repaired. After repairs were complete she continued in service until 1966, rather longer than the other 'Cr' class ships in the Royal Norwegian Navy. She played a part in a number of NATO exercises, visited foreign ports to 'show the flag' and served as a training ship for midshipmen from the naval academy.

Like *Bergen*, *Stavanger* was fitted with the Terne rocket-fired depth charge system. The launcher was fitted to a superstructure, containing the re-load magazine, replaced the torpedo tubes forward of 'X' mounting which was retained. Presumably she was also refitted with one of the USN SQS series sonars which provided target information for the system.In 1967 she was used as a target vessel for development firings of the Kongsberg Penguin air-to-surface missile. Approval was eventually given for her disposal in March 1972 and she was sold to Staubo and Son A/S and subsequently broken up in Belgium.

HNoMS Stavanger *late in her career, fitted with the Terne ASW system. Terne was a Norwegian anti-submarine weapon system, which used rocket-thrown depth charges.* *(National Museum of the Royal Navy)*

The 'Ce' Class
The 15th Emergency Flotilla

There was considerable momentum behind the Emergency Destroyer Programme in September 1942 and for a while it was assumed that there would be a further group of destroyers within the class to be given names beginning with 'Ce'. The Admiralty Ship's Name and Badge Committee allocated two such names to ships that were to be ordered in April 1943. These were *Celt* and *Centaur*, both ordered from J. Samuel White of Cowes.

In the event, however, the Admiralty decided that the 'C' class had reached the design limit and that all future construction should concentrate on the larger and more capable 'Battle', 'Weapon', 'Daring' and 'G' classes. The order with White was therefore amended to procure two 'Weapon' class ships before any steel work on the 'Ce's had actually taken place. The resulting ships were *Sword*, ex-*Celt*, which was cancelled after the end of hostilities and scrapped on the slipway in October 1945 and *Tomahawk*, ex-*Centaur*, which was renamed *Scorpion* after her launch in 1946. She was eventually completed but her service is beyond the scope of this book. The name *Centaur* was subsequently given to a light fleet carrier.

Design effort after the 'Cr' class concentrated on the later 'Weapon', 'Daring' and 'G' classes and a 'Ce' was only ever a remote possibility. Had it been built, the ships would have been repeat 'Cr's with similar details.

'Ca' Class Destroyers

Technical Data

	Builder	Laid Down	Launched	Completed
Caesar	John Brown Ltd, Clydebank	03.04.43	14.02.44	05.10.44
Cambrian	Scotts SB & E Co Ltd, Greenock	14.08.42	10.12.43	17.07.44
Caprice	Yarrow & Co Ltd, Scotstoun	28.09.42	18.09.43	05.04.44
Carron	Scotts SB & E Co Ltd, Greenock	26.11.42	28.03.44	06.11.44
Carysfort	J.S. White & Co Ltd, Cowes	12.05.43	27.07.44	20.02.45
Cassandra	Yarrow & Co Ltd, Scotstoun	30.01.43	29.11.43	28.07.44
Cavalier	J.S. White & Co Ltd, Cowes	28.02.43	07.04.44	22.11.44
Cavendish	John Brown Ltd, Clydebank	19.05.43	12.04.44	13.12.44

Technical details:

Displacement (standard)	1,915 tons (*Caesar, Cavendish*); 1,781 tons (Remaining Ships)
Displacement (full load)	2,530 tons (*Caesar, Cavendish*); 2,510 tons (Remaining Ships)
Dimensions	362 ft 9 ins x 35 ft 9 ins x 10 ft
Armament	*Caesar, Cambrian, Carron, Carysfort, Cavalier, Cavendish*
	4 x 4.5-inch DP; 2 x 40mm AA; 6 x 20mm AA; 8 x 21-inch Torpedo Tubes; 4 x Depth Charge Thrower (48/108 Depth Charges)
	Caprice
	4 x 4.5-inch DP; 4 x 2-pdr AA; 6 x 20mm AA; 8 x 21-inch Torpedo Tubes; 4 x Depth Charge Thrower (48/108 Depth Charges)
	Cassandra
	4 x 4.5-inch DP; 2 x 40mm AA; 8 x 20mm AA; 8 x 21-inch Torpedo Tubes; 4 x Depth Charge Thrower (48/108 Depth Charges)
Machinery	Two shaft Parsons single-reduction turbines
	Two Admiralty three-drum boilers
	40,000 shp giving up to 34 knots
Oil fuel:	588 tons FFO plus 27 tons diesel
Endurance:	1,450 miles @ 31 knots
	3,900 miles @ 20 knots
	5,500 miles @ 15 knots
Complement:	186 (wartime maximum 225 in a leader)

Trials:

Caesar	34.294 knots	Displacement 2,400 tons
Cambrian	33.028 knots	Displacement 2,290 tons
Caprice	32.02 knots	Displacement 2,272 tons
Carron	32.036 knots	Displacement 2,232 tons
Carysfort	32.02 knots	Displacement 2,355 tons
Cassandra	33.10 knots	Displacement 2,209 tons
Cavalier	30.01 knots	Displacement 2,327 tons
Cavendish	32.71 knots	Displacement 2,336 tons

Design Notes:

Repeats of the 'Z' class and also fitted with the Mk 1K combined high angle and low angle director. The designed armament was 4 x 4.5-inch DP; 2 x 40mm AA (twin Hazemeyer mounting fitted amidships between the two quadruple torpedo tube mountings); 8 x 20mm AA (four twin mountings, two on the bridge wings and two abaft the funnel); 8 x TT and 4 x DCT. The 4.5-inch guns were the Mk4 quick firing, dual purpose model, fitted on Mk 5 CP mountings, having a maximum elevation of 55°. They were the last hand-worked guns to be fitted in RN destroyers as the main armament, although they were semi-automatic. As with the 'Z' class, the increased weight of the director created topweight problems and only *Cassandra* completed with the designed armament. The secondary armament of the remainder varied.

Caesar; Carron; Cavalier; Cavendish
   2 x 40mm AA; 6 x 20mm AA (two twin mountings on the bridge wings and two singles abaft the funnel)

Cambrian; Carysfort
   2 x 40mm AA; 6 x 20mm AA (two single mountings on the bridge wings and two twin mountings abaft the funnel)

Caprice
   4 x 2-pdr AA (Quadruple mounting amidships in lieu of the twin 40mm AA Hazemeyer); 6 x 20mm AA (two twin mountings on the bridge wings and two single mountings abaft the funnel)

The class was insulated for service in Northern latitudes and, with the exception of *Cassandra*, they were 'de-arcticised' when allocated to the Eastern Fleet in 1945. *Caesar* and *Cavendish* were completed as Leaders.

Appearance Notes:

Single funnel. Raked bow. Sloping face to 4.5-inch gunshields. Single director fitted on the bridge roof.

Caprice completed with a short lattice foremast (remaining vessels having a taller foremast). All fitted with a stump mast, carrying air warning RDF, at the forward end fo the after shelter deck. *Caprice*, as completed, was distinguished from the remainder of the class by the shorter foremast and the quadruple 2-pdr AA mounting amidships.

Nomenclature:

When the class was ordered in February 1942 they were given spare names for the earlier flotillas, but when it was decided to give the class 'C' names, they were renamed in November 1942. *Cambrian* and *Caprice* were laid down under their original names. The original names for the whole class were:

Caesar (ex-Ranger); Cambrian (ex-Spitfire); Caprice (ex-Swallow); Carron (ex-Strenuous); Carysfort (ex-Pellew); Cassandra (ex-Tourmaline); Cavalier (ex-Pique) and Cavendish (ex-Sibyl).

Building Note:

Carysfort and *Cavalier* were originally ordered from Cammell Laird & Co Ltd, Birkenhead, but due to difficuties in that Company fulfilling the contracts, they were switched to J. S. White & Co Ltd, Cowes, in November 1942. Heavy German air raids on Cowes delayed their construction and *Carysfort* was not completed until February 1945.

Armament Changes:

1945   *Caesar*

      Two twin 20mm AA on the bridge wings landed and replaced by two single 2-pdr AA. Single 40mm AA Bofors Mk3 fitted in the superfiring position abaft the funnel in lieu of the searchlight.

      Cavendish

      Two twin 20mm AA on the bridge wings and two single 20mm AA abaft the funnel landed. Two single 2-pdr AA fitted in the bridge wings and a single 2-pdr AA fitted in the superfiring position abaft the funnel in lieu of the searchlight.

      Cambrian, Carron, Carysfort, Cavalier

      Twin 20mm AA mountings and single 20mm AA mounting landed from the bridge wings and abaft the funnel. Four single 2-pdr AA fitted, two on the bridge wings and two abaft the funnel.

HMS CAVALIER - 1946 'CA; CLASS FLEET DESTROYER

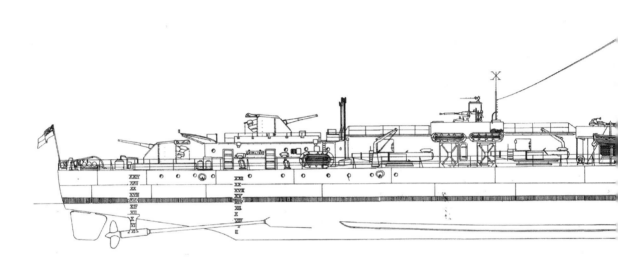

HMS CAVALIER - 1972

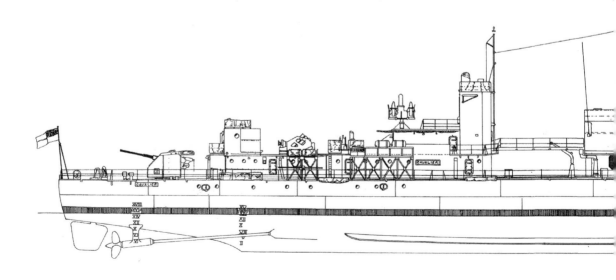

'CA' GROUP [11TH EMERGENCY FLOTILLA]

'K' TYPE GUNNERY DIRECTOR
4 - 4.5" Q.F. MARK IV C.P.V. 55° MOUNTINGS
1 - TWIN 40mm BOFORS MARK IV MOUNTING
3 - 2 PDR MARK XVI POWER OPERATED MOUNTINGS
(DUE TO SHORTAGE OF 40mm BOFORS GUNS)
2 - QUADRUPLE 21" MARK VIII TORPEDO TUBES.
FULL OUTFIT OF SHIPS BOATS

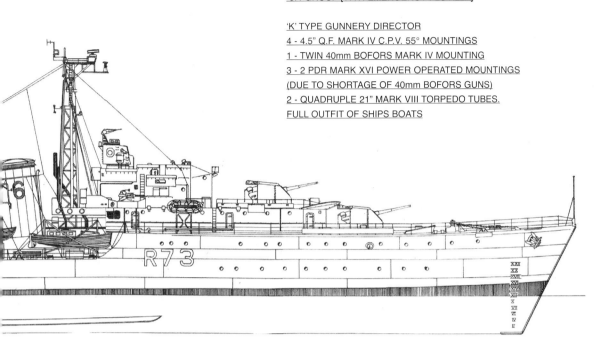

DRAWN BY JOHN LAMBERT

'CA' GROUP - AFTER MODERNISATION AT THORNYCROFT'S
SOUTHAMPTON 1955-57.   GIBRALTAR - 1966

MODIFIED BRIDGE, MAST AND AERIALS
3 - 4.5" MARK V MOUNTINGS WITH R.P.C. 50
2 - SQUID MARK IV AHEAD THROWING WEAPONS
2 - 40mm BOFORS ON MARK VII MOUNTING
1 - QUADRUPLE SEACAT SURFACE TO AIR MISSILE LAUNCHER
       [THE TWIN 40mm MARK V MOUNTING BEING DELETED]
REDUCED OUTFIT OF SHIPS BOATS

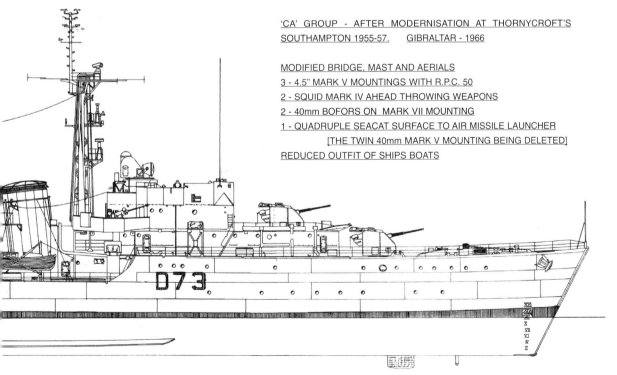

DRAWN BY JOHN LAMBERT

Caprice

Quadruple 2-pdr AA mounting amidships landed and replaced by a twin 40mm AA Hazemeyer mounting. Two single 20mm AA in the bridge wings and two twin 20mm AA mountings abaft the funnel landed. Four single 2-pdr AA fitted, two on the bridge wings and two abaft the funnel.

1952   *Caesar, Cambrian, Cassandra*

All 20mm AA mountings landed from *Cassandra*. Two single 2-pdr AA landed from bridge wings in *Caesar* and *Cambrian* and two abaft the funnel in *Cambrian*. Single 40mm AA Bofors and two single 20mm AA abaft the funnel landed from *Caesar*. All fitted with four single 40mm AA Bofors Mk3, two on the bridge wings and two abaft the funnel.

Anti-Submarine Destroyer Modernisation:

Caesar	Rosyth Dockyard	11.57 - 12.60
Cambrian	Devonport Dockyard	03.58 - 01.63
Caprice	Yarrow & Co Ltd, Scotstoun	09.56 - 03.59
Carron	Chatham Dockyard	03.53 - 08.55
Carysfort	Portsmouth Dockyard	02.56 - 09.57
Cassandra	Yarrow & Co Ltd, Scotstoun	03.57 - 11.59
Cavalier	J.I. Thornycroft & Co Ltd, Woolston	04.55 - 02.57
Cavendish	Vickers Armstrong Ltd, Tyne	01.54 - 04.56

Revised Details:

Displacement	2,053 tons (standard), 2,675 tons (full load)
Armament	3 x 4.5-inch DP; 4 x 40mm AA; 4 x 21-inch TT; 2 x Squid AS Mortar.

Design Note:

Extensively modernised as specialist anti-submarine vessels. The after 4.5-inch gun in 'X' position on the after shelter deck, the after quadruple torpedo tube mounting, all secondary armament and the depth charge throwers were removed. The after shelter deck was extended forward to amidships. New bridge-work was fitted, the first four to complete the modernisation received a modified Daring type open bridge, the remainder were fitted with an enclosed frigate type bridge.

The Mk 1K director was replaced by a Mk 6M combined high angle/low angle type and remote power control was provided for the main armament. Two single 40mm AA Bofors Mk 3 were fitted on the bridge wings and a twin 40mm AA Bofors Mk 5 mounting was fitted amidships. Two Squid anti-submarine mortars were installed on the after shelter deck and a deckhouse for projectile handling built at

the after end of the shelter deck. Projectile stowage was sufficient to enable ten double salvos to be fired from the mortars.

In 1962 it was decided to fit the Seacat surface-to-air missile system in *Cambrian, Carysfort, Cavalier* and *Cavendish* and the forward end of the after shelter deck was built up to provide a missile handling room and a platform for the launcher. To compensate for the additional topweight the remaining quadruple torpedo tube mounting and the twin 40mm AA Bofors Mk 5 mounting were landed. In the event only *Caprice* and *Cavalier* received the Seacat and the remaining threee were fitted with a single 40mm AA Bofors Mk 7 abaft the new superstructure.

Armament Changes:

1956   *Carron* (as Dartmouth Training Ship)

     4.5-inch gun in 'B' position on the forward shelter deck landed and replaced by a deckhouse for classroom accommodation

1958   *Carysfort*

     4.5-inch gun in 'B' position on the forward shelter deck landed.

1959   *Carysfort*

     4.5-inch gun in 'B' position refitted.

1960   *Carron* (as Navigation Training Ship)

     4.5-inch guns in 'A' position on the forecastle and 'Y' position on the quarterdeck and two Squid AS mortars landed.

1963   *Cavendish*

     Fitted for, but nor with, Seacat missile system. Twin 40mm AA Bofors Mk 5 amidships and quadruple 21-inch torpedo tube mounting landed. Single 40mm AA Bofors Mk 7 fitted amidships.

1964   *Carysfort, Cavalier*

     Fitted for, but nor with, Seacat missile system. Twin 40mm AA Bofors Mk 5 amidships and quadruple 21-inch torpedo tube mounting landed. Single 40mm AA Bofors Mk 7 fitted amidships.

1965   *Cambrian*

     Fitted for, but nor with, Seacat missile system. Twin 40mm AA Bofors Mk 5 amidships

and quadruple 21-inch torpedo tube mounting landed. Single 40mm AA Bofors Mk 7 fitted amidships.

1963   *Caprice, Cavalier*

Twin 40mm AA Bofors Mk 5 mounting amidships landed from *Caprice* and the single 40 mm AA Mk 7 amidships landed from *Cavalier*. Quadruple 21-inch torpedo tube mounting removed from *Caprice*. Quadruple Seacat surface-to-air missile launcher fitted to both amidships.

Subsidiary Roles:

Caprice   Seagoing Training Ship for Engineer Officers, attached to RNEC *Manadon*, Plymouth, 02.71-03.73.

Carron   Training Ship, Dartmouth Training Squadron 08.56-06.60.
Navigation Training Ship, attached to HMS *Dryad*, Portsmouth, 07.60-03.63

Displacement Note:

By 1967 the dispplacement of *Cambrian, Caprice Carysfort* and *Cavalier* had risen to 2,106 tons (standard), 2,749 tons (full load).

Disposal Details:

Caesar   Sold to Hughes Bolkow & Co Ltd, and arrived at Blyth, Northumberland for demolition 6 September 1967.

Cambrian   Sold to Thomas Ward & Co Ltd, and arrived at Briton Ferry, South Wales for demolition 12 September 1971.

Caprice   Sold to Shipbreaking (Queenborough) Ltd and arrived at Queenborough, for scrapping 5 October 1979.

Carron   Sold to Thomas Ward & Co Ltd, and arrived at Inverkeithing for demolition 4 April 1967.

Carysfort   Sold to J. Cashmore and Co Ltd, and arrived at Newport for demolition 18 November 1970.

Cassandra   Sold to Thomas Ward & Co Ltd, and arrived at Inverkeithing for demolition 28 April 1967.

The former 'Ca' class destroyers Cassandra *(above) and* Carron *(below) during the breaking up process at Thomas Ward and Co Ltd, Inverkeithing.* (T. Ferrers-Walker)

Cavalier   Sold for commercial conversion to a permanent museum ship. Arrived at Southampton in October 1977. Later towed to, and displayed at, Brighton. Resold to a Tyneside consortium and left Brighton under tow for Newcastle for a planned further use as a museum ship at Hebburn on Tyne 14 July 1987. This never happened. In 1998 the ship was bought by Chatham Historic Dockyard Trust for display as a museum ship. Arriving on at Chatham on 23 May 1998, she now resides in No. 2 dry-dock and is open to the public.

Cavendish   Sold to Hughes Bolkow & Co Ltd, and arrived at Blyth, Northumberland for demolition 17 August 1967.

'Ch' Class Destroyers

Technical Data

	Builder	Laid Down	Launched	Completed
Charity	J.I. Thornycroft & Co Ltd, Woolston	08.07.43	30.11.44	10.11.45
Chaplet	J.I. Thornycroft & Co Ltd, Woolston	29.04.43	18.07.44	24.08.45
Chequers	Scotts SB & E Co Ltd, Greenock	04.05.43	30.10.44	28.09.45
Cheviot	A. Stephen & Co Ltd, Linthouse	27.04.43	02.05.44	11.12.45
Chevron	A. Stephen & Co Ltd, Linthouse	18.03.43	23.02.44	23.08.45
Chieftain	Scotts SB & E Co Ltd, Greenock	27.06.43	26.02.45	07.03.46
Childers	Wm Denny & Co Ltd, Dumbarton	27.11.43	27.02.45	19.12.45
Chivalrous	Wm Denny & Co Ltd, Dumbarton	27.11.43	22.06.45	13.05.46

Technical details:

Displacement (standard)	1,940 tons (*Chequers, Childers*); 1,900 tons (Remaining Ships)
Displacement (full load)	2,555 tons (*Chequers, Childers*); 2,535 tons (Remaining Ships)
Dimensions	362 ft 9 ins x 35 ft 9 ins x 10 ft
Armament	*Childers* 4 x 4.5-inch DP; 2 x 40mm AA; 2 x 20mm AA; 4 x 21-inch Torpedo Tubes; 2 x Depth Charge Thrower (35 Depth Charges) *Chevron, Chieftain* 4 x 4.5-inch DP; 6 x 40mm AA; 2 x 20mm AA; 4 x 21-inch Torpedo Tubes; 2 x Depth Charge Thrower (35 Depth Charges) *Chaplet, Chequers* 4 x 4.5-inch DP; 2 x 40mm AA; 4 x 2-pdr AA; 4 x 21-inch Torpedo Tubes; 2 x Depth Charge Thrower (35 Depth Charges) *Charity, Cheviot* 4 x 4.5-inch DP; 2 x 40mm AA; 2 x 2-pdr AA; 2 x 20mm AA; 4 x 21-inch Torpedo Tubes; 2 x Depth Charge Thrower (35 Depth Charges) *Chivalrous* 4 x 4.5-inch DP; 6 x 40mm AA; 4 x 21-inch Torpedo Tubes; 2 x Depth Charge Thrower (35 Depth Charges)
Propulsion Machinery	Geared turbines SHP 40,000 = 36.75 knots.

Trials:

Charity	31.01 knots	Displacement 2,312 tons
Chequers	32.22 knots	Displacement 2,250 tons
Cheviot	32.32 knots	Displacement 2,312 tons
Chevron	32.02 knots	Displacement 2,260 tons
Chieftain	31.69 knots	Displacement 2,310 tons
Childers	31.60 knots	Displacement 2,315 tons
Chivalrous	31.60 knots	Displacement 2,375 tons

Design Notes:

Similar to the 'Ca' group but fitted with the new Mk 6 combined high angle/low angle director, and remote power control for the main armament. The designed armament was to have been 4 x 4.5-inch DP; 2 x 40mm AA (a twin Hazemeyer mounting amidships); 8 x 20mm AA (four twin mountings, two on the bridge wings and two abaft the funnel); 8 x 21-inch torpedo tubes (two quadruple mountings); four depth charge throwers and 70 depth charges. The new director was much heavier than earlier models and, with the increased electrical and radar equipment being installed, created stability problems with the additional topweight. An alternative armament was to omit the 4.5-inch gun in 'Y' position on the quarterdeck and fit two speed destroyer minesweeping gear, or four additional depth charge throwers and a further 50 depth charges. Once the stability problem had become apparent further modifications were made to the design with the omission of the forward quadruple torpedo tube mounting, single, instead of twin 20mm AA mountings on the bridge wings and depth charge stowage reduced to 35. A later amendment was to substitute two single 2-pdr AA for the twin 20mm AA mountings abaft the funnel and to omit the mainmast in favour of a stump mast aft. The designed armament was eventually 4 x 4.5-inch DP (Mk 4 models on Mk 5 CP mountings, with a maximum elevation of 55°). 4 x 40mm AA (a twin Hazemeyer mounting amidships and two single Bofors Mk 3 abaft the funnel). 2 x 20mm AA (single mountings on the bridge wings, 4 x 21-inch TT (quadruple mounting), two depth charge throwers and 35 depth charges. Due to delays in the supply of the Mk 6 director, the completion of the class was delayed and none entered service with the designed armament. The secondary armament varied between the individual vessels upon completion, as follows:

Childers
 2 x 40mm AA (twin Hazemeyer mounting amidships); 2 x 20mm AA (two single mountings in the bridge wings)

Chevron Chieftain
 2 x 40mm AA (twin Hazemeyer mounting amidships); 6 x 20mm AA (two twin mountings abaft the funnel and two single mountings in the bridge wings)

Chaplet, Chequers
2 x 40mm AA (twin Hazemeyer mounting amidships); 4 x 2-pdr AA (single mountings, two on the bridge wings and two abaft the funnel)

Charity, Cheviot
2 x 40mm AA (twin Hazemeyer mounting amidships); 2 x 2-pdr AA (single mountings abaft the funnel); 2 x 20mm AA (two single mountings on the bridge wings)

Chivalrous
6 x 40mm AA (twin Hazemeyer mounting amidships, four single Bofors Mk 3 mountings, two abaft the funnel and two on the bridge wings)

The class was not insulated for service in Northern latitudes. *Chequers* and *Childers* were completed as Leaders. *Cheviot* was fitted as a Divisional Leader.

Appearance Notes:

Single funnel. Raked bow. Sloping face to 4.5-inch gunshields. Tall lattice mast fitted in all. Stump mast, carrying air warning RDF, at the forward end fo the after shelter deck. Distinguished from the 'Ca' group by the larger director fitted on the brdge and the absence of the forward quadruple torpedo tube mounting. *Chaplet, Charity, Chequers, Cheviot, Chevron* and *Chieftain* fitted with a deckhouse at the after end of the after shelter deck 1951-55. *Chaplet* and *Chieftain* fitted with minelaying rails in 1955.

Nomenclature:

Chequers was originally to have been named *Champion*.

Minelaying Note:

Chaplet and *Chieftain* were fitted for minelaying during 1954-55, with a capacity for 50 mines. They were also given an increased anti-submarine capability and the 4.5-inch gun in 'X' position on the after shelter deck was landed to provide space for two Squid AS mortars. An ammunition handling room for the mortars was built at the after end of the shelter deck. Minelaying rails were fitted. The secondary armament was amended to a twin 40mm AA Bofors Mk 5 amidships (replacing the twin Hazemeyer mounting) and two single 40mm AA Bofors Mk 3 on the bridge wings. When carrying their full complement of mines, the 4.5-inch mounting in 'Y' position on the quarterdeck and the quadruple torpedo tube mounting were landed, as were the depth charge throwers and depth charges.

Anti-submarine Modification:

Charity, Chequers, Cheviot, Chevron and *Chivalrous* were modified (1952-53) to make them more

HMS CHEVIOT - 1958   'CH' CLASS FLEET DESTROYER

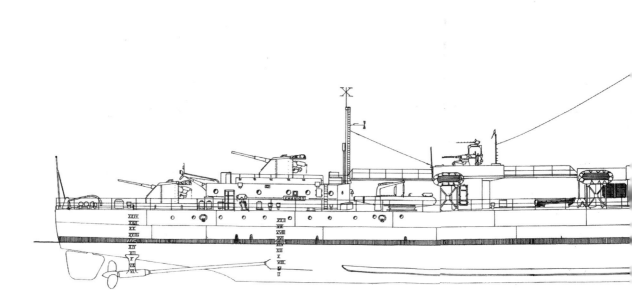

effective anti-submarine vessels. The 4.5-inch gun on the after shelter deck in 'X' position was landed and two Squid anti-submarine mortars were fitted on the shelter deck with a handling room for the mortar bombs built at the after end. The secondary armament was a twin 40mm AA Bofors Mk 5 amidships and four single 40mm AA Bofors Mk 3, two on the bridge wings and two abaft the funnel. The two depth charge throwers and the depth charges were landed. Following the modifications their displacement increased to 1,975 tons (standard) and 2,658 tons (full load).

Design Note:

Extensively modernised as specialist anti-submarine vessels. The after 4.5-inch gun in 'X' position on the after shelter deck, the after quadruple torpedo tube mounting, all secondary armament and the depth charge throwers were removed. The after shelter deck was extended forward to amidships. New bridgework was fitted, the first four to complete the modernisation received a modified Daring type open bridge, the remainder were fitted with an enclosed frigate type bridge.

The Mk 1K director was replaced by a Mk 6M combined high angle/low angle type and remote power control was provided for the main armament. Two single 40mm AA Bofors Mk 3 were fitted on the bridge wings and a twin 40mm AA Bofors Mk 5 mounting was fitted amidships. Two Squid anti-sub-

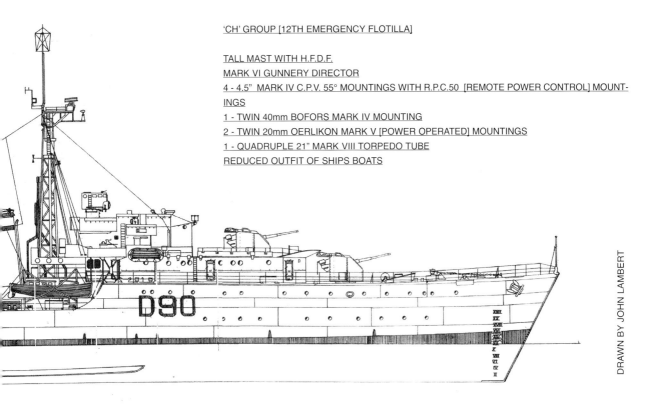

DRAWN BY JOHN LAMBERT

'CH' GROUP [12TH EMERGENCY FLOTILLA]

TALL MAST WITH H.F.D.F.
MARK VI GUNNERY DIRECTOR
4 - 4.5" MARK IV C.P.V. 55° MOUNTINGS WITH R.P.C.50 [REMOTE POWER CONTROL] MOUNT-INGS
1 - TWIN 40mm BOFORS MARK IV MOUNTING
2 - TWIN 20mm OERLIKON MARK V [POWER OPERATED] MOUNTINGS
1 - QUADRUPLE 21" MARK VIII TORPEDO TUBE
REDUCED OUTFIT OF SHIPS BOATS

marine mortars were installed on the after shelter deck and a deckhouse for projectile handling built at the after end of the shelter deck. Projectile stowage was sufficient to enable ten double salvos to be fired from the mortars.

In 1962 it was decided to fit the Seacat surface-to-air missile system in *Cambrian, Carysfort, Cavalier* and *Cavendish* and the forward end of the after shelter deck was built up to provide a missile handling room and a platform for the launcher. To compensate for the additional topweight the remaining quadruple torpedo tube mounting and the twin 40mm AA Bofors Mk 5 mounting were landed. In the event only *Caprice* and *Cavalier* received the Seacat and the remaining theree were fitted with a single 40mm AA Bofors Mk 7 abaft the new superstructure.

Armament Changes:

1946   *Chequers*

Single 40mm Bofors Mk 3 fitted in the superfiring position abaft the funnel, in lieu of the searchlight. Two single 2-pdr AA landed from the bridge wings and two from abaft the funnel. Replaced by four single 20mm AA in the same positions.

1947   *Chequers*

Two single 20mm AA on the bridge wings landed and replaced by two twin 20mm AA mountings. Single 40mm AA Bofors Mk 3 and two single 20mm AA abaft the funnel landed and replaced by two single 40mm Bofors Mk 3 fitted in echelon.

1949   *Chaplet, Charity, Chieftain*

Two single 2-pdr AA abaft the funnel in *Chaplet* and *Charity* and two twin 20mm AA mountings abaft the funnel in *Chieftain*, landed and replaced by two single 40mm AA Bofors Mk 3.

1950   *Charity, Chaplet, Chequers, Cheviot, Chevron, Chieftain, Childers*

Armament standardised for all vessels. Twin 40mm AA Bofors Mk 5 mounting fitted amidships in place of the twin 40mm AA Hazemeyer mounting. All 20mm AA mountings landed. Four single 40mm AA Bofors Mk 3 fitted, two on the bridge wings and two abaft the funnel.

1950   *Chivalrous*

Twin 40mm AA Hazemeyer mounting landed from amidships and replaced by a twin 40mm AA Bofors Mk 5 mounting.

1951   *Childers*

4.5-inch gun on the after shelter deck in 'X' position and twin 40mm AA Bofors Mk 5 mounting amidships landed.

1952   *Chevron*

4.5-inch gun in 'X' position and two single 40mm AA Bofors Mk 3 abaft the funnel landed.

1953   *Charity, Chequers, Cheviot, Chevron, Chivalrous*

4.5-inch gun in 'X' position and two depth charge throwers and depth charges landed. Two Squid anti-submarine mortars fitted on the after shelter deck.

1955   *Chaplet, Chieftain* (Modified for minelaying)

4.5-inch gun in 'X' position and two single 40mm AA Bofors Mk 3 abaft the funnel, and two depth charge throwers and depth charges landed. Two Squid anti-submarine mortars fitted on the after shelter deck.

1959   *Chaplet*

              4.5-inch gun in 'Y' position on the quarterdeck landed.

Subsidiary Roles:

Chaplet   Training Ship, Portsmouth, 02.59-09.61
              Harbour Training Ship, attached to HMS *Caledonia*, Rosyth, 1962-64, 02.71-03.73.
Cheviot   Harbour Training Ship for Engine Room Artificers, attached to HMS *Caledonia*, Rosyth
              11.59-06.62.
Chevron   Accommodation Ship at Rosyth 07.60-03.63, 1964-10.69,

Transfers:

Charity   Transferred to the Pakistan Navy 16.12.58. Renamed *Shah Jahan*.

Chivalrous Transferred to the Pakistan Navy 29.06.54. Renamed *Taimur*.

Cheviot (centre), Concord *(left) and the cruiser* Swiftsure *(right) at various stages of scrapping at Inverkeithing. Note the close range weapons and Squid mountings still in situ under canvas.* (T. Ferrers-Walker)

Disposal Details:

Chaplet Sold to Hughes Bolkow & Co Ltd, and arrived at Blyth, Northumberland for demolition 6 November 1965.

Charity Transferred to Pakistan Navy as *Shah Jahan*. Paid off for disposal in June 1982 and scrapped from 1984-85.

Chequers Sold to J. Cashmore and Co Ltd, and arrived at Newport for demolition 23 July 1966.

Cheviot Sold to Thomas Ward & Co Ltd, and arrived at Inverkeithing for demolition 22 October 1962.

Chevron Sold to Thomas Ward & Co Ltd, and arrived at Inverkeithing for demolition 12 December 1969.

Chieftain Sold to T. Young & Co Ltd, and arrived at Sunderland for demolition 20 May 1961.

Childers Sold to Italian shipbreakers and arrived at La Spezia, Italy, for scrapping 22 September 1963.

Chivalrous Transferred to Pakistan Navy as *Taimur*. Sold to Hughes Bolkow & Co Ltd, and arrived at Blyth, Northumberland for demolition 10 October 1961.

'Co' Class Destroyers

Technical Data

	Builder	Laid Down	Launched	Completed
Cockade	Yarrow & Co Ltd, Scotstoun	11.03.43	07.03.44	29.09.45
Comet	Yarrow & Co Ltd, Scotstoun	14.06.43	22.06.44	06.06.45
Comus	J.I. Thornycroft & Co Ltd, Woolston	21.08.43	14.03.45	08.07.46
Concord	J.I. Thornycroft & Co Ltd, Woolston	18.11.43	14.05.45	20.12.46
Consort	A. Stephen & Co Ltd, Linthouse	26.05.43	19.10.44	19.03.46
Constance	Vickers Armstrong Ltd, Tyne	18.03.43	22.08.44	31.12.45
Contest	J.S. White & Co Ltd, Cowes	01.11.43	16.12.44	09.11.45
Cossack	Vickers Armstrong Ltd, Tyne	18.03.43	10.05.44	04.09.45

Technical details:

Displacement (standard)	1,910 tons (*Cossack*); 1,890 tons (Remaining Ships)
Displacement (full load)	2,525 tons (*Cossack*); 2,505 tons (Remaining Ships)
Dimensions	362 ft 9 ins x 35 ft 9 ins x 10 ft
Armament	*Cockade, Constance, Contest, Cossack*
	4 x 4.5-inch DP; 2 x 40mm AA; 2 x 2-pdr AA; 2 x 20mm AA; 4 x 21-inch Torpedo Tubes; 2 x Depth Charge Thrower (35 Depth Charges)
	Comet
	4 x 4.5-inch DP; 2 x 40mm AA; 4 x 2-pdr AA; 4 x 21-inch Torpedo Tubes; 2 x Depth Charge Thrower (35 Depth Charges)
	Comus, Concord, Consort
	4 x 4.5-inch DP; 4 x 40mm AA; 2 x 20mm AA; 4 x 21-inch Torpedo Tubes; 2 x Depth Charge Thrower (35 Depth Charges)
Propulsion Machinery	Geared turbines SHP 40,000 = 36.75 knots.

Trials:

Cockade	32.17 knots	Displacement 2,204 tons
Comet	31.767 knots	Displacement 2,200 tons
Comus	31.10 knots	Displacement 2,174 tons
Concord	30.50 knots	Displacement 2,213 tons
Consort	31.60 knots	Displacement 2,356 tons
Constance	31.80 knots	Displacement 2,448 tons
Contest	31.81 knots	Displacement 2,376 tons
Cossack	33.01 knots	Displacement 2,558 tons

Design Notes:

Repeats of the 'Ch' group, they also suffered from the topweight problems associated with the fitting of the Mk 6 combined high angle and low angle director and the provisions of remote power control for the main armament. The original requirement was for 4 x 4.5-inch (single Mk 4 on Mk 5 CP mountings with a maximum elevation of 55°); 2 x 40mm AA (twin Hazemeyer mounting fitted amidships between the two quadruple torpedo tube mountings); 8 x 20mm AA (four twin mountings, two on the bridge wings and two abaft the funnel); 8 x TT and 2 x DCT and 70 depth charges. Weight restrictions caused this arrangement to be revised and, in an attempt to improve stability the forward quadruple torpedo tubes were removed and the depth charge capacity reduced by half. The armament was again amended and the final design was for 4 x 4.5-inch DP; 4 x 40mm AA (twin Hazemeyer mounting amidships and two single Bofors Mk 3 abft the funnel); 2 x 20mm AA (two single mountings in the bridge wings); 4 x 21-inch TT (quadruple mounting in the after position); two depth charge throwers and 35 depth charges.

As with the previous group, their construction was protracted owing to delays in the supply of the Mk 6 director and new electrical equipment. Only the last to complete, *Comus, Concord* and *Consort*, entered service with the designed armament,although a twin 40mm AA Bofors Mk 5 mounting was fitted amidships in lieu of the twin Hazemeyer that had been specified originally. The remaining five vessels of the group entered service with an amended secondary armament as follows:

Cockade, Constance, Contest, Cossack
   2 x 40mm AA (twin Hazemeyer mounting amidships); 2 x 2-pdr AA (two single mountings abaft the funnel); 2 x 20mm AA (single mounts on the bridge wings).

Comet
   2 x 40mm AA (twin Hazemeyer mounting amidships); 4 x 2-pdr AA (four single mounts, two abaft the funnel and two on the bridge wings).

The class was not insulated for service in Northern latitudes. They were of all welded construction, with *Contest* being the first RN destroyer to be built using this method of construction. *Cossack* was completed as a Leader. *Constance* was fitted for service as a Divisional Leader.

Appearance Notes:

Single funnel. Raked bow. Sloping face to 4.5-inch gunshields. Single director fitted on the bridge roof. All completed with a tall lattice foremast. All fitted with a stump mast, carrying air warning RDF, at the forward end fo the after shelter deck. No TT mounting in the forward position. *Cockade, Comet, Comus, Concord, Consort, Contest and Cossack* fitted with an ammunition handling room at the after end of the after shelter deck in 1955.

Nomenclature:

Concord was laid down and launched as *Corso*. Renamed in June 1946.

Anti-Submarine Destroyer Modernisation:

During 1953-54 *Cockade, Concord, Consort* and *Cossack* were refitted to enhance their capability as anti-submarine vessels. The 4.5-inch gun in 'X' position was landed and two Squid AS mortars fitted. A handling room for the ammunition and firing equipment was fitted at the after end of the shelter deck. The secondary armament was revised to an all 40mm AA arrangement, with a twin 40mm AA Hazemeyer mounting fitted amidships, replaced by a twin 40mm AA Bofors Mk 5 mounting. Four single 40mm AA Bofors Mk 7 were intalled, two on the bridge wings and two abaft the funnel in place of the original Mk 3 mountings. The two depth charge throwers were removed. After modernisation their displacemnt increased to 1,950 tons (standard) and 2,650 tons (full load).

Minelayer Conversions:

In 1955 *Comet* and *Contest* were converted to minelaying destroyers with a capacity for 50 mines. Mine rails were fitted port and starboard, extending from abaft the funnel to chutes at the stern. They were also given an enhanced anti-submarine capability and the 4.5-inch gun in 'X' position on the after shelter deck was landed and replaced by two Squid AS mortars and an ammunition handling room at the after end of the shelter deck. The depth charge throwers were also removed. The secondary armament was made an all 40mm installation, a twin 40mm AA Bofors Mk 5 mounting was fitted in place of the twin 40MM AA Hazemeyer. Two single 40mm AA Bofors Mk 7 were fitted on the bridge wings in place of the 20mm mountings and two single 40mm AA Bofors Mk 7 were fitted abaft the funnel in place of Mk 3 models. When serving as minelyers with a full complement of mines the 4.5-inch gun in 'Y' position on the quarterdeck and the quadruple TT mounting were landed.

Armament Changes:

1948   *Comet*

                   Two single 2-pdr AA on the bridge wings landed and replaced by two sngle 20mm AA.
                   Two single 2-pdr AA abaft the funnel landed.

1951   *Cockade, Comet, Contest, Cossack*

Twin 40mm AA Hazemeyer mounting amidships landed and replaced by a twin 40mm AA Bofors Mk 5 mounting. Two single 2-pdr AA abaft the funnel landed and replaced by two single 40mm AA Bofors Mk 3.

1952   *Constance*

4.5-inch gun in 'X' position on the after shelter deck landed. Twin 40mm AA Hazemeyer mounting amidships landed and replaced by a twin 40mm AA Bofors Mk 5 mounting. Two single 20mm AA on the bridge wings and two single 20mm AA abaft the funnel landed and replaced by four single 40mm AA Bofors Mk 7 fitted in the same positions. Single 40mm AA Mk 7 fitted on the after shelter deck.

1954   *Cockade, Concord, Consort, Cossack*

4.5-inch gun in 'X' position on the after shelter deck landed and replaced by two Squid AS mortars. Two depth charge throwers landed. Two single 20mm AA on the bridge wings landed and replaced by two single 40mm AA Bofors Mk 7.

1955   *Comet, Contest*

4.5-inch gun in 'X' position on the after shelter deck landed and replaced by two Squid AS mortars. Two depth charge throwers landed, together with two single 40mm AA Bofors Mk 3 abaft the funnel. Two single 20mm AA on the bridge wings landed and replaced by two single 40mm AA Bofors Mk 7.

1956   *Comet, Contest*

4.5-inch gun in 'Y' position on the quarterdeck landed, together with the quadruple torpedo tube mounting.

Subsidiary Roles:

Concord   Tender to HMS *Caledonia*, Rosyth. 1957-62.

Contest   Torpedo Training Ship, Portsmouth. 1951-55

Proposed Sale:

In 1957 it was proposed to sell *Comus* to Peru, but negotiations ended and the sale was cancelled.

Two views of HMS Cossack *on 15 March 1961 awaiting demolition at Troon.* (T. Ferrers-Walker)

Disposal Details:

Cockade   Sold to J. Cashmore and Co Ltd, and arrived at Newport for demolition 15 August 1964.

Comet   Sold to West of Scotland Shipbreaking Co Ltd and arrived at Troon for scrapping 23 October 1962.

Comus   Sold to J. Cashmore and Co Ltd, and arrived at Newport for demolition 12 November 1958.

Concord   Sold to Thomas Ward & Co Ltd, and arrived at Inverkeithing for demolition 22 October 1962.

Consort   Sold to Prince of Wales Dry Dock Co Ltd and arrived at Swansea for demolition 15 March 1961.

Constance Sold to Thomas Ward & Co Ltd, and arrived at Inverkeithing for demolition 8 March 1956.

Contest Sold to Thomas Ward & Co Ltd, and arrived at Grays, Essex, for scrapping 15 March 1961.

Cossack Sold to West of Scotland Shipbreaking Co Ltd and arrived at Troon for scrapping 1 May 1961.

'Cr' Class Destroyers

Technical Data

	Builder	Laid Down	Launched	Completed
Creole	J.S. White & Co Ltd, Cowes	03.08.44	22.11.45	14.10.46
Crescent	John Brown Ltd, Clydebank	16.09.43	20.07.44	31.09.45
Crispin	J.S. White & Co Ltd, Cowes	01.02.44	23.06.45	10.07.46
Cromwell	Scotts SB & E Co Ltd, Greenock	24.11.43	06.08.45	12.09.46
Crown	Scotts SB & E Co Ltd, Greenock	16.01.44	19.12.45	17.04.47
Croziers	Yarrow & Co Ltd, Scotstoun	26.10.43	19.09.44	30.11.45
Crusader	John Brown Ltd, Clydebank	15.11.43	05.10.44	26.11.45
Crystal	Yarrow & Co Ltd, Scotstoun	13.01.44	17.02.45	06.02.46

Technical details:

Displacement (standard)	1,910 tons (*Crescent, Crusader*); 1,890 tons (Remaining Ships)
Displacement (full load)	2,525 tons (*Crescent, Crusader*); 2,505 tons (Remaining Ships)
Dimensions	362 ft 9 ins x 35 ft 9 ins x 10 ft
Armament	*Creole, Crescent*
	4 x 4.5-inch DP; 2 x 40mm AA; 2 x 2-pdr AA; 2 x 20mm AA; 4 x 21-inch Torpedo Tubes; 2 x Depth Charge Thrower (35 Depth Charges)
	Cromwell, Crown, Croziers, Crystal, Crusader
	4 x 4.5-inch DP; 4 x 40mm AA; 2 x 20mm AA; 4 x 21-inch Torpedo Tubes; 2 x Depth Charge Thrower (35 Depth Charges)
	Crispin
	4 x 4.5-inch DP; 4 x 40mm AA; 2 x 2-pdr AA; 4 x 21-inch Torpedo Tubes; 2 x Depth Charge Thrower (35 Depth Charges)
Propulsion Machinery	Geared turbines SHP 40,000 = 36.75 knots.

Trials:

Creole	30.90 knots	Displacement 2,168 tons
Crescent	31.50 knots	Displacement 2,430 tons
Crispin	31.91 knots	Displacement 2,173 tons
Cromwell	31.55 knots	Displacement 2,372 tons
Croziers	32.871 knots	Displacement 2,142 tons
Crusader	31.401 knots	Displacement 2,447 tons
Crystal	32.032 knots	Displacement 2,266 tons

Design Notes:

Repeats of the 'Co' group, they also suffered from the topweight problems associated with the fitting of the Mk 6 combined high angle and low angle director and the provisions of remote power control for the main armament. The designed armament was finalised as 4 x 4.5-inch (single Mk 4 QF dual purpose models, on Mk 5 CP mountings with a maximum elevation of 55°); 4 x 40mm AA (twin Hazemeyer mounting fitted amidships and two single Bofors Mk 3 abft the funnel); 2 x 20mm AA (two single mountings on the bridge wings); 4 x 21-inch TT (quadruple mounting in the after position); two depth charge throwers and 35 depth charges.

Construction was again lengthy owing to delays in the supply of the Mk 6 director. *Cromwell, Crown, Croziers, Crusader* and *Crystal* completed with the designed armament and the remaining had various secondary armament as follows:

Creole, Crescent
2 x 40mm AA (twin Bofors Mk 5 amidships); 2 x 2-pdr AA (single mounts abaft the funnel); 2 x 20mm AA (two single mounts on the bridge wings).

Crispin
4 x 40mm AA (twin Bofors Mk 5 mounting amidships, 2 x single Bofors Mk 3 abaft the funnel); 2 x 2-pdr AA (single mountings abaft the funnel).

The class was not insulated for service in Northern latitudes. *Creole* and *Crispin* were of all welded construction. *Cromwell* and *Crown* never saw service with the RN, being transferred to the Royal Norwegian Navy whilst under construction. *Crescent* and *Crusader* were transferred to Canada upon completion. Both were fitted as Leaders.

Appearance Notes:

Single funnel. Raked bow. Sloping face to 4.5-inch gunshields. Single director fitted on the bridge roof. All had tall foremast. *Croziers* and *Crystal* fitted with a stump mast, carrying air warning RDF, at the forward end of the after shelter deck. *Creole* and *Crispin* fitted with a deckhouse on the forward shelter

deck in place of the 4.5-inch gun in 'B' position in 1947. The deckhouse was removed and the gun refitted in 1958. *Crusader* fitted with a funnel cap in 1960.

Nomenclature:

Crispin	Laid down and launched as *Craccher*. Renamed in June 1946
Cromwell	Laid down and launched as *Cretan*. Renamed in June 1946

Transfers:

Creole	Sold to the Pakistan Navy 20.06.58. Renamed *Alamgir*
Crescent	Transferred to the Royal Canadian Navy 09.45. Name unchanged.
Crispin	Sold to the Pakistan Navy 18.03.58. Renamed *Jahangir*
Cromwell	Transferred to the Royal Norwegian Navy while fitting out 12.07.46. Renamed *Bergen*.
Crown	Transferred to the Royal Norwegian Navy while fitting out 12.07.46. Renamed *Oslo*.
Croziers	Transferred to the Royal Norwegian Navy 10.10.46. Renamed *Trondheim*.
Crusader	Transferred to the Royal Canadian Navy 11.45. Name unchanged
Crystal	Transferred to the Royal Norwegian Navy 10.10.46. Renamed *Stavanger*.

Subsidiary Roles:

Creole	Advanced ASW Training Ship, Londonderry. 1946-53.
Crispin	Advanced ASW Training Ship, Londonderry. 1946-54.
Crusader	ASW weapons & sonar Trials Ship. 1960-63.

Armament Changes:

1947	*Creole, Crispin*

4.5-inch gun in 'B' position on the forward shelter deck landed and replaced by a deckhouse. Two single 2-pdr AA abaft the funnel in *Creole* landed and replaced by two single 40mm AA Bofors Mk 3. Two single 2-pdr AA on the bridge wings in *Crispin* landed and replaced by two single 20mm AA.

1949	*Crescent*

Two additional 2-pdr AA fitted abaft the funnel.

1953	*Crusader*

4.5-inch gun in 'Y' position on the quarterdeck landed. Two single 20mm AA on the bridge

wings landed and replaced by two single 40mm AA Bofors Mk 7. Two single 40mm AA Bofors Mk 3 abaft the funnel replaced by two single 40mm AA Bofors Mk 7. Twin 40mm AA Hazemeyer mounting amidships landed and replaced by a twin 40mm AA Bofors Mk 7 mounting.

1957   *Bergen (ex-Cromwell), Oslo (ex-Crown), Trondheim (ex-Croziers), Stavanger (ex-Crystal)*

Two single 20mm on the bridge wings landed and replaced by two single 40mm AA Bofors Mk 7. Twin 40mm AA Hazemeyer mounting amidships landed and replaced by a twin 40mm AA Bofors Mk 7 mounting. Two single 40mm AA Bofors Mk 3 abaft the funnel landed and replaced by two single 40mm Bofors Mk 7.

1958   *Alamgir (ex-Creole), Jahangir (ex-Crispin)*

After modernisation following sale to Pakistan. Deckhouse on forward shelter deck removed and 4.5-inch gun refitted in 'B' position. 4.5-inch gun in 'X' position on the after shelter deck landed and two Squid AS mortars fitted on the deck. Depth charge throwers landed. Two single 20mm AA on the bridge wings landed and replaced by two single 40mm AA Bofors Mk 7. Two single 40mm AA Bofors Mk 3 abaft the funnel landed and replaced by two single 40mm AA Bofors Mk 7. Twin 40mm AA Hazemeyer mounting amidships replaced by a twin 40mm AA Bofors Mk 5 mounting.

1960   *Crusader* (as Trials Ship)

Two depth charge throwers landed. Variable depth sonar fitted at the stern.

1964   *Bergen (ex-Cromwell)*

Quadruple torpedo tube mounting and two depth charge throwers landed. Tern anti-submarine missile launcher fitted.

1965   *Stavanger (ex-Crystal)*

Quadruple torpedo tube mounting and two depth charge throwers landed. Tern anti-submarine missile launcher fitted.

Displacement Note:

The displacement of *Bergen, Oslo, Tronheim* and *Stavanger* had increased to 1,966 tons (standard) and 2,640 tons (full load) by 1957.
The displacement of *Alamgir* and *Jahangir* increased to 1,955 tons (standard) and 2,650 tons (full load) following their modernisation refits in 1957-58

Destoyer Escort Conversion:

Crescent   Esquimalt Dockyard   1955-56

Revised Details:

Displacement   2,140 tons (standard), 2,825 tons (full load)
Armament   2 x 4-inch AA; 2 x 3-inch AA; 2 x 40mm AA; 2 x Limbo AS Mortar.

Design Note:

Converted to a specialist anti-submarine vessel on similar lines to the Royal Navy's Type 15 fast anti-submarine frigates, but with a differing armament and a larger bridge structure. All the existing armament and superstructure were removed and the hull was plated up to the forecastle level aft to have a short quarterdeck. The hull plating was also extended upwards amidships for the new superstructure, and the bridgework was extended to the ships sides. A twin 4-inch AA Mk XVI, fitted on a CP XVIII mounting, giving a maximum elevation of 80°, was positioned on the forecastle and a twin 3-inch 50 cal US pattern mounting fitted aft of the new mainmast. Two single 40mm AA Bofors Mk 7 were sited abreast the foremast, port and starboard. The anti-submarine armament of two Limbo AS mortars were mounted in echelon at the end of the forecastle deck, abaft the 3-inch AA mounting, and a handling room for the mortars and firing equipment room was built aft. Variable depth sonar was fitted at the stern. A new lattice foremast and mainmast were stepped. Following the conversion she was re-rated as a Destroyer Escort.

Appearance Note:

Long forecaste extended aft to a short quarterdeck. Distinguished from the RN conversions by the heavier, block bridge structure, extending to the ship sides and the twin 4-inch AA mounting positioned on the forecastle. Cap fitted to the funnel. Shield fitted to the twin 3-in AA mounting aft. Lattice masts fitted fore and aft. Bulky installation for the variable depth sonar fitted at the stern.

Armament Change:

1962   *Crescent*

              Two single 40mm AA Bofors Mk 7 abreast the foremast landed, together with one Limbo AS mortar. Triple 12.75-inch TT for AS torpedoes fitted amidships on the centreline.

Disposal Details:

Creole   As *Alamgir* paid off for disposal 1982 and scrapped during 1983-84.

Crescent   Sold to Eastern Shipbreakers and left Victoria, British Columbia for scrapping in Taiwan 21 May 1971.

Crispin   As *Jahangir* paid off for disposal 1982 and scrapped during 1983-84.

Cromwell   As *Bergen* paid off for disposal in 1964. Sold to Norsk Shipbreakers and arrived at Grimstad for scrapping 21 July 1968.

Crown   As *Oslo* paid off for disposal in 1964. Sold to Norsk Shipbreakers and arrived at Grimstad for scrapping 6 July 1968.

Croziers   As *Trondheim* paid off for disposal 1961. Sold to Belgian shipbreakers and arrived Ghent for scrapping 12 December 1961.

Crusader   Paid off for disposal during 1970. Sold to Italian shipbreakers and arrived at La Spezia for scrapping in September 1971.

Crystal   As *Stavanger* paid off for disposal 1966. Sold to Dutch shipbreakers and scrapped in Holland during 1967.

'Ce' Class Destroyers

Technical Data

	Builder	
Celt	J.S. White & Co Ltd, Cowes	Cancelled 1943
Centaur	J.S. White & Co Ltd, Cowes	Cancelled 1943
Un-named	Yarrow & Co Ltd, Scotstoun	Cancelled 1943
Un-named	Yarrow & Co Ltd, Scotstoun	Cancelled 1943
Un-named	J.I. Thornycroft & Co Ltd, Woolston	Cancelled 1943
Un-named	J.I. Thornycroft & Co Ltd, Woolston	Cancelled 1943
Un-named	Scotts SB & E Co Ltd, Greenock	Cancelled 1943
Un-named	Scotts SB & E Co Ltd, Greenock	Cancelled 1943

Technical details:

Displacement (standard)	1,890 tons
Displacement (full load)	2,505 tons
Dimensions	362 ft 9 ins x 35 ft 9 ins x 10 ft
Armament	4 x 4.5-inch DP; 4 x 40mm AA; 2 x 20mm AA; 4 x 21-inch Torpedo Tubes; 2 x Depth Charge Thrower
Propulsion Machinery	Geared turbines SHP 40,000 = 36.75 knots.

Notes:

In late 1942 it was proposed to order a further flotilla of 'C' class vessels and orders were placed in February 1943. They were to have been repeats of the Cr group with the Mk 6 director and remote power control for the main armament. The topweight problems of the three previous groups had now become apparent and it was accepted that the 'standard' type was no longer capable of accommodating the new weapons and equipment which were becoming available. A decision was taken to discontinue the type and concentrate future construction on the larger designs which were then being produced. The orders were cancelled in March 1943 by which time only two of the class had received names

The eight vessels were re-ordered from the same builders on 7 April 1943 to a new design, rsulting in the initial batch of the Weapons class. *Celt* was laid down and renamed *Sword* in September 1943. She was subsequently cancelled on 5 October 1945 after launching and then scrapped. *Centaur* was laid down and renamed *Tomahawk* in September 1943. Subsequently renamed *Scorpion* she was completed in 1947.

The six previously un-named vessels were re-ordered as follows:

Yarrow & Co Ltd: Laid down as *Battleaxe* and *Broadsword*. Both completed.

J.I. Thornycroft & Co Ltd: Laid down as *Crossbow* and *Culverin*. *Crossbow* was completed in 1948. *Culverin* was launched in March 1946. She was cancelled and sent to the shipbreakers immediately after launching.

Scotts SB & E Co Ltd: Laid down as *Carronade*. She was cancelled, but launched in April 1946 to clear the slips. She was sent to the breakers immediately after launching. The second vessel, *Grenade*, was never laid down, being cancelled on 23 December 1944.

Pennant Numbers

Ship	pre-1948	post-1948	Later
Caesar	R 07	D 07	
Cambrian	R 85	D 85	
Caprice	R 01	D 01	
Carron	R 30	D 30	
Carysfort	R 25	D 25	
Cassandra	R 62	D 10	
Cavalier	R 73	D 73	
Cavendish	R 15	D 15	
Chaplet	R 52	D 52	
Charity	R 29	D 29	164
Chequers	R 61	D 61	
Cheviot	R 90	D 90	
Chevron	R 51	D 51	
Chieftain	R 36	D 36	

HNoMS Bergen *displaying the pennant number D304. She had earlier used J04 and, prior to transfer, had been assigned R35.*
(National Museum of the Royal Navy)

Ship	pre-1948	post-1948	Later
Childers	R 91	D 91	
Chivalrous	R 21	D 21	
Cockade	R 34	D 34	
Comet	R 26	D 26	
Comus	R 43	D 20	
Concord	R 63	D 03	
Consort	R 76	D 76	
Constance	R 71	D 71	
Contest	R 12	D 48	
Cossack	R 57	D 57	
Creole	R 82	D 82	160
Crescent	R 16	DDE 226	
Crispin	R 68	D 168	162
Cromwell	R 35	J 03	D 304
Crown	R 46	J 02	D 303
Croziers	R 27		D 305
Crusader	R 20	DDE 228	
Crystal	R 38		D 306